DIVIDED CITIES

Studies in Urban and Social Change

Published by Blackwell in association with the *International Journal of Urban and Regional Research*. Series editors: Chris Pickvance, Ivan Szelenyi, and John Walton

Published

Divided Cities
Susan S. Fainstein, Ian Gordon, and Michael Harloe (eds)

Fragmented Societies
Enzo Mingione

The City Builders
Susan S. Fainstein

Forthcoming

Post-Fordism
Ash Amin (ed.)

The Resources of Poverty
Mercedes Gonzalez de la Rocha

Social Rented Housing in Europe and America
Michael Harloe

Cities after Socialism
Michael Harlow, Ivan Szelenyi, and Gregory Andrusz

Urban Social Movements and the State
Margit Mayer

Free Markets and Food Riots
John Walton and David Seddon

DIVIDED CITIES

NEW YORK & LONDON IN THE CONTEMPORARY WORLD

Edited by
Susan S. Fainstein, Ian Gordon, & Michael Harloe

BLACKWELL
Oxford UK & Cambridge USA

Contents

Figures

Tables

Contributors

Nicholas Buck is Chief Research Officer at the ESRC Research Centre on Micro-Social Change in Britain, University of Essex. His recent research focuses on the impacts of economic change on the social structure in large cities. He is a co-author of *The London employment problem* (1986).

Malcolm Cross is Principal Research Fellow at the Centre for Research in Ethnic Relations, University of Warwick. He has recently co-edited *Racism, the city and the state* (1981), *Work and the enterprise culture* (1981), and *Beyond law and order* (1991). He is also the editor of *New Community: A Journal of Research and Policy on Ethnic Relations*.

Matthew Drennan is Professor of Economics at the Wagner School, New York University, although currently working in Cornell University. He has written extensively on the role of producer services in the transformation of US metropolitan areas, particularly New York. His publications include *Modeling metropolitan economies for forecasting and policy analysis* (1985).

Norman Fainstein is Professor of Sociology in the Graduate School and Dean of Arts and Sciences, Baruch College, City University of New York. He has published extensively on the political economy of urban development, racial stratification, social movements, and public policy.

Susan S. Fainstein is Professor of Urban Planning and Policy Development at Rutgers University. Among her books are *Urban political movements* (1974), *Urban policy under capitalism* (1982), and *Restructuring the city* (1986). She is currently working on a book entitled *The city builders*, which is a study of the political economy of real estate development in New York and London.

Ian Gordon is Professor of Geography at the University of Reading. He has published extensively on migration, and urban and regional labor market issues. His recent publications include *The London employment problem* (with N. Buck and K. Young). He is currently working on a comparative study of teritorial competition within the Single European Market.

Michael Harloe is Professor of Sociology and formerly Dean of Social Sciences at the University of Essex. Editor, *International Journal of Urban and Regional Research*. Recent books include *New ideas for housing: the experience of three countries* (with Maartje Martens, 1990) and *Place, policy, and politics: do localities matter?* (co-edited with C. G. Pickvance and John Urry, 1990).

John R. Logan is Professor and Chair of the Department of Sociology at the State University of New York at Albany. His recent books include *Urban fortunes: the political economy of place* (co-authored with Harvey Molotch, 1987) and *Beyond the city limits: economic restructuring and urban policy in comparative perspective* (co-edited with Todd Swanstrom, 1990).

Peter Marcuse is Professor of Urban Planning at Columbia University. Formerly President of the City Planning Commission of Los Angeles, he is now active in housing and community affairs in New York City. He has published extensively on European and American housing and urban development. His most recent book, *Missing Marx* (1991), is an account of the last days of communism in East Germany.

Kenneth Newton is Professor of Government at the University of Essex, and Executive Director of the European Consortium for Political Research. His recent publications include *The politics of local expenditure* (1987) and *Does politics matter?* (with L. J. Sharpe, 1986).

Monika Reuter completed her doctorate in the Department of Sociology at the State University of New York at Albany, in 1991 and is currently conducting post-doctoral research in Germany. Her thesis was a study of the influence of technological change on the work experience of women.

Saskia Sassen is Professor in the Graduate School of Architecture and Planning, Columbia University. Her recent publications include *The global city* (1991).

Neil Smith is Professor and Chair of Geography at Rutgers University.

His research interests include space and social theory and housing. Author of *Uneven development* (2nd edn, 1991), he has written extensively on gentrification, the subject of a forthcoming book, *The uses of gentrification*.

Peter Taylor-Gooby is Professor of Social Policy at the University of Kent. He is the author of *Social, welfare, social change and social policy* (1991), *The public provision of private welfare* (1987), and *Public opinion, ideology and state welfare* (1985). He is currently carrying out research on dependency among social security claimers in Brixton, London.

Roger Waldinger is Professor of Sociology at the University of California, Los Angeles. He is the author of *Through the eye of the needle: immigrants and enterprise in New York's garment trades* (1986) and co-author of *Ethnic entrepreneurs: immigrant business in industrial societies* (1990).

Ken Young is Professor of Politics at Queen Mary College, London University. His research interests are in urban politics and government. His books include *Metropolitan London: politics and urban change* (with P. L. Garside, 1982), *Managing the post-industrial city* (with L. Mills, 1983), and *The London employment problem* (with N. Buck and I. R. Gordon, 1986).

Preface

This book represents, we believe, a unique effort in social scientific cooperation. While comparative urban studies has recently become a flourishing industry, efforts at comparison have either been carried out by a single author who has studied several places or have been the product of a group effort wherein each author contributes a case study of a single place. Here we have sought a genuine transatlantic cooperation in which the authors of each chapter have met together and produced an integrated piece, then the group of pieces has been tied together to create a volume intended to be read as a single document and not an edited collection of papers. In the process a number of scholars, many of whom did not know each other initially, have learned of their common interests and have educated each other.

The genesis of this work lies in two sources. First, in 1987 Ivan Szelenyi, then chair of Sociology in the Graduate Center of the City University of New York, along with Ray Pahl and Michael Harloe in the United Kingdom, decided to convene a group of British and American scholars with the aim of developing a social survey of New York to be compared with a counterpart effort in London. Subsequently, however, Szelenyi's move to Los Angeles and, even more significantly, the transformation of Eastern Europe distracted him from his earlier aims. Pahl's own heavy commitments also meant that he had to drop out of the project.

Second, the Committee on New York City of the US Social Science Research Council (SSRC), in a number of meetings on various topics related to the city, convened many of this book's contributors. Under the academic leadership of John Mollenkopf and the administrative guidance of David Szanton, the SSRC committee both stimulated new interest in New York among a number of urbanists and brought them into contact with researchers who had already devoted considerable time to examination of the city. We are particularly grateful for the financial support from SSRC which enabled Michael Harloe and Ian Gordon to participate in these meetings.

When we began this project, both cities were on the upward trajectory of a boom based on extremely rapid expansion of the financial, business services, and real estate industries. Our concern was to cut through the illusion of prosperity and demonstrate the extraordinarily uneven impacts of growth and restructuring on the populations of the two cities. During the course of research and writing, New York's economy turned sharply downward, and its government received a significant change of leadership; at the same time London entered a serious real estate slump and, along with the rest of the United Kingdom, began to show signs of economic weakness. Relative to the rest of their respective countries, however, London was doing considerably better than New York. These events do not contradict our underlying analysis concerning social division, since they in no sense involve a reversal of the underlying processes of economic restructuring. They have, however, called into question some of our initial assumptions concerning the stability of an economy based on "advanced" industries.

We wish to acknowledge with thanks the support of the Economic and Social Research Council and the Joseph Rowntree Foundation of the United Kingdom, the University of Essex Fuller Fund, the University of Kent Research Committee, the Social Science Research Council of the United States, Baruch College of the City University of New York, the Rutgers University Research Council, and the Rutgers University President's Council on International Programs.

Susan S. Fainstein, New York City
Ian Gordon, Reading
Michael Harloe, Colchester

1

Introduction: London and New York in the contemporary world

Susan S. Fainstein and Michael Harloe

On both sides of the Atlantic global forces have been transforming the economic bases of metropolitan areas. The new logic of production, employment, and distribution has engendered changes in land-use and social occupation; it has caused a reordering of the urban hierarchy and of the economic links between places. Common trends in the developed capitalist countries include declines in manufacturing and increases in service employment; the rapid growth of the producer services sector within cities at the top of the global hierarchy; and, along with the concentration of economic control in multinational firms and financial institutions, decentralization of their manufacturing and routine office functions. Greater flexibility of production and spatial fragmentation of industry have heightened the requirement for coordination among economic sectors and between geographically far-flung sites of production and distribution. The financing needs of the modern corporation have become both more vast and more complex.

Cities have felt the impact of global restructuring differentially. Rather than there being a single model of the capitalist city, there is instead a system of cities performing different functions and thereby occupying different niches within a hierarchy (Noyelle and Stanback, 1983; Allen and Massey, 1988). In order to understand how particular places interact with global forces, we need to compare those that occupy similar niches. For cities performing unique functions at the apex of national urban hierarchies, the obvious comparative cases are their counterparts in other nations. London and New York are thus conspicuous subjects for such an exercise.[1] The point of the comparison is to hold economic roles as constant as possible so as to determine their importance relative to other variables in producing social outcomes, and to investigate the sources of difference in national traditions and public policies.

Coordination needs, negotiation of financial packages, speculation, the treatment of firms as themselves negotiable assets, and the creation of new markets for the exchange of arcane financial instruments have led to an enlarged aggregation of command and control activities in global cities (Friedmann, 1986; Friedmann and Wolff, 1982). In London and New York (along with Los Angeles and Tokyo the premier global cities) these increased command and control functions have combined with other traditionally dominant roles that the two cities have played in their national systems. New York and London are also the capitals of culture and information production in their respective countries; they are magnets for world tourism; they contain the principal settlements of recent immigrants; they continue to be major manufacturing centers, cores for wholesale and retail distribution, and ports for air and sea traffic, even while these functions continue to decline relatively or absolutely. Their metropolitan areas remain the largest in population in their respective nations, and thus they also comprise the largest markets for consumer products.

During the last two decades both New York and London have passed through periods of economic decline and revival; the stability of the latter condition is, however, not assured and, during the course of the writing of this book, became increasingly fragile. Both cities are suffering through severe property slumps and are feeling the effects of national recessions. New York's economy, which displayed recessionary symptoms before the nation's, is undergoing severe job loss as well. Whether this new phase is temporary and the city will simply follow the course of the country (if indeed a recovery is on the horizon for the US as a whole), or whether it represents the beginning of long-term contraction, is unclear at this point. London's current downturn appears more closely tied to Great Britain's overall economic health; its fortunes will therefore more likely rebound in tandem with the national economy.

The authors of this book have been struck by the extent to which similar economic processes have been accompanied by similar socio-political outcomes despite quite different political and institutional traditions. Although we note some important continuing differences, we nevertheless find that in both metropolises the political triumph of conservative regimes resulted in an approach to development led by the private sector. We attempt in the following chapters to delineate the forces that produced this outcome but also to show the social costs that ensued. We premise our analysis on the belief that privatization and individualism are not the solutions to economic stagnation.

Gourevitch (1986), in a comparison of national responses to economic crisis, has contended that, historically, some crises have provoked similar reactions among advanced capitalist countries whereas others have not. The implication is that worldwide economic forces need not stimulate identical policies in countries similarly affected. We accept this implication and assume that, with different political leadership, London and New York could have followed different courses. Like Gourevitch, however, we do not consider political leadership an autonomous factor and recognize that its underpinnings rest in a social structure that itself traces back to economic forces. Gourevitch asserts that the five nations he studied all pursued a similar rightward course during the seventies and eighties despite different political commitments; the extent to which they veered in a conservative direction, however, varied. This variance marks the presumed leeway available to government in these times. New York and London, reflecting the policies of their national governments, both went very far toward a market-led model. We do not think that the policies of their regimes were simply compelled by circumstances. Rather we argue that these policies worsened the condition of a large proportion of their populations and may have contributed to long-term instability. At the time of writing both cities are undergoing property recessions; New York is suffering from fiscal crisis and heavy job loss as well. Thus, the expansion of the eighties has ended, and its underlying weaknesses have become more apparent.

This volume investigates the economic and social conditions of the London and New York metropolitan areas, roots political mobilization in those conditions, and analyzes existing policies. Its descriptive focus moves back and forth between the levels of region and core area (these are further described in the appendix to this chapter). Cheshire and Hay (1989, p. 15) define a functional urban region as an area whose "boundaries are determined on the basis of economic relationships rather than history or political divisions." They argue that for comparative urban research it is necessary to employ a functional rather than a jurisdictional delineation of an urban area since the arbitrariness of the latter would make comparisons of such variables as employment or population growth meaningless. Nevertheless, consistent application of their definition also presents serious methodological problems since, in the absence of strong regional governments, regions do not have politics, policies, social structures, and data sets in the same sense as do cities. Therefore, when our analysis shifts from underlying economic processes to social and political questions, our focus tends to move to the core city, as traditionally defined. This is particularly the case in discussions of New York, where the enormous number and variety of local government units within the region make discussion of the whole virtually impossible. Even the rough breakdown that we use for London —

dividing it into Inner London, the outer boroughs, and the Outer Metro-politan Area and assuming considerable homogeneity within these three categories – does not work for New York, where the region contains old central cities as well as an extremely variegated set of suburbs.

These comparative difficulties apart, our examination of just two urban regions raises the usual question of case study analysis – what is the wider significance of our findings? In particular, what generalizations can be derived from a study of two places chosen precisely for their atypicality? We have identified unique aspects to global city status and do not expect that very many other places will wholly emulate the pattern of development characterizing New York and London. We have, however, also argued that, in terms of both spatial formation and social structure, London and New York display dynamics similar to other regions that do not contain global cities. Moreover, given the size and dominance of the two regions, what happens to them is important in itself.

NEW YORK AND LONDON IN THE WORLD URBAN SYSTEM

London and New York, as discussed above, resemble each other both in the economic and political forces affecting them and in the position they occupy within the international economic system. These in turn have shaped spatial form and social structure. To summarize the argu-ment: London and New York have been affected by the internationaliz-ation of capital and the rise of new technologies that have caused the outflow of manufacturing from old urban centres to peripheral areas at home and abroad. They have at the same time profited from the increas-ing importance of financial and coordinating functions, as well as of tourism and cultural production, saving them from the fate of "rust belt" areas with no compensating economic role. Continuing economic importance, however, takes place within new spatial and social circum-stances.

Intense controversy surrounds the question of how the linkages between new patterns of industrial location and the changing nature of industrial organization are to be conceived. The recent development of the two regions can possibly be understood as connected to the reconcentration of industry in a new form of agglomeration. Scott (1988a, ch. 4) contends that there has been a change in the overall technology of production away from hierarchical to market forms of control. He argues that: "The net effect will be an intricate labyrinth of externalized transactions linking different producers, many of whom will coalesce in geographical space to form clusters and subclusters of agglomerated economic activity" (Scott, 1988, p. 54). The tight agglomeration of the old urban core was produced by the need to lower the costs of internal transactions; the looser connectedness of the new urban region, based on modern transportation and communication technologies, results from the same dynamic. However, Scott's belief that a new regime of "flexible accumulation" is leading to the reagglomeration of industry in "marshallian industrial districts" has been criticized by Lovering (1990, 1991) as theoretically and empirically deficient (see Scott 1991a, 1991b, for a response to this critique). Lovering suggests that Scott's theory is economistic and deterministic, ignoring nationally and locally specific processes, which involve differing mixtures of "fordist" and "postfordist" organizations of production, in order to present a general theory of industrial reagglomeration.

Scott's analysis focuses on the needs of manufacturers rather than the financial, business service, and cultural industries that dominate the cores of the New York and London regions. However, Lovering (1990, p. 168) comments, in the case of the City of London, that it is perhaps the nearest that the UK has to an "industrial district" – although he adds, "what is remarkable is its vintage – it is hard to see how this could be described as post-fordist in any useful sense." In contrast, Sassen, like Scott, argues that changing forms of economic control have produced new spatial patterns, and applies this logic to the industries that dominate the London and New York core economies:

> There is a new logic for concentration. . . . There is a new system of "coordination," one which focuses on the development of specific geographic control sites in the international economic order. (*Sassen*, 1991*a*, *p.* 5)

She further assserts that global cities are sites for production as well as coordination:

> They are sites for a) the production of specialized services needed by complex organizations for running a spatially dispersed network of factories, offices, and service outlets; and b) the production of financial innovations and the making of markets, both central to the internationalization and expansion of the financial industry. (*Sassen*, 1991*a*, *p.* 5)

Both the New York and London regions during the 1980s proved magnets for economic activity that arrayed itself throughout their territories at differing intensities of concentration. The metaphor has been used of milk in a bottle as representing the earlier mode of economic agglomeration and spilled milk, or perhaps more accurately spilled mercury, as denoting the new model. Fishman (1987) coins the term "technoburb" to capture peripheral zones within metropolitan areas that now contain the complete gamut of productive and reproductive functions and goes so far as to claim that these areas operate independently of the core city around which they have developed.

Within the New York and London regions the old central cities still exert an enormous pull on their surrounding areas; certain principal industries – finance, advanced services (Schwartz, 1989), and entertainment have not decentralized significantly. Nevertheless, the portions of the region outside the old core (that is, London outside the Green Belt and the New York metropolitan area minus New York City) conform to Fishman's (1987, p. 185) description of areas that "are often in more direct communication with one another – or with other techno-cities [i.e. metropolitan areas] across the country – than they are with the core." Peter Hall, in predicting the lives of a family living in Kent in the year 2001, comments: "The people of Hamstreet live lives that are not circumscribed either by the boundaries of their new community or even by the greater Ashford area, a mini–conurbation of some 150,000 people. They commute freely across south-east England, to London, to other locales in Kent, even across to France" (Hall, 1989, p. 9).

The London and New York regions as a whole therefore conform to a spatial patterning that characterizes expanding regions elsewhere and which some theorists envision as ultimately universal (Hall, 1988). Their cores, however, maintain a unique importance that no longer pertains to the central business districts of most other metropolitan regions.

DUALITY, SOCIAL POLARIZATION, AND THE UNDERCLASS

At least as much controversy surrounds the question of the changing social structure of major urban areas as surrounds the changing geography of production. Even during the peak of the boom of the eighties economic revival did not reproduce the old social ecology or the economic stability and homogeneity that the working and middle classes experienced during the earlier postwar growth period. Instead a more complicated social structure emerged with a lower class unable to find work within the prevailing occupational hierarchy; a working class employed as clerical personnel in large offices or as low-level service workers in hospitals, hotels, and retail establishments; a technically trained middle class that acted as the support structure for the major firms and government; a disparate group of aspirants for fame in the entertainment industry; an astonishingly affluent upper class that occupied the top echelons of the big law partnerships, real estate development firms, investment banks, security brokerages, and media companies; and in New York a largely immigrant stratum working in the old manufacturing sector and frequently also forming its managerial ranks.

These groups inhabited a city where former manufacturing buildings and dockland sites housed the affluent, recent immigrants imparted life to decayed neighborhoods, formerly sound housing deteriorated as a consequence of low-income occupancy and inadequate or nonexistent government subsidies, and parks and abandoned buildings became the dormitories of squatters. Increasing land values in the urban core encouraged the dispersal of mobile middle-class residents and back office functions, even as professional and managerial personnel gentrified centrally located housing. Private market forces wrought this physical and social restructuring of the two cities, but the state encouraged the process by relaxing planning controls and underwriting development costs.

Harking back to the England of Disraeli's two nations and Jacob Riis's other half, many commentators on these processes have identified a social duality wherein one part of the population experienced affluence and success while the other suffered degradation. Economic growth in both cities has been accompanied by sharp increases at both the top and bottom ends of the income distribution. Social inequality manifested itself spatially, as income groups became increasingly segregated. As in the Victorian era, it is above all the concern about, and even fear of, the growth of an urban "underclass" in cities like London and New York which has transformed a sociological concern about the emergent class structure into a wider topic for public and political debate.

Uneven development

As already mentioned, a key starting-point for the research on which this book is based was the perception, widely held by the late 1980s, that London and New York had "turned the corner." In both cities many policy-makers and, more cautiously, some academics saw changes like the upturn in population and investment in the built environment as marking the end of an era of decline – now seen perhaps as a necessary if painful adjustment to a new economic basis for urbanization. In both places those in power strongly linked this transition to a switch in governmental emphasis – away from policies which attempted to compensate vulnerable sections of the population for the "diswelfares" of a market-dominated urban system to those which focused on supporting the further growth of the most advanced and dynamic sections of the urban economy, and to those sections of the population who worked and invested in these industries. Of course, it was clear that many of those in the two cities' labor markets, and most of those outside them, had little to gain directly from these changes. However, if addressed explicitly at all, the principal argument was that the benefits of renewed growth would eventually "trickle down" to such sectors of the population. Moreover, it was claimed, previous compensatory policies had failed to deliver much that was of real and lasting value to those on whom they were purportedly targeted. Instead, they had spawned a large-scale bureaucracy and a high level of public expenditure, much of the latter devoted to paying the salaries of the former.

However, there were other voices to be heard. Those at the bottom end of the urban "renaissance" – community-based activists in still declining neighborhoods or in those disrupted by the impact of the new economic growth, and the politicians who represented such areas – pointed to the persistence of many characteristics of the 1970s, including high levels of unemployment and poverty, deteriorating housing, declining public and private services, and so on. From such a perspective the trickle down effects appeared to involve the costs rather than the benefits of urban revival. Moreover, as public expenditure and employment were slashed, these trends intensified.

This was the context which some commentators sought to encapsulate in the image of the "dual city" – the suggestion that London and New York each contained, in the same urban and regional space, two increasingly separate economies, inhabiting increasingly segregated neighborhoods and social systems. Features such as the juxtaposition of homogeneously low- and high-income areas, the occupation of the sidewalks of well-to-do districts by the homeless, and the simultaneous broadening of employment opportunities for some and the foreclosure of them for others have encouraged many to use this two city metaphor when referring to New York or London. The contrast has perhaps been heightened by a rather selective perception of the inhabitants of these two worlds and a narrow geographic focus. From such a viewpoint the observer saw, on the one hand, the expansive economy, environment, and life style of the "new service class" inhabiting a "reconquered," gentrified inner city, and, on the other hand, the misery of those at the margins of the labor market and outside it, living in close spatial proximity to this first group but a world away in social and economic terms. The continued existence of the "middle mass" of the population, predominately located in the suburbs and toward the periphery of the two city regions, hardly rated a mention in such scenarios. Instead, the concern has been that a process of social and economic polarization is occurring, a shift away from what Pahl (1988) has described as a pyramidal social structure toward an hour-glass pattern. In such a structure, in principle at least, economic and social mobility from the base to the apex is possible. However, in the polarizing cities of London and New York (and elsewhere) such mobility may be increasingly inconceivable for those trapped in marginal jobs or dependent on state benefits – cut off from the new opportunities opening up in the growth sectors of the urban economies.

However, bimodality is an inadequate descriptor of the complicated social and spatial patterns which subsequent chapters in this book describe.[2] In a recent analysis of the effect of industrial restructuring on social organization Mingione points to the significance for the contemporary social structure of increased international economic competition. This has forced producers to increased flexibility in the utilization of labor, especially in the tertiary sector. As a consequence, social stratification has become increasingly complex, and individuals with similar occupational positions may have strikingly different living conditions and long-term prospects. He comments:

> White-collar jobs . . . are extremely and increasingly diversified in terms of pay and conditions of work. This heterogeneity is also reflected in different socialization arrangements depending on the fact that the casual, part-time, temporary or badly paid job is done by a married woman or a pensioner to complement an inadequate household income, by a young man or woman in a transitory phase or by a "breadwinner" in life-long poverty and emargination [sic] from the mainstream of the labour market. Think, for instance, of the wide gap separating what are apparently the same associative interests of two badly paid part-time waiters employed in a fast food establishment or coffee shop in an American city when one is a white college student and the other is an adult black "breadwinner." (*Mingione*, 1991, *p.* 427)

In discussing the situation of global cities, Mingione (1991, p. 461) discerns an even greater tendency toward polarization and fragmentation than elsewhere, caused by the pressure of extraordinarily high-priced real estate markets on stable, middle-income families, forcing them out of the city.

The underclass debate

As Mingione notes, recent sociological accounts contain different and conflicting accounts of this polarization (Mingione 1991, pp. 441–5). For some it entails the loss of middle-income groups from the social structure. Others stress the growth of an affluent middle class alongside an impoverished, marginalized group. But what both conceptions share is the belief that economic restructuring and social change result in the creation of an increasingly isolated mass of impoverished people, whose chances of upward social and economic mobility are minimal. The term "underclass" is now widely used, both sociologically and in public life, to refer to this group.

This term has a long and confused history. When coined by Myrdal in 1962 it referred to those on the margins of the economy. It was frequently used by sociologists to refer to low–paid, nonwhite, mainly migrant workers at the bottom of the US labor market (Giddens, 1973, pp. 215–19). However, in the past 15 years, when unemployment has been at a much higher level than hitherto, the definition of the underclass has shifted and its geographical focus has widened, so that it is now used to refer to all (or some) of those whose attachment to the formal labor market is tenuous or nonexistent in a number of advanced capitalist societies. It has also taken on a wider range of value-laden meanings in "quality" journalism and in public debate. In this context, as Fox (1982) has written (reviewing Auletta, 1981):

> [t]he underclass, or synonyms for it, has a long history as a useful abstraction. The word caricatures a segment of humanity and provides a license to exempt them . . . from the same standards and opportunities as the rest of us . . . Auletta speaks for numerous relatively prosperous Americans who seem to need an underclass. Racists and conservatives need one to explain the inadequacies of affirmative action. Advocates of social scientism – of variations on the venerable theme of a culture of poverty – need one to explain the genealogy of intergenerational misery . . . proponents of an underclass have wanted us to believe that American society was endangered by unassimilable creatures who suffered defects in both their heredity and their environment. (*p.* 62)

It is in such terms that the concept has been taken up by neo-liberal critics of social policy and so become irremediably incorporated in the continuing debate between these commentators and their opponents. Debates on the nature and causation of the underclass have become ever more complex, often shedding more heat than light. Essentially, the right uses the term to refer to what the Victorians called the "undeserving poor" – that group, apart from the "respectable poor," whose poverty supposedly results from individual fecklessness and immorality, aided, according to this modern version of the old thesis, by the enabling nature of the welfare state (Mead, 1986; Murray, 1984; 1990). These individuals create, and are created by, a deviant subculture, most evident in the decaying inner city neighborhoods at the center of the great conurbations. The account stresses the cultural causation of the underclass and is heavily moralistic. It has helped legitimate the national urban policies which right-wing governments have imposed on both London and New York in the last decade.

In opposition to such accounts, sociologists such as William Julius Wilson (1980, 1987) and John Kasarda (1990) adopt a broader, structurally defined conception of the underclass. The decline of manufacturing employment and the rise of new jobs in the services, some of which require high levels of education but many of which require few skills and offer fewer prospects, has left those with only minimal education – notably blacks and Hispanics in the US – outside the formal labor market altogether (though many are involved in the growing informal or criminal sectors) or in a highly insecure and marginal position within it. At the same time better educated minorities have been upwardly mobile – aided by anti-discrimination laws and policies – both economically and geographically and have moved out of the ghetto towards suburbia. The new "disorganized" ghetto of the underclass has taken the place of its "organized" predecessor. Wilson and others who share this analysis utterly reject the cultural determinism, moralism, and right-wing policy conclusions of the first view which has been outlined.[3] Indeed, Wilson has recently (1991) suggested that the term is now so laden with moralistic overtones that the phrase "ghetto poor" may be preferable. However, his continuing contention that this group is largely the product of a "mismatch" between labor supply and demand and that racially constructed divisions, unlike those of class, are of declining significance in the labor market (he believes they are still significant elsewhere in the social system) has been heavily criticized (see, for example, N. I. Fainstein, 1987).

These debates have largely occurred in the USA, where, whatever their other differences, most protagonists have in mind, when they refer to the underclass, the concentrations of nonwhite ethnic minority populations living in the inner city ghettos. Although the British sociologist John Rex has used the term to refer to some sections of UK inner city minority populations,[4] the association of the underclass with inner city ethnic minorities self-evidently makes far less sense, given the absence of such racially segregated inner city neighborhoods in Britain. Instead, while Murray (1990) has attempted to convince his British readers that his analysis of the culturally conditioned underclass in the USA holds good for the UK too (although here it is not racially bounded), other commentators and social scientists, most of whom prefer structural to cultural explanations, have offered a range of alternative definitions.[5] Many of these extend the notion of the underclass to include not just people of working age who are excluded from, or who only have an insecure connection with, the labor market but also those beyond retirement age, for example, who are dependent for their income on state welfare benefits. Like Wilson, most of these writers utterly reject the neo-liberal policies that frequently accompany "culturalist" theories of the underclass.

These views on polarization and the underclass have much in common with the debates surrounding the varyingly defined concepts of "marginality," "modernization," and the "culture of poverty" in Third World cities – and the policy implications that were drawn from them – from the 1950s to the 1970s.[6] Here too, there were structurally and culturally based analyses. The latter suggested that two separate economies and societies – the "marginal" and the "modern" – were emerging in Third World cities, although in the particular circumstances, not paralleled by London or New York, of hypertrophic, "overurbanized" urban systems. Together with these images went the contention that the development of the "modern" sector under the impact of advanced multinational and local capital had virtually no impact (except as a source of attraction for migrants) on the growth and dynamics of the "marginal" sector, nor did the latter act as anything other than a drag on the progress of the former. One of the most dramatic material and policy-related consequences of such a view was the penchant of governments for the physical elimination of the areas of marginal squatter housing in such cities, and the forced relocation of their inhabitants beyond the city boundaries. However, these dualistic theories of "modernization" were eventually found to have little basis in reality and the "myth of marginality" (Perlman, 1976) was exposed. The linkages between the growth of the "modern" and the "marginal" sectors, both under the tutelage of international capital, aided by the international agencies, was evident.

Of course it would be a mistake to make too much of the parallels between the analyses now being applied to cities such as London and New York and those which were adopted to explain the evolution of Third World cities (in many ways the parallels can also be drawn across time in these two cities, comparing the discourses which surrounded their later nineteenth-century transitions and the current situation – some materials for this will be found in the next chapter). However, especially in the crucial matter of policy prescriptions, particularly those coming from the political right, there are some interesting and even alarming similarities. Compare, for example, the policy of "triage" (or "planned shrinkage") adopted in New York in the late 1970s – the neglect of whole areas of the city which were written off as irremediable until living conditions got so bad that even the poor left them, allowing the remaining buildings to be razed and redevelopment to occur – with the policy of squatter clearances in Third World cities (Marcuse et al., 1982). Or compare the belief which some have that large cities such as London and New York have become centers for a welfare-dependent population, with a lack of relevant skills for employment in the urban economy – which is thought to justify policies such as cutting welfare benefits or even the discouragement of urban settlement in such places – with the view among Third World policy-makers that the marginal population ought to be discouraged from migration to the cities, or even removed, because it was unable to participate in the "modern" economy.

However, the failure of this earlier example of an attempt to apply a simplistic theory of the "dual city" to urban systems undergoing profound processes of social and economic restructuring serves to draw our attention to the need for a far closer examination of the actual processes which have been at work since the 1970s in London and New York. The images of a dual or polarized city are seductive, they promise to encapsulate the outcome of a wide variety of complex processes in a single, neat, and easily comprehensible phrase. Yet the hard evidence for such a sweeping and general conclusion regarding the outcome of economic restructuring and urban change is, at best, patchy and ambiguous. If the concept of the "dual" or "polarizing" city is of any real utility, it can serve only as a hypothesis, the prelude to empirical analysis, rather than as a conclusion which takes the existence of confirmatory evidence for granted.

THE RESEARCH AGENDA

Despite the considerable volume of academic research, official reports and data, and so on which exists on London and New York, this is insufficient to test the validity of the proposition that lies behind the "dual city" hypothesis, namely that economic revival and urban renaissance have been accompanied by accelerating social and economic polarization. The first problem – reflecting academic and policy-oriented divisions of labor and interest – is that relatively few attempts have been made so far to bring together the mass of separately conceived and executed social, political, economic, and other studies of the two cities in order systematically to explore the causes and consequences of economic restructuring and their urban impacts. However, the second problem becomes evident as soon as one embarks on such a project. This concerns the lack of existing primary research and data collection regarding many aspects of the urban transformation. Just to take one example, there is still too much reliance on cross-sectional data when attempting to study and draw inferences regarding dynamic processes which can be fully understood only by longitudinal surveys.

Within the confines of the time and resources available to the research project on which this book is based, it was not possible to make a major contribution to filling the gaps left by the lack of primary research. However, the research project has been able to achieve more in relation to the first problem outlined above, bringing together within a common research framework, strategy, and team a more integrated analysis of what the existing corpus of research and data can tell us about the contemporary situation in the two cities. A central outcome of this effort, developed throughout the subsequent chapters and considered in more detail in the conclusion, is the recognition that the "dual" or "polarizing" image of the two cities partly obscures a more complex reality. One consequence is that policy prescriptions derived from such an image may be misguided and even damaging to the interests of the majority of the populations of both cities.

The above mentioned research limitations are, of course, combined in this study with the familiar difficulties encountered by most comparative research, made worse in this case by our reliance on the secondary analysis of data and research collected in differing national cultures and contexts, with differing objectives and not by a unified team of researchers. Many such problems are described by the authors of the subsequent chapters. How successfully they have been surmounted is for the reader to decide. However, despite these difficulties, evidence for some clear patterns of similarity and difference between the two places does seem evident, as well as for an assessment of the specific impact made by the global city role discussed earlier in this introduction.

Given the need to penetrate beneath the superficialities of the "dual city" image, the research strategy aimed to examine five key questions concerning economic restructuring and urban revival in these two "global" cities. These were as follows.

1   *In what sense, if any, was there an urban revival?* The three changes, noticeable from the early 1980s in both cities, which are most frequently associated with renaissance are the reversal of population decline, the creation of new jobs in certain sectors of the economy, and new investment in offices, retailing, and housing. Such developments are documented in the chapters to follow, along with more detailed analyses of the nature of these changes. This analysis, considering, for example, just which sectors of the population have been moving to or remaining in the two cities and which continue to move out, which types of jobs have been created and which types of investment in the built environment have occurred, is an essential precursor to the second set of questions to which the research was oriented.

2   *For whom was there an urban revival?* Answering this question involves linking changes in the urban economies, labor and housing markets, and in the production of the built environment, and relating

the whole process to specific sectors of the population. In addition, a crucial issue is to identify for whom there was not an urban revival, why this did not occur and what connections, if any, exist between the advantages which accrue to the beneficiaries of urban change and the disadvantages which persist and even intensify among those who have lost out. A particular concern is the extent to which the costs of change appear to be a necessary accompaniment of the types of benefits and instabilities which renaissance has generated. The comparison of the two cities would, it was hoped, enable us to draw some tentative conclusions about this question which could not be gained from a single city study. As already discussed, the choice of the two cities as suitable comparators was based on the observation that both now play leading roles, as global or world cities, in the organization of the international economic system. So, looking outwards from each city as it were, a third question was posed.

3 *To what extent was the revival of the eighties a consequence of the fact that London and New York are global cities?* There are several important matters to be considered when attempting to answer this question. First, the need to specify in general terms, not simply in relation to the two cities, what are the major changes in the international economic order which form the substance of claims about the growth of a global economy, together with the distinctive types of productive organization, structure, and location which are emerging. Second, the need to have regard to the particular nature of London and New York as they have historically evolved. Obviously the effect of global changes is likely to be modified or perhaps mediated by the particular social, demographic, political, and other features of the particular places where they impact, and the outcome of this interaction forms the second area for research and analysis. Third, the need to account not just for the direct impact of changes in the global economy, in terms, for example, of the jobs gained and lost, but the indirect effect on matters such as housing, the social ecology of the city, political and institutional structures, and so on.

Much of the work required under this heading involves studies of the working out of market-led processes. However, state policies are always deeply implicated in market activities, sometimes helping to shape and support them, at other times acting to restrain them, most often perhaps attempting to do both at the same time. So the fourth question to be considered was as follows.

4 *What role have public policies played in urban revival?* Implicitly or explicitly the attempt to assess whether such policies have been market supportive or market compensatory runs through most of the discussion of this question and is closely linked to the issue of who has

benefited and who has lost out in the process of urban change. In this part of the research we have scrutinized the claims that changing state policies have played a central role – for good or evil – in the upturn in the fortunes of the two cities. Answers about the size and nature of state involvement in urban revival may also indicate what the potential scope for different future policy mixes may be, for example policies which aim to sustain many of the benefits of growth without incurring some of the costs. This leads on to the final, more speculative, set of questions with which we are concerned.

5   *Is the revival of the two cities sustainable and can its distributional consequences be modified, by state or other action?* The first of these questions has become increasingly salient as our research has proceeded. Recession and cutbacks in employment in the leading growth sectors of the two cities and depressed conditions in the real estate industries have provided a severe check to the unbridled optimism that both cities had "turned the corner" which existed in the mid-eighties. At the time of writing it is unclear whether these reversals are more than a temporary phenomenon, but they do serve to illustrate just how fragile the "renaissance" may prove to have been when viewed in the longer term. At the same time, as we show later in the book, the costs of revival have become ever more apparent, not just in terms of the worsening circumstances of many whom it never benefited, but also, for example, through generally high housing and land prices and the degradation of the environment, transport, and public services, resulting in a significant deterioration of the material basis for urban life of wider sections of the urban population. Such consequences suggest that, even if the current setbacks of both cities are purely temporary, continuing growth may not be sustainable without increasingly heavy costs which are not limited to a marginalized minority. In these circumstances the locational and other advantages which have helped to elevate London and New York to global city status may transfer to other, less burdened cities. Finally, such considerations must enter into any assessment of the role that public policies might play in modifying the consequences of continued growth and/or avoiding the loss of these locational advantages.

THE POLICY DEBATE

Policy analyses of British and American metropolitan development for the last 30 years have stressed crisis.[7] During the 1960s few doubts were expressed concerning the general economic health of the New York and London regions, but first in New York then later in London serious concern was evinced over the plight of the inner city (N. I. Fainstein and S. S. Fainstein, 1974; Lawless, 1989). Governments in both places responded with targeted programs aimed at improving the life chances of poor people disproportionately living in the aging residential areas located within the boundaries of the turn-of-the century city. Even at that time critics on the left contended that urban poverty resulted from the larger context of social inequality rather than the particular deficiencies of poor people and their neighborhoods.[8] But these left critics tended to relate inequality to failures of the welfare state and to domestic social and political domination by large corporations and wealthy individuals rather than to global economic processes.

Later, however, there was a shift from a focus on the potential for social explosion created by politically mobilized communities of poor people to diagnoses of more generalized economic crisis. The sudden rapid decline of manufacturing and port activities in Inner London and New York City, expanding unemployment in all economic sectors, cyclical downturns in real estate markets, and shortfalls in governmental revenues all contributed to a view of the urban problem as a failure of economic growth. Within conventional analyses it was argued that the government had to shift resources from social service and welfare provision to economic development initiatives (Morris, 1980). More progressive thinkers traced economic decline to long-term tendencies within capitalism and in particular to the new international division of labor (Rees and Lambert, 1985). Both tendencies accepted that a restructuring of capital was necessary to revive the aggregate economies of old urban areas: the right regarded such an effort as generally beneficial if painful in the short run; the left saw it as an effort to increase the exploitation of labor.

Neither the economic boom of the eighties nor the sharp downturn that inaugurated the nineties has fundamentally changed these policy orientations. In both cities, however, there is renewed attention to issues of public finance. In London the downfall of Margaret Thatcher, largely attributable to her efforts to impose the poll tax, has caused a Conservative reformulation of local taxation, the outcome of which remained unclear at the time this was written. In New York renewed fiscal crisis has led in the short run to severe cutbacks in public spending and widespread calls for long-term restructuring of the municipal government. In London the tax collection problem is closely tied to the fate of the national government and is essentially a political crisis; in New York the city's faltering economy is the direct cause of its financial woes. The policy debate in both cities over local government finances ultimately boils down to conservative support for reduced levels of taxation, privatization of services, and cutbacks in social welfare spending facing opposition from supporters of a larger and more benevolent public sector. The great unpopularity of increased taxation in a period of stagnation, however, puts the defenders of public-service provision in an extremely vulnerable position.

THE ANALYTICAL FRAMEWORK

The general rationale for the contents of the book has already been outlined, ending with a discussion of the five key questions to which the research has tried to provide some answers. However, the structure of the volume and the historical period with which it is concerned require some further explanation.

The first of these concerns, the structure of the volume, has been shaped by the initial framework for the research project upon which it is based. Our starting-point was the hypothesized similarity – under the impact of globally organized changes in capitalism – in recent economic changes in the two cities. Conversely, we thought it likely that there would be a greater variation in the patterns of unequally distributed life chances which resulted from such changes. What, we suggested, linked the (possibly) broadly similar economic "inputs" to the two urban systems with their (probably) more differentiated outcomes for the two populations were a number of distinctively constituted further features of the two places. The ones we have chosen to examine in some detail are labor market structures, housing and social ecology, race/ethnicity, and planning/urban politics. Obviously this list is not a complete one; issues such as transportation, education, and differing cultural character-istics are also likely to be significant, but the limited resources available for the project have meant that only passing attention has been paid to such concerns.

An important additional dimension to the research framework resulted from the self-evident fact that in both cities contemporary social and economic change has taken place within a context set by their previous histories. In both cities the recent revivals have been built on the histori-cal legacy of past rounds of investment, social and political structures, public- and private-sector institutions and processes, and so on. There-fore, the essential starting-point for the book is a consideration of the impact of this longer-term context on the current situation.

Of course, the rather linear model linking common economic changes with differentiated outcomes provided no more than a point of departure for the research. The causal linkages between the various factors outlined above are complex and not unidirectional. Each of the subsequent chapters seeks to unravel and describe in a more realistic way than the model proposes the nature of these linkages. In the course of this work it has become apparent that there are in fact some important similarities and some equally striking differences between the two cities in every aspect of their current constitution, including the specific roles which they play, as global cities, in the international economy. Nevertheless, the motive force which has been supplied in both locations by broadly similar global economic changes to a whole range of urban processes is amply illustrated by the chapters which follow.

The main focus of the book is, of course, on developments between the late 1970s and the late 1980s, the period when the public and political concerns of the previous decade or more, with the seemingly irreversible decline in the two cities' economic and urban fortunes, gave way to a growing optimism, at least among those who had benefited from economic restructuring. However, the decline of the 1970s and the selective growth of the 1980s can best be seen as two aspects of a single process. Indeed, even in the era of decline, significant areas of the two urban economies began the expansion which was to accelerate as the 1970s gave way to the 1980s. Likewise, the processes of decline, evident in the 1970s, affecting other economic sectors have not ceased in the last decade. These considerations resulted in the decision that each chapter (apart from that which provides a longer-term historical overview) should analyze changes over the past two decades. However, there is some necessary variation in the exact period covered by each chapter and within them as well. This is for two reasons: first, the lack of complete synchronicity between, for example, developments in economic factors, on the one hand, and changes in politics or the social structure, on the other; and, second, detailed differences in the timing of parallel changes in such factors between the two cities.

The following seven chapters deal in turn with the historical framework, the evolution of the two metropolitan economies, consequential changes in their labor markets, the patterns of inequality which largely result from such changes, the key role of "racially" and ethnically constituted social and economic divisions, the impact of economic change on housing and social ecology, and, finally, the changes in urban politics and policies in response to economic and social restructuring.

In the final chapter we bring together the salient findings from the seven previous chapters in order to reconsider the five key questions outlined in the previous section of this introduction. We discuss the implications of these changes for the social structures of the two cities and for the broader analytical and theoretical issues regarding world or global cities and their supposed characteristics which have been mentioned above. Finally, we discuss the role that public policies might play in sustaining the growth and prosperity which both cities experienced in the 1980s, while distributing these benefits in a more equitable manner. The limitations of current pro-market policies are summarized but a critical view is also taken of the failure, so far, to develop coherent and viable alternative approaches. Such alternatives are unlikely to emerge without a considerable mobilization of political support in their favor.

NOTES

1 Other recent efforts at comparing either London and New York or British and US urban policy include Savitch, 1988; Sassen, 1991a; Barnekov et al., 1989; Hall, 1988; Judd and Parkinson, 1990.
2 An extensive discussion of the use of the dual city metaphor as applied to New York City is contained in the introduction to Mollenkopf and Castells, 1991. Despite the title of this book (*Dual city: restructuring New York*), its contributors emphasize fragmentation rather than duality as the defining characteristic of contemporary New York society. Marcuse (1989b, p. 698) subjects the general concept of duality to criticism as "either wrong or badly incomplete, and its use, though often well-intentioned, does more political harm than good." Although the title of his paper refers to the "quartered city," he, in fact, suggests that there are five main divisions in New York City's urban social structure.
3 However, both sides in this debate have, to an extent, shifted ground as it has continued. For example, in later work Wilson agrees that the structurally determined social isolation of the underclass does lead to the development, among some of the ghetto population, of a deviant subculture, however,

> [u]nlike the concept of culture of poverty, social isolation does not postulate that ghetto-specific practices become internalized, take on a life of their own, and therefore continue to influence behavior even if opportunities for mobility improve. Rather, it suggests that reducing structural inequality would not only decrease the frequency of these practices; it would also make their transmission by precept less efficient. (*Wilson*, 1990, *p.* 186)

Interestingly, Charles Murray has also now attempted to distance himself from this concept of the culture of poverty: "The burden of my argument is that members of the underclass are *not* sunk in a cultural bog; that all people who are poor do *not* repeat the cycle of disadvantage, whereas others do, and the interesting question is why the latter group . . . in the industrialised west seems, in recent years, to have grown rapidly" (Murray, 1990, p. 69). Murray's answer to this question is that the young men who mainly form the underclass are "essentially barbarians" (p. 23) who are civilized only by marriage. The majority of the poor become integrated in mainstream society by this means. However, a minority do not do so. In contemporary urban societies tolerance of illegitimacy, the failure to detect and punish crime, and liberal welfare policies combine to encourage an ever greater section of the poverty population to follow what he evidently sees as their natural barbaric propensities – hence the growing underclass. Nevertheless, the structural causes of this poverty are still ignored and more than a hint of the culture of poverty thesis remains in Murray's concern about the transmission of morally reprehensible attitudes and behavior to the illegitimate children of single mothers, who, he claims, suffer from the absence of "responsible fathers and husbands" as role models (pp. 10–11).

4   Rex used the term to refer to a section of black, mainly Afro-Caribbean, youth in the inner city which was not only structurally separated from the majority population as a result of racial discrimination in the labor and housing markets, in education, and so on, but which was also developing a degree of separate class consciousness as a result – in short, becoming a "class for itself," to use the Marxist terminology (Rex and Tomlinson, 1979). Subsequent debate on the UK "underclass" – while it may initially have been partly influenced by Rex's formulation, has, in practice, largely ignored his special and limited use of the term.

5   See, for example, the British critics of Murray, such as Field, Brown, Walker, and Deakin (Institute of Economic Affairs, 1990). Townsend (1990) also defines the underclass much more widely, to include all those at the bottom of the labor market as well as those outside it, such as retirement pensioners. However, according to Runciman, "the term must be understood to stand not for a group or category of workers systematically disadvantaged within the labour market . . . but for those members of British society whose roles place them more or less permanently at the economic level where benefits are paid by the state to those unable to participate in the labor market at all" (1990, p. 388). Sociologically speaking, there is considerable justification for this latter definition, if one accepts that in capitalist societies social classes are largely determined by occupational position within the productive sphere, as did Marx and Weber. The term underclass, then, clearly denotes a group which is not so engaged. However, theories of *social stratification* which define different social "strata" in terms of unequally distributed life chances, social prestige, etc. have less difficulty in applying a label like "underclass" to denote those groups of the very poor, whether they be inside or outside the labor market, who comprise the "bottom" stratum of society. In part the now almost terminal state of confusion into which the underclass debate has fallen results from a pervasive lack of clarity concerning the theoretical grounding of the concept.

6   Lloyd (1980) contains a brilliant dissection of the many ambiguities which surrounded the concepts of dualism and marginality as applied to Third World development. There are close parallels between this confused debate and that concerning the urban underclass.

7   Cheshire and Hay (1989) and Scott (1988a) discuss the ways in which the content of urban analysis changed along with trends in the world economy. Regarding this shift, Scott (1988a, p. 4) comments:

> This is not to say that the old [urban] theory was necessarily false or incoherent; I mean, rather, that if social theory is to be viable and relevant, it must not only adhere to purely formal criteria of truth, however conceived, but it must also . . . shift its focus as the pertinent questions and human predicaments of the lived world change their shape and form.

8   This took the form of the culture versus structure argument concerning the causes of poverty. See Valentine (1968). Contemporary debates about the "urban underclass" have given this controversy a new lease of life – as discussed above.

APPENDIX: THE LONDON AND NEW YORK REGIONS

As noted in this chapter, there are difficulties in adopting the suggestion that the type of comparative urban research presented in this book should employ functional rather than official or jurisdictional definitions of regions. Accordingly, when we refer to New York City we are employing the latter definition and explicitly note when we intend to specify the larger, functional definition by using the term "the New York region." When discussing London, we generally mean the area bounded by the Green Belt ("Greater London") that, until its abolition, had been governed by the Greater London Council (GLC).

London

For official purposes England is divided into eight *standard regions*. London lies at the heart of, and dominates, the *South East region* (see figure 1.1). The population census recognizes three main subdivisions of this region – *Greater London*, the *Outer Metropolitan Area*, and the *Outer South East*. In addition, a further subdivision is recognized, within Greater London, that of *Inner London* and *Outer London*, and for some purposes the separate area of *Central London* within Inner London is also recognized. In varying places this book therefore makes reference to:

– South East region. Consists of Greater London and the adjacent counties of Essex, Hertfordshire, Bedfordshire, Buckinghamshire, Oxfordshire, Berkshire, Surrey, West and East Sussex, Kent, and the Isle of Wight. In 1981 this area contained just over 17 million persons.
– Outer South East. Consists of those parts of the South East region most distant from Greater London, roughly lying in a band between 45 and 65

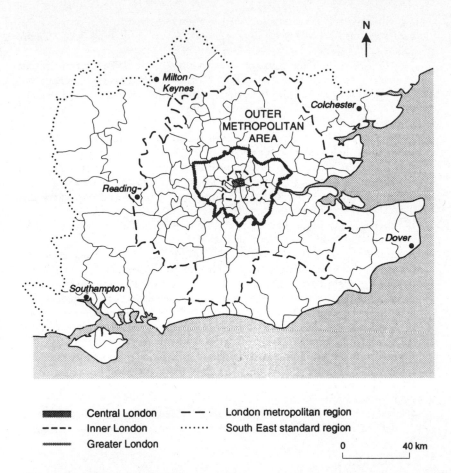

N
↑

Figure 1.1 The London region

miles from the metropolitan center. It consists of large free-standing towns and smaller settlements which have faced heavy development pressures in the last 20 or so years. It includes the whole of East Sussex and the Isle of Wight and parts of Kent, Essex, Bedfordshire, Buckinghamshire, Oxfordshire, Berkshire, Hampshire, and West Sussex. In 1981 this area contained around 4.7 million persons.

– Outer Metropolitan Area (OMA). The area which lies between Greater London and the Outer South East, roughly between 15 and 45 miles from the metropolitan center and separated from Greater London by the metropolitan Green Belt (and whose inner border runs close to the line of London's orbital M25 motorway). There are still considerable areas of open countryside in this subregion, where substantial development has occurred in the postwar years. It includes the whole of Surrey and those parts of the other counties

24   *Susan S. Fainsein & Michael Harloe*

noted above which are not included in the Outer South East. In 1981 this
area contained around 5.5 million persons and covered about 3,800 square
miles.
- Greater London. The London conurbation, until 1986 (when it was
  abolished) the area of jurisdiction of the Greater London Council, but
  subdivided into 32 London boroughs plus the City of London. In 1981 this
  area contained just over 6.8 million people (see table 1.1) and covered 610
  square miles.
- Outer London. The suburban boroughs of Greater London. Until the establishment of the Greater London Council in the early 1960s most of this area
  was under the jurisdiction of the surrounding counties (plus the county of
  Middlesex, which was wholly abolished in this reform). It covers an area
  where continuous urbanization developed in the inter- and postwar years.
  Two slightly different definitions of Outer London exist. In 1981 the "group
  B" boroughs (19 in all) had a population of 4.25 million; "Outer London"
  boroughs (20 in all) had a population of 4.46 million.
- Inner London. This consists of the 13 ("group A") or 12 ("Inner London")
  central boroughs in Greater London plus, in both cases, the City of London
  (which has special arrangements of its own for local government purposes).
  In broad terms this covers the area of London which was built up pre-1914
  and "Inner London" is identical to the area which came under the jurisdiction
  of London's first metropolitan government, the London County Council
  (LCC). The LCC was abolished to make way for the Greater London
  Council and, until its more recent abolition, the special purpose Inner London
  Education Authority (ILEA). In 1981 the "Inner London" boroughs had a
  population of 2.35 million; the "group A" boroughs had a population of
  2.55 million.
- Central London. This approximates to London's Central Business District.
  As defined in the 1971 population census, London's "conurbation center"

Table 1.1   Greater London population (thousands)

		Percent born in New Commonwealth and Pakistan
1931	8,110	
1951	8,197	
1961	7,992	
1971	7,452	13
1981	6,696	18
1986[a]	6,775	

[a] Estimated
Note: "New Commonwealth" includes Carribbean, India, Pakistan,
Bangladesh, Cyprus, Gibraltar, Malta, Gozo, and the Far East.
Source: Central Statistical Office, 1987, table 2.8; Clout and Wood,
1986, table 18.1.

roughly follows the line of the main railway termini, lying mainly to the north of the river Thames but with a small extension south of the river. It includes the City of London, the major shopping and entertainment center (the "West End"), and the center of government and high-income residence to the west. In 1971 this area had a resident population of about 230,000, but this included large numbers of temporary residents (for example, in hotels), a daily workforce of 1.24 million (20 percent of the total workforce in the GLC and OMA), and covered about 10.5 square miles. The 1981 census contains no data on this area but its population level has probably not altered greatly.

Betweeen 1966 and 1981 the fastest growth in population and employment (just under 25 percent in each case) occurred in the Outer South East (Buck et al., 1986, p. 41). Indeed, this growth has now spilled out beyond the South East altogether, so that parts of the surrounding regions (South-West and East Anglia) have also been growing rapidly and, in functional terms, are increasingly integrated in the South-East (although note that the South East space economy is not simply focused on London; a more complex pattern of linkages between Greater London and major centers, elsewhere in the South East has developed – see Champion et al., 1987, pp. 1–16, for a discussion of the division between that part of the region mainly dominated by London's economy and that which is linked to free-standing Local Labour Market Areas in the rest of the region). In this same period the Outer Metropolitan Area grew at about half the rate of the Outer South East. Greater London as a whole lost population and employment, there was a loss of around 4.5 percent for both of these in Outer London, but a drop of 18 percent in population and 23 percent in employment in Inner London. In the later 1970s the outflow of population from Greater London began to slow down and, as discussed later in this book, in the 1980s a marginal increase in the capital's population probably occurred. Some population projections suggest that a further small increase in population may occur in the 1990s; a further rapid decline now seems unlikely.

New York

As in London, there are differing functional and administrative definitions of the New York region (see Schwartz, 1989). These include the following:

- The area in which the Port Authority of New York and New Jersey operates. It covers 3,900 square miles, contains 17 counties, and in 1987 had a population of 15.6 million.
- The functionally defined US Census Consolidated Metropolitan Statistical Area (CMSA). It covers 7,659 square miles, contains 24 counties, and in 1987 had a population of 17.9 million. Many of the regional statistics collected by the federal government and used in this book cover this area.

- The Regional Plan Association (RPA) study area — "the tri-state region." It covers 12,757 square miles, contains 31 counties and in 1987 had a population of 19.8 million, with some 11 million jobs.
- The regional core (as defined by Hughes and Sternlieb, 1989). It covers about 600 square miles, including New York City plus its counterpart across the river in New Jersey. In 1986 this contained 9.2 million people and over 5 million jobs. (See figure 1.2 for regions and table 1.2 for New York City population figures.)

The RP study area provides the broadest and most adequate definition of the New York region, because it includes those areas into which population and industry have decentralized in the postwar era. It includes more than 500 very diverse municipalities — old cities, suburbs of various vintages, suburban office centers, holiday resorts, etc.

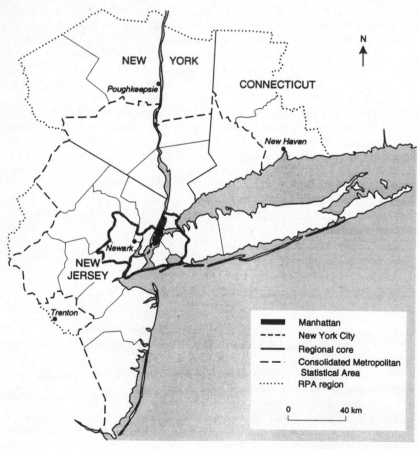

Figure 1.2 The New York region

Table 1.2 New York City population (thousands)

	1940	1950	1960	1970	1980	1990
New York City	7,455	7,892	7,782	7,895	7,072	7,323
% white	94	90	85	NA	61	52
Manhattan	1,890	1,960	1,698	1,539	1,428	1,456
% white	83	79	74	NA	59	59
Brooklyn	2,698	2,738	2,627	2,602	2,231	2,301
% white	95	92	85	NA	56	47
Bronx	1,395	1,451	1,425	1,472	1,169	1,173
% white	98	93	88	NA	47	36
Queens	1,298	1,551	1,810	1,986	1,891	1,911
% white	97	96	91	NA	71	58
Staten Island	174	192	222	295	352	371
% white	98	96	95	NA	89	85

Notes: Figures for 1990 do not include an adjustment for the undercount. At the time of writing the Bureau of the Census was still considering whether to adjust the numbers upwards to reflect estimates of undercounting.

Individuals of Hispanic origin are included in both white and nonwhite categories depending on how they identified themselves. The city contained 21 percent of Hispanic origin in 1980 and 25 percent in 1990. Percentage white is not supplied for 1970 because the treatment of those of Hispanic origin in that year differed from the rest of the series. Groups not included in the "white population" are blacks, native Americans, Asian/Pacific Islanders, and "others."

Sources: Rosenwaike, 1972, pp. 121, 133, 136, 141, 197; US Bureau of the Census, 1986, p. 202, table A; Fiske, 1991.

There was a period of rapid suburban expansion in the 1920s, linked to commuting by train and trolley cars. Counties such as Westchester, Greenwich, Bergen, Essex, and Nassau, centered on public transport interchanges, developed at this time. The Depression and the war meant that rapid growth did not resume until the late 1940s. Increasing car ownership and the intensive development of radial and orbital highways made the construction of widely dispersed, low density suburbs possible.

A central area surrounded by three concentric rings of development can be identified, the products of this history. These are as follows:

- The core of the region, the boroughs of Manhattan, Brooklyn, the Bronx, and Queens in New York City and Hudson County, across the river from New York City, in New Jersey. This is the oldest and most densely populated part of the region.
- The adjacent inner ring which consists mainly of the older, pre-Second World War suburbs and smaller industrial cities such as Newark and Elizabeth. This includes Nassau, Westchester, Bergen, Passaic, Essex, Union, and Richmond counties in New Jersey and New York State.
- An intermediate ring, where most development began after the Second World

War. This includes the rest of Long Island (i.e. Suffolk county) plus New Haven, Fairfield, Rockland, Morris, Somerset, Middlesex, Mercer, and Monmouth counties, stretching out into that part of Connecticut adjacent to Long Island Sound and along the New Jersey coast south of New York City and into the east of this state. These first three divisions comprise the tri-state region (New York–New Jersey–Connecticut).

– The outer ring, which has begun to be affected by the decentralization of population and economic activity in the most recent years. This includes Litchfield, Dutchess, Putnam, Ulster, Orange, Sullivan, Sussex, Warren, Hunterdon, and Ocean counties, covering the whole of eastern Connecticut, the southern sector of New York State, and all of New Jersey except the most southern counties which lie between Philadelphia and Atlantic City.

2

A comparative history, 1880–1973

Nick Buck and Norman Fainstein

In this chapter we examine the comparative histories of New York and London during the century that precedes the most recent restructuring of the international economy and consequent reorganization of urbanism. Doing so allows us to understand the origins of the built environments, social geographies, economies, and political institutions of the two cities. More than that, however, historical comparison over a relatively long duration helps us to identify what is distinctive about the national milieus of these capitals of capital, to see the typical ways in which rather similar economic forces play themselves out over time through different political cultures and institutions.

A review of a century of development in two places necessarily forced us to construct a highly synthesized essay based mainly on the primary research of others. Our method for comparing New York and London has been to identify critical periods in the political economies of each city. Because the two occupied similar nodal positions in a capitalist world economy centered in the North Atlantic, we have been able to assume that the cities passed through the same stage of development simultaneously. Thus, we believe that a comparison of New York and London between 1880 and 1914 (our first period) analyzes the effect of the industrial revolution on places undergoing similar restructuring processes and occupying similar positions in the world urban hierarchy. Under the same assumption we have chosen two other periods for comparison: (1) the years of the Depression and the Second World War, when capitalism experienced a crisis that resulted in the political incorporation of the "mature" working class, and (2) the "long 1960s" (1960–73), when both cities began to experience the "problem of the inner city" that was a reflection, in part, of the new realities of economic and spatial restructuring. In each period we examine similar topics: flows of capital and people that redefined the cities' social economies and built environments; major political actors and their agendas; and unresolved tensions and conflicts that helped shape later events. We conclude the chapter with a brief summary of the lessons of this exercise in comparative history.

THE RISE OF THE DOMINANT MANUFACTURING CITY: 1880–1914

By the last part of the nineteenth century London and New York had become the largest cities in the world and the greatest centers of manufacturing. They were also financial and industrial control points for an international economy dominated first by Britain, and then jointly by Britain and the United States. They housed the world's largest working classes under some of the world's worst conditions for human existence. The possibility of rebellion appeared omnipresent to their ruling classes, as the political stability of capitalism seemed by no means assured.

New York

Flows of people and capital

During the years between 1880, when the then new immigration commenced from Southern and Eastern Europe, until the First World War, New York was transformed socially, economically, and spatially. Its population in 1880 of 1.9 million[1] grew substantially, reaching 4.8 million in 1910. By then, the city comprised about 5 percent of the US population; about half its residents were concentrated in Manhattan (Lampard, 1986, table 5).[2] Throughout these years New York was a city of immigrants, with more than 50 percent of its labour force foreign-born (Lampard, 1986, table 6).[3] But while the foreign-born at the start of the period were mainly Irish and German (a small minority of whom were Jewish), the new entrants were southern Italians and Jews from Russia and Poland.[4] These newcomers crowded into the Lower East Side of Manhattan at densities comparable to the highest in the world, roughly 800 per acre or 500,000 per square mile (Regional Plan Association, 1929, p. 73), while the Irish and the Germans now found somewhat better quarters in a tenement district that in 1910 encompassed most of Manhattan east of Third Avenue, the Midtown West Side, the South Bronx, and parts of Harlem and Brooklyn. The most salient fact about the New York of 1914 was that it was a proletarian city, and that this proletariat was overwhelmingly comprised of first- and second-generation European immigrants drawn from socially and politically diverse nationalities. As a result, ethnicity established fundamental lines of division within the lower classes.

The economic base of the city was transformed in several ways. In 1880 New York was a low-rise mercantile city centered geographically around its port, with its workforce "engaged in the financial, commercial, and manufacturing activities appropriate to the entrepot that handled the lion's share of America's trade with the outside world" (Hammack, 1982, p. 33). Thirty years later manufacturing was more concentrated among industries that reflected the city's comparative advantage in immigrant workers and active ethnic entrepreneurs – most notably in the garment trades, which employed about 250,000 or 36 percent of manufacturing workers (Lampard, 1986, table 4). Concurrently manufacturing's economic share contracted (although the number of manufacturing workers increased greatly). White-collar employment now expanded to about 35 percent of the workforce,[5] both because of the rapid growth of industries like insurance, publishing, and communication over which the city was dominant, and because of the rise around 1900 of modern business corporations, most of which located their headquarters in Manhattan. All the while the port of New York maintained its leading position.[6]

Thus, by 1910 New York was a dominant manufacturing city in the sense of its large manufacturing base, its corporate domination over US manufacturing activities located elsewhere, and its major role in the shipment of both goods and capital around the world.[7] Its manufacturing, however, usually took place in small firms (rather than the giant factories of Chicago and Cleveland). The city had a strong base in financial and service industries as well. Except that it had a smaller workforce and was not a capital city, New York generally replicated London's diversified, manufacturing-based economy.

The economic expansion of New York required the development of its built environment. The growth of office industries stimulated the construction of office buildings, at first only downtown as manufacturing and residential uses were displaced, then, after 1900, with the opening of the modern railroad stations, in midtown. The commercial city of the previous century was razed and rebuilt. Faced with the need for new plants that had to be proximate to working-class residential districts, manufacturers erected high-rise factories (called lofts); these rapidly expanded in size and domain until they were huge structures of 10 to 20 stories that extended northward to midtown.[8] Many of these loft buildings remained to take on new uses with economic restructuring in the last quarter of the century.

Political actors and their agendas

The decades around the turn of the century are usually called the Progressive period in both national and urban politics. In these years governmental bureaucracies and methods of administration first became institutionalized, usually at the behest of the "public spirited" wing of the upper class, and over the opposition of other business interests and the partisan political organizations (rings and machines) with whom they symbiotically coexisted. Still, before the First World War the scope and scale, not to mention professionalization, of all levels of government in the US were quite limited. The federal government was almost entirely disconnected institutionally, financially, and programmatically from states and localities. National political parties operated from the bottom-up, with state organizations sovereign. The Congress was ascendant and controlled by state party organizations that were themselves commonly in collusion with powerful capitalists.

During the Progressive period, as local governmental institutions were reformulated and insulated from ward-level politics, municipalities were granted expanded powers. In New York City the transformation was especially notable because a unified municipal government, with a popularly elected mayor and legislative body, was established in 1898 over its entire modern territory. This government in the first decades of the twentieth century monopolized police, firefighting, sanitation, health care, parks, water supply, public education, including a municipal college, and, not of least importance, the granting of contracts and franchises for transportation, electrification, sewers, and streets. Both the range of functions and the scale of physical expansion of the city made its local government the most powerful in America. Nonetheless, the extent of social control and economic intervention from all levels of government was much weaker than in Western Europe at this time. The economy and the built environment were privately owned and comparatively unregulated. Moreover, even after 1898, the unified government of the city could not cross the state line that ran through New York harbor, and thereby excluded nearby urban centers in New Jersey.

Politics in the period amounted mainly to the mediation of competing interests within the upper class and the provision of benefits to party organizations: the Democrats, who had incorporated the Irish and the Germans, had a somewhat more proletarian class base than the Republicans, who included most of the old Yankee aristocracy, but also the Americanized German population. The Jews remained outside the "regular" party system until the latter part of the period, and the Italians never entered at all before the First World War. The Democratic Party, controlled most of these years by the Tammany Hall machine, penetrated deeply to the communal level, and operated a substantial system of patronage in both the public and private sectors (especially over construction and the docks, where the party and organized criminal gangs were intertwined). It was "by combination of the party machine, the utilities, and the underworld that control of the city could be gained, and by that control each segment of the power combination could obtain what it wanted" (V. O. Key, as quoted in Lowi, 1963, p. 82). The Republicans, for their part, remained less of a mass party organization and eventually lost control over New York City government, retreating instead to the state capital, where they often carried out the direct will of leading capitalists, particularly the railroad and banking interests.

Under two astute leaders, Croker and then Murphy, the Tammany Hall machine established a stable partisan regime for much of the period, especially the latter years. By then the machine had made peace with the skilled trade unions in the American Federation of Labor (AF of L) and even supported weak forms of labor legislation. It also routinely provided symbolic benefits to the immigrant Germans, Irish, and, to some extent, the Jews. But it remained implacably opposed to labor unions that sought to enter politics, and successfully kept out of the arena of local politics any programmatic issues that might be identified with collective working-class interests. In this way it effected and reproduced the segmentation between – on the one side – the politics of the workplace waged between workers and unions and bosses (then extremely conflictual though never referred to as politics) and – on the other side – the politics of the community played out through competing parties and candidates in municipal elections that rarely dealt with policy issues and never addressed the social question.[9]

While the failure of socialism in America appears overdetermined in retrospect, it hardly seemed inevitable to the contemporary elite. Dominant groups – which changed in composition over the period with the rise of managers and professionals – were united in their terror of a radically organized proletariat, a distinct possibility many thought, given the dual society that had emerged in New York. The economic misery of the foreign-born masses, the apparent social disorganization and criminality of immigrant neighborhoods, the squalor of tenement life – all were the subject of endless popular treatments, government reports, and learned articles in the new academic disciplines of sociology and political science. The combination of poverty, foreignness, and political agitation posed a grave threat to the American political and economic system.

The response of the propertied classes was multiple and fragmented, particularly with regard to local conditions. As economic elites, businessmen managing national corporations had no interest in city politics, while others accommodated themselves to the necessary corruptions of the political machine. As citizens, the bourgeoisie shifted from a dominant laissez-faire position early in the period, to a conservative, statist approach later. In the American context statism meant expansion of local government functions, public provision of capital infrastructure for economic development and effective competition with rival cities (most notably Chicago), and a limited effort to deal directly with social conditions, mainly through provisions to regulate public health and to Americanize immigrant children in public schools.

Programmatic innovations and unresolved conflicts.

These fell into two arenas. The first involved the strengthening and professionalization of the municipal government. As previously noted, the political boundaries of modern New York were established in 1898 with the amalgamation of the cities of Brooklyn and New York and the annexation of several other towns. Metropolitan government provided the region with a single effective government, the boundaries of which encompassed the entire urbanized area east of the Hudson River,[10] including a vast territory of farmland in Queens, eastern Brooklyn, and the northeast Bronx where expansion could take place. With a unified tax base the city could now finance the physical infrastructure critical to deconcentration and, thereby, to its growth.

   If decentralization of population and economic activity was one route to defusing the potentially explosive immigrant social problem, social integration was the other. The paramount American mechanism to that end was already established as public education. The schools created a common culture and also provided sufficient human capital for individual social mobility, or so it was hoped by the Progressive advocates of schooling. Early in the century newly professionalized educators along with Progressive elites combined in New York to take the schools "out of politics," to expand their mission, and to insulate them from popular control. The latter required an end to the highly decentralized system of neighborhood school boards then in effect. After years of conflict the New York City school system was unified, teachers and principals were appointed by a centralized bureaucracy based on professional credentials, and the danger of "un-American" influences penetrating from immigrant neighborhoods was removed for half a century,[11] until blacks and Hispanics again demanded "community control."

   The construction of the physical infrastructure for a greatly expanded city, along with modest advances in housing and land-use regulation, constituted a second arena for innovation. Besides grading and paving hundreds of miles of streets, the most important public investments were the construction of two new bridges from Lower Manhattan to Brooklyn. Along with the Brooklyn Bridge opened in 1882, the Manhattan and Williamsburgh Bridges provided access to Manhattan lofts from Brooklyn tenements. By 1914 the bridges to Brooklyn carried tracks for the new rapid transit system. The opening of the subways, publicly funded but privately owned and operated at this time, further decentralized working- and middle-class housing in the pre-automobile city. Newly constructed tenement districts followed the lines northward through Manhattan and the South Bronx and east through Brooklyn. The subway fare was fixed at 5 cents, where it remained until 1948. Through this mechanism, the municipal government subsidized worker transportation directly, and indirectly subsidized housing by allowing its construction on relatively cheap land that had previously been remote from the downtown manufacturing and port district.

Before the turn of the century there was little regulation of housing and land-use.[12] The most important statute was the Tenement House Act of 1879. It required a limited number of indoor toilets, running (cold) water, and some ventilation. It also established a uniform design, the so-called dumbbell tenement,[13] a five-, six-, or even seven-story walk-up that typically housed 20 to 30 large families and their boarders in two- and three-room flats. More than 10,000 of these "urban caves" were produced by a class of small businessmen and operated privately. Sufficient levels of crowding were maintained to make the "old law" tenements profitable, so that housing production kept apace with population expansion. In 1901 a new tenement law required considerably better plumbing, ventilation, and, by now, electrification. But implementation was staged, and enforcement was weak. Consequently the effects of improved housing were not felt by the working class for more than a decade. By that time increased prosperity along with cheaper decentralized locations permitted better-off working-class households to afford the rents of the "new-law" tenements. While there were numerous reports about horrible housing conditions throughout the period, the alternative of public production gained little support, even from working-class political organizations and unions.

The period ended with the promise of political stability and a rising standard of living for the city's working class. Immigration was cut off during the war, restricted afterwards, and effectively ended in 1924, thereby reducing the endless supply of low-wage workers. The American urban economy prospered during the First World War and the following decade. Conservative regimes were in power locally and nationally. It would take the Depression to produce the political realignments necessary for another wave of major programmatic innovations in New York.

London

Flows of people and capital

The late nineteenth century was the period of London's dominance of the world system. It was the largest city in the world, and it was the political and administrative center of a major imperial system. London's markets controlled large parts of the flows of trade and capital, and it was a major source of capital for industrial development throughout the world. A measure of the significance of the financial flows is the net income on overseas investments, managed by the City of London; this amounted to 8.6 percent of GNP by 1913, a level which has not been attained in any other large country in modern times, and which was nearly two-thirds the share of gross profits companies earned within Britain (Feinstein, 1972).

In consequence the London economy depended significantly on activities associated with trade, finance, and administration. The Port of London and the City of London were the focus for the first two of these, while government and the associated concentration of headquarters services underpinned the third. Together they also supported London's economic role as a major center of consumption. This was reinforced by the residence for at least part of the year of the wealthiest fraction of the national population. They in turn stimulated a large manufacturing sector specializing in consumer goods.

Like New York, London also had a large and diversified manufacturing sector. It had more manufacturing workers than any other city in the world. Of approximately 1.9 million employed residents in the narrowly defined County of London in 1891, around 600,000 or 32 percent were working in manufacturing industries. (The resident workforce in New York was a little over a million in 1890, of which 35 percent was employed in manufacturing – Lampard, 1986, table 6; thus, the sectoral structure of employment was remarkably similar in the two cities.) The largest sector, as in New York, comprised the garment trades (260,000); printing and paper (87,000) and wood and furniture (68,000) were second and third. Also as in New York, manufacturing tended to be located in relatively small workshops, with a considerable amount of home work. The physical structure of the metropolis inhibited the introduction of large-scale factory production, except on the periphery, and the majority of employers worked with very little capital. Much of London's industry faced competitive pressure from more efficient provincial factories.

The combination of this unstable manufacturing sector with port-related activities that underwent considerable fluctuations of employment meant that a large segment of the working-class labor market was subject to extremely casual conditions of employment. This had a number of consequences, including very insecure working-class standards of living, and substantial difficulties in political and trade union organization. In these respects too, London and New York were similar.

London, like New York, had a markedly divided social structure, formed by a combination of the large employment in relatively highly paid administrative, professional, and clerical activities, a relatively affluent fraction of the working class in some of the craft industries, such as printing, and a large and much more impoverished fraction of the working class trapped in the casual labor market. In comparison with other British cities, it had a particularly large upper- and middle-class population, and a comparatively small fraction of its proletariat employed in big mills and factories. Here, too, it resembled New York.

The population of the city expanded significantly faster than the national population throughout the nineteenth century. London with its suburbs increased from just over 1 million in 1801, or around 12 percent of the national population, to 4.7 million in 1881, or 18 percent of the total, and to 7.2 million, or around 20 percent in 1911 (cf. New York, 4.7 million and 5 percent in 1910). Britain, unlike the United States, was losing population through emigration, rather than gaining it from immigration, and the bulk of London's population growth came from domestic sources.[14] Immigration from Ireland and the rest of Europe made only a minor contribution to the structure of London's population. Except for a relatively small Jewish concentration in the East End, London was overwhelmingly British and English-speaking.

In contrast to New York the emergent pattern was not one of a succession of waves of immigrants arriving at the center and driving the previous ethnically distinct waves outwards, but, rather, a continuous process of inflow from around Britain, into available space both in the inner areas and newly developing suburbs, combined with a movement outward of those able to afford more space and costlier journeys to work. One consequence was that, unlike New York, where the central social problem appeared to be assimilating newcomers, in London the problems were those of the long-term residents and the London-born, and policy discourse revolved around the degenerative effect of urban living and its conflicting interpretations (Stedman Jones, 1971).

In the later nineteenth century London's spatial patterning was becoming increasingly class-divided. The lines of segregation were sharpening as redevelopment schemes in the City and West End drove out some of the remaining working-class concentrations in these areas (Dyos, 1955). Low-wage workers were increasingly concentrated in a broad arc to the east and south of the City of London. It is significant, and in sharp contrast with the ethnic patterning of New York, that Booth (1892), in carrying out his survey of life and labor in London in the late 1880s, should characterize streets solely on the basis of a relatively complex gradation of the income and labor market position of their residents.

The concentration of poorer sections of the working class was reinforced by hiring practices in the casual labor market, which meant that workers were obliged to live within reasonably close walking distance of possible places of work. They therefore could not take advantage of the new house-building on the periphery of the city, even if the rents there had been affordable. Moreover, since the stock of housing in Inner London was being reduced by conversions to industrial and commercial uses and railway-building, and, unlike New York, there was little new construction of housing at higher densities, working-class housing conditions were deteriorating, particularly in the eastern half of the inner area.[15]

Clerical and other lower-middle-class workers, as well as some manual workers, were using this rapid suburban growth as a means of escape from the housing conditions of Inner London. Suburbanization was markedly shaped by transport developments. In particular the policy of railway companies had a considerable impact on the long-term social geography of the suburbs (Kellett, 1969). Government sought to impose an obligation on railway companies to provide services at fares accessible to the working classes in compensation for destroying inner area housing. To the northwest and south of London this was resisted, and these areas developed as more uniformly middle-class suburbs, while to the northeast the Great Eastern Railway actively encouraged this type of traffic. Thus workers in relatively secure and better-paid employment were able to escape to the new working-class suburbs such as Leyton, Stratford, and Tottenham (areas comparable to the boroughs of New York reached at this time by the city's subsidized rapid transit lines). The result was increased concentration of those in poverty in the inner East End, which came to be seen as the central social problem of London.

Political actors and their agendas

The political power of London stemmed from its role as national and imperial capital, and as core city in the world financial system. But in contrast to its national and international political significance, its local politics was parochial and weakly developed. Historically, London had ineffective and divided local government in comparison with other British cities, and did not obtain a single, multi-purpose authority until 1889. One consequence of this institutional fragmentation was a very low level of poliltical mobilization, reinforced by the centralization of the British political system.[16]

There were other reasons for the political disorganization of both London's elite and its proletariat. Indeed, there remains a considerable problem in defining what the urban elite in London was – and what political, social, and economic problems it faced. Industrial capital acted as the social base for urban reform movements in other British cities, but it was almost absent from London, and its interests were subordinated. Financial and commercial capital was politically insulated from the issues of the remainder of the metropolis within the archaic structures of the City of London. While London as capital city monopolized national elite institutions – government, the legal system, the press – and was the major consumption center for the rich, national elites had only the most peripheral interests in the problems of London as a production center; their main concern seems to have been with social stability (Stedman Jones, 1971).

The threat to social order posed by the lower strata of the working class was both political and social. The example of revolutions in Paris and other continental capitals fed perceptions that London might be next, and the riots of the unemployed which swept Central London in 1886 reinforced ruling-class anxiety. For this reason, the expansion of labor union power – manifested, for example, in the successful dock strike of 1889 – was grudgingly welcomed by a significant component of the governing class as evidence that disorganized workers were becoming incorporated into political structures.

The concern over a social threat involved a long-standing struggle on the part of middle-class London to protect its spaces from working-class intrusion, particularly from the perceived "rough" element of the working class. The relative fixity of the urban form should not disguise the fact that there were rapid changes in the social status of neighborhoods, and a leading thread of middle-class politics involved defense from the working class. This was to be a major element in Conservative resistance to London-wide government, which might seek to pursue redistributive social and spatial policies.

Together, these perceived threats led to an identification of the central problems of working-class London as pathological individual behavior – disorder, crime, drunkenness, vice. For the political right the solutions were to find economic and, more particularly, social disciplines to "moralize" the working class, for example by a controlled use of charity, as exemplified by the Charity Organization Society. For progressives the problems lay more in underlying social and economic deprivations – and particularly slum housing and low and irregular incomes. Housing tended to take the highest priority in reformers' agendas, and there were attempts in this period to develop subsidized municipal housing as a solution to the problem. Though limited in scale before the First World War, these efforts set the agena for the postwar housing program (Wohl, 1977).

Programmatic innovation and unresolved conflicts

The problems of physical management of the city became a major spur to institutional and programmatic innovation toward the end of the nineteenth century.[17] Central to these innovations was the attempt to resolve the question of metropolitan government. The structure of government was seen to be inadequate to meet the needs of a modern city. London had no single directly elected local government body up to 1889. From 1855 the physical problems of the development of the city had been managed by the Metropolitan Board of Works (MBW), itself selected by the lowest level of London government, the Vestries – bodies which already had proved quite incapable of managing the problems of urban growth. The weakness of local authority, the absence of electoral accountability, and growth in signs of corruption caused considerable political pressure, particularly from middle-class progressives, for a local government organization capable of taking control of the development of urban infrastructure and providing municipal services more adequately. London's movement for municipal government reform thus resembled New York's in the same period in its formal objectives. It was not, however, driven by the same social purpose as its New York counterpart, which was determined to wrest control of government from the immigrant-dominated political machine.

The issue of municipal reform in London raised the underlying conflicts between proponents of a single governing authority, who generally came from the left and were at that time associated with the progressive wing of the Liberal Party, and those who favored a more localist and fragmented pattern of government. The latter tended to have allies in the Conservative Party and the national level, which had no desire to create a countervailing – and likely radical – center of power to Westminster (Young and Garside, 1982). In New York no upper-class counterpart to Tory localism existed.

In 1889 the reformers prevailed, and the creation of the London County Council (LCC) led to the consolidation of a progressive coalition of Liberals and Fabian socialists. This grouping sought to expand the role of local government in housing, in regulation of urban development, and in the provision of municipal services. The consequence was conflict over the scope of LCC powers between the progressive-dominated LCC (up to 1907) and Conservative national governments, supported by

Conservative local movements within London. One of the major issues was the preservation of middle- and upper-class enclaves within London. The central government, once more under Conservative control, reduced the powers of the LCC by creating in 1899 a lower tier of government, the metropolitan boroughs. Nevertheless, the LCC was able to undertake an expanded provision of municipal services, particularly by beginning a house-building program.

While in the 1880s London's concerns had a major salience in national debates about social policy, the effects on legislation in this period were very limited. By the time a reform-minded Liberal government returned to power in 1906, the social policy agenda had widened greatly. The reforms of the Asquith government that arguably laid the foundations for the British welfare state, such as old age pensions and national insurance for sickness and unemployment, did not have any particular application to London, and in the latter case were almost irrelevant to the problems of the lower reaches of the working class. This was to set a pattern: given that in Britain social policy, as distinct from physical urban policy, was set entirely at the national level, the distinctive social problems of London were unlikely to be adequately addressed.

Comparisons

In summarizing this first period, we find considerable economic similarity between London and New York. Their industrial and occupational structures were nearly identical. However, differences in patterns of land tenure and perhaps in culture resulted in London spreading further outward than New York, with sufficient working-class housing construction a perennial problem. In New York the deconcentration of the city was accompanied by continual physical reconstruction of the central core and extensive private construction of working-class housing at high densities within walking and then rapid transit access to the Lower Manhattan manufacturing district.

The significant distinction between the cities lay in the socio-political realm. Immigration in New York interplayed with the extremely decentralized political system to establish ethnically organized machine politics. Machine politicians continuously struggled with middle-class reformers over control of relatively strong municipal government. This displacement of class conflict undermined any programmatic working-class consciousness. In Britain a much stronger central government became the arena for class-organized political parties. The rise of the Liberal Party resulted in the first elaboration of a national welfare state. Municipal reform toward the end of the period made the London boroughs into relatively strong and modern units of administration just when the comparable level of government in New York was being eliminated. At a time when ethnic and class antagonisms in New York played themselves out within urban politics and within a unified municipal government, neither local politics nor the local state had a significant role in stabilizing the political economy of industrial capitalism within Britain.

STABILIZING THE WORKING-CLASS CITY: 1929–1945

By the 1930s the political incorporation of the immigrant and migrant workers of the turn of the century had been completed. But once again capitalism was in crisis. The world economic downturn threatened stability, particularly in New York, where its impact was much more severe than in London. In both countries national governments responded to economic crisis with policy innovation – the welfare state and planning. During the Second World War there was a halt in the development of domestic policy, and the different effects of the war on the two cities laid the basis for their postwar trajectories. However briefly, at the end of the war London reigned along with New York as the center from which the Anglo-American economies dominated the world.

New York

Flows of people and capital

Immigration ended, but the city continued to grow in population, from 6.8 million in 1930 to 7.5 million in 1940. New York still comprised about 64 percent of the region's 10.6 million population,[18] only marginally lower than its 68 percent share in 1910 (Lampard, 1986, table 10). Even with the flow stopped, foreign-born whites constituted 42 percent of the resident workforce (cf. a peak of 53 percent in 1910). The black population had more than doubled since the First World War, and reached about 7 percent of the resident workforce by 1940.[19] Puerto Ricans added about 1 percent more (Lampard, 1986, table 6). As of 1930, about 33 percent of New York's 3.18 million workers were employed in manufacturing (only a little less than the maximum proportion of 38 percent in 1880 – Lampard, 1986, table 6). New York maintained America's largest manufacturing base, and continued as a city characterized by European immigrants working at blue-collar jobs, even as its white-collar workforce and service sector slowly expanded during the first three decades of the century.[20]

The Depression that began in 1929 and continued until 1941 created severe labor dislocations in New York City. Nevertheless, although unemployment reached levels of 25 percent, the city's economy was not relatively hard hit compared to the rest of the country. Manufacturing employment recovered during the war from a 9 percent decline in the 1930s, and the city's share of regional manufacturing employment remained steady, as did the region's position nationally, the latter hardly changing between 1919 and 1947 (Tobier, 1988, pp. 97–9).[21] Like manufacturing, white-collar employment remained relatively steady. The office real estate market collapsed, with a peak vacancy rate of 34 percent in 1934, but it too recovered. The boom of the war years left the city with fully utilized manufacturing plant and port facilities, with little vacant office space, and a severe shortage of housing.

Political actors and their agendas

The LaGuardia administration, which came to power in 1934, was the first municipal regime to ally itself directly with industrial labor unions. But when LaGuardia took office, he inherited a fiscal crisis that forced him to lay off thousands of municipal workers, reduce wages, and cut services. His regime cloaked itself in popular symbols (legitimizations for Italians and Jews, labor unions, the "down and out"), even while its budgetary behavior was conservative and closely monitored for several years by a committee of bankers, who had imposed an "austerity plan" on New York in return for continued lending.

LaGuardia achieved left-oriented objectives because he was able to command intergovernmental resources at a level unparallelled in US history. During the Depression, New York State government – under the governorship of liberal Democrat Herbert Lehman – greatly expanded its programs for social welfare, improved working conditions, and housing. It provided many of the models for the federal New Deal. By 1934 the New Deal was in full force. The Roosevelt administration, with which LaGuardia was allied, now supplied the city with substantial resources intended to reduce unemployment; most of this money was for capital expenditures. LaGuardia allowed Robert Moses – a conservative Republican estranged from Tammany and Roosevelt, who had established a reputation as a highway builder in the 1920s – to direct the city's expenditures of intergovernmental funds for infrastructure, parks, and housing. Moses also organized and commanded the Triborough Bridge and Tunnel Authority. Along with the Port Authority of New York and New Jersey, it built public works and employed thousands. Using these new vehicles and resources, the city embarked on redevelopment and

housing programs. LaGuardia and Moses shared credit for these generally popular efforts.

The period ended in 1946 with Tammany again winning office in the
wave of red-baiting which swept the country in the mid-1940s. The
O'Dwyer regime continued LaGuardia's commitment to symbolic ethnic
representation. European ethnic groups were represented in governmental appointments, and, wherever possible, the Democrats ran "balanced" tickets, including Irish, Italian, and Jewish candidates (Lowi,
1963). Tammany accommodated itself to the gigantic empire established
by Moses. Even as the neighborhood organizations of the Democratic
Party atrophied, the party elite intertwined with real estate, banking,
and construction interests to feed off of intergovernmental and public
authority revenue streams. After a lag in the war years, large-scale
redevelopment commenced again in New York, now fully under the
direction of Robert Moses, with the city government primarily a vehicle
for legitimizing the process (Caro, 1974).

Programmatic innovations and unresolved conflicts

These fell into two main categories. The first involved the reorganization
of the built environment. During the 1930s, New York began a program
of bridge, tunnel, and highway construction that would prepare the city
for the automobile age. Except for completion of a major addition to
its transit system (the "IND" subway), there would be no improvement
of public transportation until the mid-sixties, and even then little was
accomplished. Highways were built largely along the lines established
in the 1929 Regional Plan, which envisioned a less dense city surrounded
by residential suburbs and industrial centers. The Regional Plan was
the product of a private good-government group and had no building
authority; there was no official comprehensive planning, and little political discussion of alternatives.[22]

Public housing programs were now established for the first time.
Private charities and New York State were the only source of funds
until the 1937 federal Housing Act; federally supported public housing,
however, was not important until the 1950s. Public housing construction
was used as a basis for slum clearance. During the 1930s most of the
housing was built in the Lower East Side, and it was occupied by
European immigrants. As of 1940, public and publicly assisted housing
still amounted to only 15,000 units, less than 10 percent of the private
housing constructed during the Depression and a trivial percentage of
the 2.5 million unit housing stock (N. I. Fainstein and S. S. Fainstein,
1988, table 7.4). New York was nevertheless the largest producer of
public housing in the country.

The building of new political institutions constituted the second legacy of the period. The scope of local government once again expanded. The 1930s and war years witnessed the establishment, inter alia, of the New York City Public Housing Authority, the Transit Authority, the Triborough Bridge and Tunnel Authority, and the City Planning Commission; social welfare agencies were greatly expanded in function and rationalized in organization; and the bi-state Port Authority emerged as a powerful planning and construction bureaucracy responsible for the trans-Hudson tunnels and George Washington Bridge, Newark and LaGuardia (and later Idlewild – now Kennedy) Airports, and other facilities. The powerful public authorities were self-financing and largely independent of elected municipal officials, who were neither fiscally nor politically responsible for development projects that affected hundreds of thousands of people. At the same time, neighborhood representation in local government weakened as the Democratic Party ceased to be a grassroots organization, and the American Labor Party and other socialist groups were kept off the City Council with the Legislature's elimination of proportional representation in 1945. Thus, just as local and regional governmental agencies became more powerful, the political capacity of the city's working-class majority declined.

London

Flows of people and capital

The interwar years saw a transformation of London's economy. In spatial terms we can identify three components. The first was a Central London economy, including the City of London and its financial and commercial services, as well as government and related services. The second component, the Inner London transport and manufacturing sectors, maintained itself with a pool of Inner London labor. But alongside these extant sectors was added a third – suburban, factory-based manufacturing – which had only a limited existence before the First World War.

The growth of suburban manufacturing is reflected in Greater London's share of national industrial output, which rose from 17 percent in 1924 to 25 percent in 1935. The Greater London region accounted for around 44 percent of all new factory openings in the period 1932–8. London's net increase of 532 factories contrasts with a net increase of 112 in the rest of the country. Sectors such as engineering, which had been particularly weak in the Inner London economy before the First World War, formed a major part of this growth (Llewellyn Smith, 1931). The inter-war developments laid the groundwork for the postwar position of the wider London region as the most technically advanced segment of British manufacturing.

The strength of Outer London manufacturing is the major explanation for the contrast in the economic fortunes of London and New York during the Depression. While New York was seriously affected, *in common* with the rest of the US, London was barely touched at all, *in contrast* to the rest of Britain. It experienced both relative and absolute economic growth through the 1930s, and its unemployment rates were markedly below national levels. In fact, the Depression and war reinforced regional disparities in the UK, with London and the South East furthering their economic hegemony,[23] as compared to New York, which managed only to retain its relative position within the nation.

The population of Greater London continued to grow slowly through these years, peaking at 8.7 million in 1939, but declining to 8.3 million by 1951, as wartime destruction accelerated decentralization. Within this overall figure there was an increasingly sharp contrast between change in the inner area – that covered by the LCC – which lost around 350,000 in the 1930s, and the outer areas of the conurbation, which gained 850,000.

In the interwar period, and particularly the 1930s, the pace of physical expansion of Greater London accelerated. The average radius of the built-up area increased from around 7 miles in 1914 to over 12 miles in 1939. Government policies encouraged a suburban building boom, with the emergent pattern consisting of semi-detached houses following the logic of public transportation routes. New housing prices fell relative to incomes, and this also encouraged suburbanization of the skilled working-class and middle-income white-collar workforce (Johnson, 1964; Hall, 1989). In all of these respects London and New York were quite similar, with the exception that in London British Rail developed the radial system established by the "subways" in New York.[24]

In contrast there was relatively little physical redevelopment of Central and Inner London, except for some development of higher-income flats in the western part of the center, and a limited program of redevelopment for public housing by the LCC. The spatial lines of class division were becoming more accentuated as the process of population decentralization removed much of the better-off population of Inner London.

The slow pace of local authority housing redevelopment, combined with physical deterioration and the persistence of low wages and casual labor in proletarian boroughs, led to a continuing problem of social order, but it no longer had the threatening character of the pre-First World War period. White's (1986) account of social change in the "worst street in north London" shows how, even in a street possessing all the most acute housing and labor market characteristics of prewar inner London, suburbanization and a more regular labor market were leading to stabilization.

Political actors and their agendas

Local government elections of 1919 had seen a significant political advance by Labour, but in subsequent elections in the 1920s the party was reduced to a narrow base in the East End. In this area a radical political movement developed around the problems of unemployment. Known as Poplarism, after the Borough in which it was concentrated, it created intense conflicts between central and local government, which in the long term led to defeats for the movement. These conflicts were essentially around the question of whether social policy was to be defined at the national or the local level. Poplarism also created a cleavage within the London Labour Party (LLP) between George Lansbury and other radicals and Herbert Morrison, who dominated the LLP (Branson, 1979; Jones and Donoughue, 1973). Morrison pursued a strategy which could appeal to middle-class London. He sought a more developed organization of the party, of which the LLP was itself an example, and an approach to local government which focused on more efficient administration and the development of higher levels of municipal services. He also fought for the extension of municipal control in fields such as transport. In this sense Morrison inherited much of the political agenda of prewar LCC Progressivism.

With Morrison triumphant, Labour enjoyed a steady political advance in London in the 1930s, although it remained stagnant nationally. Morrison's approach appeared to be paying off, with an increasing number of metropolitan boroughs falling under Labour control, and the LCC itself after 1934. In this period the postwar political geography of London became recognizable, with Labour organization established in the eastern half of Inner London, and extending into parts of inner south London. Many of the London boroughs in these areas fell under continuous one-party control. Political change tended to follow the social shift in the inner residential boroughs as the middle-class population moved out to the suburbs. Labour advance in the newer industrial suburbs tended to be slower, and before the Second World War was largely concentrated in areas of local authority housing.

So far our discussion of politics has focused on the LCC area, but, as suggested earlier, much of the change and activity in London in this period was taking place in the suburbs, which were largely beyond LCC influence. These suburbs were mainly Conservative-dominated, but they were also in the process of organizing basic services, and some developed a limited amount of council housing. They began, however, to come into conflict with the LCC over the latter's attempt to resolve some of the housing problems of Inner London by building local authority estates in the suburbs. There was considerable resistance in some counties to such development, which was perceived to be threatening to the social status of middle-class suburbs. Toward the end of the 1930s resistance to development of any kind was beginning to grow among interests on the periphery, concerned at the loss of agricultural land, and the declining amenity value of their areas. This was one of the major factors underlying a new approach to London planning which developed around the time of the Second World War.

Programmatic innovation and unresolved conflicts

While party politics largely went into abeyance during the period of war, paradoxically the level of active debate over distributional issues and the physical problems of London became much more intense than it had been during the 1930s when programmatic innovations remained relatively slight. In the context of total war, planning solutions to problems had much greater salience. London's growth itself began to be seen as a political problem at both the national and the regional level. There was an increasing perception that London was becoming overcongested and was absorbing too large a proportion of the nation's growth, and that planning was a necessary tool to contain this growth, promote national industrial efficiency, prevent the despoliation of the countryside around London, and bring about more socially harmonious development.

In the late 1930s restraints on urban development on the periphery of London were introduced through the Green Belt, and there were limited steps to encourage industrial development away from London in the depressed regions. It was during the Second World War itself, however, that a series of major reports set the framework for postwar London regional planning and national regional planning: the Barlow Report on the distribution of the industrial population (Royal Commission, 1940), which laid the foundations for regional industrial policy, and Abercrombie's Greater London plan of 1944.

Abercrombie's strategy was to reinforce the Green Belt by general restraints on converting rural land to urban uses in the wider London region, and to combine this with concentrated development in new towns within the region which were to take overspill population from London. In this way population densities could be reduced in Inner London, while preserving the recreational opportunities of Londoners and the existing rural character of much of the South East. The long-term significance of the Green Belt and wartime and immediate postwar planning policy is that they imposed constraints on the outward spread of London for the first time since the industrial revolution. The political and economic consequences of these constraints and conflicts over their implementation became one of the central themes of the history of postwar London.

Attempts to resolve the housing problems of Inner London before 1939 were largely through the LCC policy of building local authority housing in the suburbs, including, for example, the very large estate at Dagenham in Essex. In the face of considerable resistance from wealthier suburban authorities, the estates tended to be concentrated in lower social status suburban areas. The wartime planning innovations sought to reinforce this policy through planned decentralization to new towns in the wider London region, combined with a policy of public redevelopment in the suburbs. The need for this redevelopment was increased by the extent of wartime destruction.

The problems of the transport system were now recognized, but not seriously addressed. As suggested earlier, there was substantial private-sector investment in railways, and this had underpinned the growth of the suburbs. There had, however, been little road-building, and there was an emerging problem of adapting London to the growing use of the car, given that its urban structure had largely been built on the basis of public transport. A considerable emphasis in London wartime planning was devoted to road proposals, but in the postwar period they were to remain a relatively intractable problem.

The wartime period also saw major developments in social policy, though, as in previous periods, these developments were under national control. Two are particularly significant for our account. First, the social policy innovations were to lead to a very significant increase in the scale of state social provision, and its extension to wider areas of people's lives. One particular consequence was a significant growth in the responsibilities of local government bodies. The LCC and the London boroughs took on increasingly wide-ranging roles, which included both social provision and control over the built environment. In the case of the LCC, some of this development occurred before the war, as Morrison sought to expand its activities after Labour gained control in 1934.

Secondly, the Education Act of 1944 at last extended free secondary education to the whole population. This somewhat mitigated the class-divided nature of the preceding education system, which had depended heavily on parents' resources. The school-leaving age had only been raised to 14 in 1918, and the resources to implement this had been extremely stretched and unevenly available. Moreover, the public system was becoming divided between grammar schools, which promoted academic achievement, technical schools, and other secondary schools. In spite of this, in the twentieth century mobility rates in Britain as a whole do not appear to have been lower than in the United States (Cutright, 1968; Tyree et al., 1981), which had a much more egalitarian school system. Social mobility seems to have been generated primarily by the expansion in the number of middle-class jobs. This itself was significantly promoted by the growth of state services.

Comparisons

In sum, then, we find a good deal of similarity in political and social developments between London and New York. In both cities the local welfare state expands and the indigenous working class becomes more powerful, if not dominant, in municipal politics. The main differences lie first in the increasing ascendancy of Greater London and the South East region in the British national economy. Second, public intervention in housing and planning establishes the basis for a much more rational pattern of greenbelts, new towns, and decentralized council housing estates in London. In part for this reason, the construction of public housing never becomes the vehicle in London for large-scale redevelopment of the central city. Nor does London produce a Robert Moses capable of developing infrastructure that would transform the pattern of metropolitan development. Instead London builds few new roads and remains committed to a transit-based pattern of decentralized development.

PROBLEMS OF THE INNER CITY: 1960–1973

Decentralization of manufacturing and suburbanization now strongly affected New York and London, but particularly New York, given the city's dependence on its own tax base. So, too, did sharp declines in the ports of New York and London. These processes constituted the first stages of the massive economic restructuring that would accelerate with the Organization of Petroleum Exporting Countries (OPEC) embargo of 1973. They left the population of the two inner cities increasingly disadvantaged economically. In addition, and particularly in New York, immigration and migration changed the racial composition of the lower classes and introduced a racial politics which could not be contained by the institutional arrangements that had successfully incorporated the white working class during the mid-century. The period ended in a politically induced fiscal crisis in New York, and with collapse of the manufacturing economies of both cities.

New York

Flows of people and capital

By 1969 New York could look back at three decades of economic prosperity.[25] Although manufacturing had lost a quarter million jobs after its 1953 peak, other sectors compensated. Riding the national wave of economic expansion in the 1960s, and driven by finance, insurance, real estate (FIRE), and other service industries, the city reached an historic employment high of 3.75 million in 1969 (cf. 3.47 million in 1949).[26] Whereas in 1949 30 percent of city employment was in manufacturing (1.04 million jobs), 20 years later almost 300,000 jobs had been lost, with 20 percent now employed in that sector. Conversely, employment in FIRE and other services increased from 844,000 (24 percent) to 1.26 million (33 percent). Partly in response to minority group pressure, government employment (mainly municipal) also expanded in the two decades from 11 percent to 15 percent of total employment, adding almost 200,000 jobs (Temporary Commission, 1976, table 1). The rest of the New York region remained virtually unchanged in manufacturing, and expanded sharply in the growth sectors of FIRE and service industries. Thus, the pattern of change was similar in the city and the region to the nation as a whole.[27]

At the beginning of the decade few would have predicted that most of the 1970s would be marked by economic contraction. Yet the combination of suburbanization and regional shift decimated manufacturing, with the decline growing more precipitous once international restructuring intensified after 1973 (N. I. Fainstein and S. S. Fainstein, 1988, table 7.2). Moreover, the service economy also went into recession, and government employment was sharply cut with the fiscal crisis of the seventies. On average, the city lost 80,000 jobs per year between 1970 and 1977, a toll that reached roughly one-sixth of its employment base. Economic growth, however, was not the central problematic of public discourse until well after decline set in. Rather, public and private elites concerned themselves with managing what was expected to be a gradual transition to an office-based economy under attack from racial minorities demanding political power and social services.

The political mobilization of blacks and Hispanics (then almost entirely Puerto Rican) was predicated upon wholesale transformation of the city's demographics. Rapid suburbanization after the war along with sharply increased standards of living encouraged an exodus of more affluent white households (the descendants of the European immigrants of the previous period).[28] The non-Hispanic white population declined by more than 800,000 during the 1950s, by another 1.2 million in the sixties, and by another 120,000 each year during the seventies (N. I. Fainstein and S. S. Fainstein, 1988, table 7.1). Aggregate contraction of the white population, and particularly of middle-income families, was accompanied by a shift in its center of gravity to the more recently developed areas of Queens and Staten Island, and of course to suburban municipalities. The black and Hispanic population expanded from about 1 million in 1950 (or 12 percent of the total) to 3 million (or 37 percent of the total) by 1970 in a highly segregated residential pattern (Sternlieb and Hughes, 1975, p. 105, ex. 2). By then ghettos occupied large expanses of previously white central Brooklyn and southern Queens, as well as the South Bronx and northern Manhattan.[29]

Political actors and programs

Politics in New York City was greatly affected by interrelated national forces that pushed the country toward the left in the 1960s. The civil rights movement turned northward and became increasingly radicalized as the decade progressed. Partly in response to this danger in the streets, liberal Democratic regimes expanded the US welfare state. Seeking to incorporate recently urbanized blacks into its electoral base, Democratic Party elites in the Kennedy and Johnson administrations elaborated a series of urban programs that at once channeled resources to local governments and helped to mobilize the black population. The contradictions of these reforms from the top produced a tumultuous urban politics as cities became the contested sites for alternative visions of how minority groups would be incorporated into the political system (see Marris and Rein, 1973; N. I. Fainstein and S. S. Fainstein, 1974). At the same time, and for these reasons, local governments greatly grew in size and functional responsibility.

In New York City the orientation of the governing regime had begun to shift by 1960. Mayor Robert Wagner, himself a product of the Tammany Hall Democratic political machine, was under increasing pressure from middle-class liberal reformers and a nascent cast of civil rights leaders. In running for the last of his three terms (1962–5), Wagner opposed and defeated the regular Democratic Party organization, defining himself as a programmatic leader committed to expansion of governmental services and civil rights (see Shefter, 1985).

The second and more radical stage of reorientation of the city's governing regime began with the election of John Lindsay, a liberal Republican Congressman who represented the so-called silk stocking constituency of Manhattan's Upper East Side.[30] His inauguration as a "fusion" mayor (in the tradition, he claimed, of LaGuardia), signaled a political alliance between the progressive wing of the business elite and restive minority groups. Lindsay was one of the mayors who established, in the words of Robert Salisbury (1964), a new convergence of power in American cities. He and his colleagues sought simultaneously to modernize city government through emulating private-sector management techniques, to attract private development capital and upper-middle-class residents to the central city, and to increase the share of the urban poor in the proceeds of an affluent society. Lindsay, more than most, stressed this third aim (Yates, 1974).

Like his predecessor, Lindsay strongly supported housing programs for low- and moderate-income groups. Until 1950 public housing in New York was mainly a white program with some racial integration, a consequence of the link between public housing and slum clearance that was largely restricted to white Lower Manhattan. But in the next two decades inmigration of blacks and Puerto Ricans, white prosperity, and government placement of welfare families in the projects dramatically changed the racial composition of tenants, with a consequent loss of the program's electoral popularity. New York State bond referenda for public housing were defeated in 1964 and 1965. Combined with white communal opposition and cutbacks in federal funds under President Nixon, the loss of state aid ground the nation's largest effort at social housing to a halt during Lindsay's first term (1966–9). Of the 41,000 units built during the 1960s, two-thirds were legacies of the Wagner administration (N. I. Fainstein and S. S. Fainstein, 1988, table 7.4). Thus, while various anti-poverty programs like Community Action, Model Cities, Legal Services, and Job Training channeled resources into the city's ghettos, the much more important redistributive and planning capacity provided by social housing was lost just as it was most needed, and precisely because of the increasing significance of race in local and national politics.

The decline of the public housing program meant that publicly supported housing became increasingly dependent on subsidized nonprofit and private developers. This housing was targeted to the mainly white, upper working and lower middle classes (see chapter 7). The most important efforts were sponsored by a nonprofit corporation, the United Housing Foundation, founded by local labor unions, and a New York State program reinvigorated by liberal Republican Governor Nelson Rockefeller. Many subsidized units were built on land in Manhattan previously cleared by urban renewal projects, thereby replacing vast tracts of inexpensive tenement housing with more costly units and precluding reoccupancy by the black and Hispanic poor (who increasingly moved into the South Bronx and downtown Brooklyn).

The mindset of liberal elites in the mid-sixties was that one of the causes of urban poverty was the rigidity and inefficiency of the civil service bureaucracies established earlier in the century. These problems were compounded by the entrenched interests of social groups that had used public employment as a source of mobility – in New York, Irish and Italian Catholics and Jews. Lindsay's governmental strategy was consistent with this analysis as well as with the new federal programs based upon it.

Shefter's (1985, p. 88) formulation in terms of three broad dimensions succinctly captures what at first glance might appear to have been contradictory emphases. Lindsay sought to centralize the city's proliferation of departments, commissions, and boards into modern administrative agencies, rationally organized and directed by a cadre of professional managers, often drawn from elite business and academic positions. He also circumvented bureaucracies out of his control by establishing parallel institutions performing similar functions; the Community Action and Model Cities programs are cases in point. Finally, he sought to elaborate new structures to facilitate direct community participation in governmental service delivery, bypassing the inadequate route of elected officials, and empowering bureaucratic clients. Thus, he supported decentralization and community control of public education (thereby reversing the outcomes of "reform" at the turn of the century), citizen boards for hospitals and other health care agencies, "little city halls" to monitor government agencies, and a civilian review board for the Police Department.

> It is only a slight simplification to say that centralization was a technique with which the administration sought to influence its upper and middle class allies and decentralization was a technique for enhancing the influence of its nonwhite allies. The Lindsay administration, however, was unable to control the political forces that its decentralization proposal unleashed. (*Shefter*, 1985, *pp.* 89–90)

Space precludes a detailed discussion here of the endless demonstrations, sit-ins, and conflicts associated with the urban social movements of the sixties and early seventies (for which, see N. I. Fainstein and S. S. Fainstein, 1974). Suffice it to say that the demands of minority groups, especially blacks, for an increased share of public jobs, governmental services, and political power met quickly with opposition from white voters and the government employees under attack. Lindsay's strategy and personal charisma prevented a major civil disturbance in New York, when every other big city was beset with riots. Yet it probably contributed to increased racial polarization and a sense among working-class whites that they were being asked to pay the material costs of social justice while the city's business elite remained insulated, sent its children to private schools, and lived in expensive white neighborhoods or suburban jurisdictions.

Even as the Wagner and especially the Lindsay administrations increased their spending on the poor, they continued to support major efforts at restructuring the built environment of Manhattan, converting the southern half of the island from a centre of manufacturing and shipping to offices, shops, and housing for the city's upper classes. David Rockefeller and his Chase Bank established the Downtown-Lower Manhattan Association (DLMA) in 1957. DLMA acted as a private planning and development agency advancing the program of financial institutions in Lower Manhattan to redevelop an area suffering from industrial abandonment and inadequate new office construction. The Port Authority, with the help and guidance of Governor Nelson Rockefeller, reshaped and expanded DLMAs proposal for a "world trade center"; when the facility opened in 1972 it represented a public investment of more than $1 billion and added more than 10 million square feet of office space. Lindsay supported two other critical elements of the DLMA plan, the Lower Manhattan Expressway (which ironically would have destroyed the then unfashionable and unnamed manufacturing district of SoHo) and the Second Avenue Subway, though neither got built.

Lindsay encouraged New York State agencies to invest heavily in the Manhattan core and to target benefits to upper-income residents. Thus, the New York State Urban Development Corporation constructed more than 2,000 housing units on Roosevelt Island, adjacent to the midtown eastside, 70 percent of which were rented to middle- and upper-income households (Brilliant, 1975, p. 79); the Port Authority, as noted, developed the World Trade Center; and the Battery Park City Authority issued bonds for construction of millions of square feet of office space and luxury housing on the Hudson River landfill created by excavation for the World Trade Center. One of the reasons for the fiscal crisis of the mid-seventies was the strain on resources caused by Lindsay's attempt simultaneously to assist the lower classes and to establish the Manhattan infrastructure necessary for office-based production and managerial-class consumption.

Legacies of the period

The fiscal strains which eventually reached crisis proportions in 1975 were directly rooted in the simultaneous expansion of the scope of New York City's governmental responsibilities and in its inability to control regional and national forces that determined its financial capacity. Each of the city's major ventures in the sixties expanded its expenditure base. The establishment of decentralized institutions drained the budget because reformers lacked the capacity to dismantle the redundant central apparatus. In the city the growth of the US welfare state was translated into a sharp increase in welfare, health care, and educational expenditures. While a major proportion of these local activities was funded through intergovernmental transfers, New York locally financed a greater share than did other cities. When the federal government moved away from addressing the urban crisis under Nixon and Ford, the city was politically unable to cut expenditures sufficiently. Furthermore, reorganization of the built environment added substantially to debt service. Thus, the city's bankruptcy originated both in major and largely successful efforts to modernize its built environment and in programs that directly benefited capital rather than the poor.

The capacity of the city to realize gains from regional development was markedly reduced. Economic expansion during the period was much greater in the region than within the city itself. Because there was no effective mechanism for regional planning, vast areas of New York City could lie abandoned, while new factories and warehouses were constructed in outlying areas. Middle- and upper-income white households moved to the suburbs, where they could encapsulate themselves in self-financed political jurisdictions, even while the city became the home of the region's poor, with their high demands on services and extremely low tax payments. The more New York was perceived as dominated by minority groups, the greater were the efforts of other jurisdictions in the region to protect themselves fiscally and socially from the city's "undesirable" population.

Whatever the perception, however, the fact was that minority empowerment had not proceeded very far by 1973. For a variety of reasons minority-based social movements were demobilizing, so pressure in the streets sharply abated. Electoral representation of blacks and Puerto Ricans remained limited to a few members of the city council and sometimes the Manhattan borough president. While a cadre of civil rights leaders had moved into government employment, and various anti-poverty agencies had been transformed into political machines, the political incorporation of an expanding minority population remained an unfulfilled legacy of the sixties.

London

Flows of people and capital

London's economy in this third period had more in common with the economic structure of the first period than with the years in between.

Although it no longer enjoyed a hegemonic role in the world economy, as Britain had largely divested itself of its empire, the City of London experienced an absolute increase in its significance due to the growing scale of the international economic system. Moreover, the wider complex of corporate services in Central London was expanding rapidly. In aggregate the Central London economy experienced considerable growth, at a much higher level than in the interwar period. There was a significant increase in demand for office space, and construction and redevelopment continued rapidly even after the initial surge created by repair of wartime damage. This represented the first major redevelopment wave in Central London since the mid-nineteenth century. In part it was a response to demands to reshape London as a center for international business, but it was an essentially unplanned process, which took on increasingly the character of a speculative property boom.

By contrast, and in parallel with the first period, manufacturing in the core area of the conurbation entered a prolonged period of decline, which was only partly compensated by growth on the periphery. The decline, concentrated in Inner London in the 1960s, encompassed the whole of Greater London in the 1970s, and led to a more rapid rate of manufacturing job loss than in any other British conurbation. Greater London lost around 500,000 manufacturing jobs (or about a third of its original total) between 1961 and 1974. The Port of London within the boundaries of Greater London, with much of its related warehousing and wholesaling activities, was also declining rapidly. Both contractions paralleled those of New York. Long-term growth in employment in publicly funded health, education, and welfare services and the cushioning effects of fiscal transfers from central government meant, however, that the contraction did not take on the features of a combined social, economic, and fiscal crisis like that experienced by New York in the 1970s. Nevertheless, this radical restructuring of the economy undermined many of the features which had served to stabilize the labor market in the interwar period. It also left large derelict industrial areas, which were to prove an intractable problem for planners in the 1970s who sought socially balanced redevelopment under pressure from Labour local authorities.

By the 1960s Inner London was also experiencing rapid population decline. It lost 460,000 people between 1961 and 1971, while the outer area of Greater London lost 80,000. At the same time a ring including much of the Green Belt and the towns beyond was growing rapidly, gaining 800,000 in the decade. This area sent 450,000 commuters into London by 1971, and was also a recipient of considerable industrial and office decentralization from London of firms still tied to a wider London economy.

Population decentralization was distinctly socially skewed. The public-sector New and Expanded Towns Programmes accounted for only 15 percent of migrants, as the vast majority of migrants out of London were going to new private housing. The opportunities to move were very limited for those with lower incomes. A survey carried out in 1980 found that almost 40 percent of London heads of households earned less than £80 per week, but this group accounted for only 7 percent of all moves (Gordon et al., 1983). In the 1981 Census 32 percent of men in Inner London were in less skilled occupations, but this group accounted for only 10 percent of all moves out of London. Movement into public-sector housing in the New Towns was also skewed towards the skilled working class (Deakin and Ungerson, 1977). The processes of decentralization thus left behind the less skilled and those on lower incomes, or without incomes, who were increasingly trapped in the inner city.

The 1960s were the major period of overseas immigration to Britain, particularly from Commonwealth areas in the Caribbean and the Indian subcontinent. Almost a million people arrived between 1955 and 1971. Inner London was the most significant destination for that immigration. Increasingly, the "inner city problem" acquired a racial dimension and intergroup conflict intensified. At the end of the 1960s governments introduced more restrictive immigration policies.[31] By 1971 the black and Asian population represented about 6 percent of London's population. It was somewhat concentrated spatially, but did not take on the form of racial ghettos dominated by minority groups in any way comparable to those of New York.

There was intense reconstruction and redevelopment of housing, largely in the form of substantial local authority housing estates. These estates caused a single-tenure working class to concentrate in large areas of inner east London, resulting in the persistence of preexisting social and economic problems combined, in many cases, with an extremely unpopular physical form. By 1971 local authority housing accounted for 30 percent of the stock in Inner London (rising to 42 percent by 1981). In the meanwhile the 1960s also saw the beginnings of a movement back into parts of the inner city by middle-class households, renovating the better quality older housing. This gentrification was to lead to increasing political conflict in parts of London. Overall, then, the direction of population flows was similar to those of New York, but the magnitude of racial and class restructuring was much less in London, and public provision of housing accommodation was far greater. The fiscal effects were entirely different under the centralized British welfare state, which sharply expanded in this period.

Political actors and their agendas

The stabilization of London politics, built around a relatively powerful, Labour-dominated, London County Council, covering Inner London, and a set of smaller, largely Conservative, local authorities in the suburbs, began to break down in the 1960s. Within this long-drawn-out transformation of the politics of London, three main strands can be identified. The first was the declining salience of the Morrisonian Labour politics based on local government provision of a high level of social services. The second was the growth of a politics around land development issues. The third strand had older roots – the intensification of a suburban politics concerned with the protection of enclaves.

The social recomposition of London had a particularly serious effect on the traditional mode of Inner London Labour politics. The outmigration of much of the skilled working class removed some of the better organized sections of the labor movement and caused the entrenched local party organizations to become increasingly unrepresentative of the remaining population. In particular, ethnic minorities were hardly incorporated in the political process at this stage, and tended to be excluded from public housing.

Moreover, decentralization, formerly the objective of policy in London, produced new problems for the inner boroughs, faced with fiscal difficulties stemming from economic decline in Inner London. The incomes of local authorities based on rates and government grants, determined in part by population, were stagnant or contracting in real terms, while the cost of delivering services to a smaller population remained high. Pressures on public services led to declining quality in many areas, and hence to increasing dissatisfaction with government among large sections of the population, particularly given rising standards of living and expectations. Housing was especially the object of criticism, as redevelopment activity produced unpopular, high-rise housing estates. Together these factors led to a serious erosion of support for the Labour Party in Inner London in the late 1960s. This was reflected in the borough elections of 1968, when Labour lost many of its previous strongholds to the Conservatives.

Redevelopment generated a new politics of resistance. There was a growing concern on the fringes of the central business district that traditional activities and housing were being displaced to make way for office developments, and a perception that borough councils of both parties were providing inadequate representation for community views. Residential communities became increasingly alienated from local government, as they perceived it to be managerialist and unresponsive

(Cockburn, 1976). The attempt to resolve traffic congestion problems by building a large network of urban motorways generated an even higher level of protest.[32]

The attempts to resolve the housing problems of Inner London, combined with the rate of spontaneous out-migration, were responsible for generating political conflicts at the level of the whole region. The inability of the newly founded Greater London Council (GLC) to deal with its responsibility for a metropolitan housing strategy was compounded by the resistance of Outer London boroughs to the development of GLC public housing. The impasse exacerbated the spatial polarization of London between a working-class inner area and middle-class suburbs (Young and Kramer, 1978). The fragmentation of London regional government intensified the conflicts around the protection of enclaves, resulting in the problem of regional planning discussed in the next section.

Programmatic innovations and unresolved conflicts

Programmatic innovation in the 1960s and 1970s still depended on a legacy from the wartime planning reforms. Politicians and planners were working with an agenda based on regional planning and controlled decentralization to resolve the problems of Inner London. These policies, however, were running into intense political opposition, were working through an inadequate institutional structure, and often proved to have perverse results. The problems of London in this period must thus be seen in terms of both the center and the periphery. They were linked by processes of migration and urban growth and redevelopment, and by the operation of the planning system.

The British planning system succeeded in containing urban growth and in limiting the conversion of rural to urban land. The result, however, was unintended private-market suburban development, rather than planned, self-contained new communities (Hall et al., 1973). It was characterized by rapid inflation of land prices and a socially skewed pattern of settlement. The effort to address these issues through the framework of the GLC largely faltered. With the collapse of its metropolitan housing strategy and the rejection of the road proposals in the Greater London Development plan, it had little remaining positive role in the strategic planning of London. Instead the powers of the 32 London boroughs increased.

The scale of decentralization led to growing demands from surrounding counties for a means of slowing the rate at which new house-building was taking place around London. This was reinforced by projections which suggested an acceleration in the rate of population growth. This resistance led to a significant revival in the role of regional planning. A series of planning reports during this period stressed the interdependence of the whole South East region, and proposed the creation of at least four new city regions in the South East. Although the downward revision of population projections removed the perceived need for these cities, the conflicts over accommodating growth in the region were not resolved, nor were problems of Inner London really faced in the regional planning process. Regional planning itself went into decline with the onset of recession in the 1970s.

There was another strand of innovation which related more directly to the perceived problems of the inner city. These were seen very much in terms of problems of social polarization, and particularly increasing spatial segregation evidenced in the emergence of poverty ghettos. One of the key terms of the debate was "social mix." It was substantially affected by the mid-1960s riots in American cities, though equivalent events had not yet occurred in Britain (except for anti-immigration riots in Notting Hill in West London in 1958). It gave rise to a set of spatially targeted national government programs, partly based on US experience, such as the Community Development Projects. This strand was to become more significant in the 1970s with the 1977 government White Paper *Policy of the Inner Cities*, which terminated many of the decentralization policies. Nonetheless, the weakness of community development policy, particularly in the context of rapid industrial decline, combined with the collapse of the metropolitan housing strategy, meant that there were few remaining institutional means of resolving the problems of Inner London.

A CENTURY IN COMPARISON

By the onset of the recession of the mid-1970s, both London and New York were seen as cities with severe problems of adjustment to changing conditions. At that stage, however, their differences appeared greater than their similarities, with New York experiencing much more intense problems of both economic decline and political conflict (although within a far less disastrous national context). A focus on the 1980s, on the other hand, would be more inclined to stress the similarities, as both cities appeared to strengthen their roles in the world financial system, and enter a period of growth based largely on that role. Some of the political differences also diminished, as political conflict in London increased, as race came to take on a greater role in London politics, and as a planning policy much more oriented to business growth was fostered there.

Short-term comparisons, then, give us a rather confused picture of similarities and differences. This chapter, by examining a longer period, has sought to clarify the comparison and bring into sharper focus the areas where the cities share characteristics and where they diverge. It has also brought out the distinctiveness of the role of the two cities within their respective nations.

We have suggested a broad similarity of economic structure and of processes of economic restructuring. There have been differences of timing and of intensity of change, but in the main the chapter has identified similar processes operating in the two cities. These are consequences of the parallel and interlinked role the two cities have played over long periods of time. Their economies produced similar social structures comprising a substantial middle class characteristically employed by big organizations and a blue-collar population characteristically working for rather small firms. Differences in physical geography and in the processes of development of the built environment have led to differences in the spatial distribution of these classes. More important, differences in processes of population growth of the two cities, and particularly the role of international migration in New York, as well as migration from the southern US by blacks, have led the cities to have very different ethnic and racial composition, with significant consequences for politics and social policy. In London the dominant dividing line has been class, while in New York it has been race and ethnicity, and, as we have shown, this has been a substantial impediment to working-class organization.

It is in the area of political structures and patterns of governmental intervention that the differences between the cities over the long term have been most marked. The differences may be summarized under two broad heads: the greater autonomy from national political institutions of New York, as compared with London, and the greater level of state intervention in social policy and urban planning in Britain, compared to the United States.

A contrast running through this chapter has been the centrality of national government decisions to the development of London (for example, the repeated attempts to reform London government, and the Green Belt and the related postwar planning system) and the very much more independent and active role of New York City (for example, its leading role in the construction of transport infrastructure and its ability to mount a substantial public housing program in the face of niggardly federal support). Of course, there have been exceptions. For example, the London County Council did have a leading role at some periods in social welfare and housing investments, whereas developments in New York have responded to federal policies, as in the construction programs of the Depression and the fiscal crisis of the 1970s, which was in significant part federally induced. Nevertheless, the British political system is very much more centralized than that of the United States and this has been important in shaping New York and London. New York City has been a strong unitary authority, covering a large part of the core of the metropolitan area, while London's government has been characterized by fragmentation. Thus, New York could implement more or less coherent construction programs within its boundaries, while the London boroughs tended to go their own ways. Yet in Britain the national government was able and willing to intervene to manage the physical development of London over a wider geographical scale, while in New York there was no body capable of undertaking regional planning and influencing development in suburban jurisdictions.

The other major difference has been the higher level of intervention in social welfare spending and in urban planning in Britain, in part a consequence of the strength of working-class politics at the national level. Many of the interventions here, while largely national in inspiration, had significant urban effects, and they served to mitigate market inequalities. For example, the strength of support for public housing from national government before the 1970s allowed the fragmented governments of London to build a very significantly higher level of public housing than in New York City, a level sufficient for it to become the majority working-class tenure in Inner London, and to permit large numbers of skilled workers to leave Inner London to suburban public housing. Until the 1970s this intervention went a considerable distance in resolving the housing problems of Inner London, though at the expense of an increase in social segregation. But this segregation was considerably lower than that produced in the New York region by a totally dominant private housing market combined with strong suburban governments largely able to control their own social composition. International contrasts along similar lines could be traced in social services, income support, and health care.

The central social divisions in London, based on class, were largely mediated directly by national government welfare policies, or, in the case of housing, by a heavily subsidized national policy implemented by local government. In New York, on the other hand, the central social divisions around race and ethnicity were largely mediated at the level of local government policy, and hence conflicts were more explicitly focused on the city.

It would be simplistic, however, just to assert a higher level of state intervention in London, and an even greater mistake to attribute this only to ideological differences in approaches to the role of the state. The situation varies across policy domains, and in many areas the differences in ultimate results are rather small. Two areas where the outcomes were unquestionably distinct were housing and public transport. In contrast to housing, in the construction of roads the level of government intervention was very much higher in New York; the city was one of the first to develop a dense urban motorway network (although London's public transit performance exceeded New York's). By contrast road investment in London proved to be an intractable problem. We have also suggested that there was a higher commitment to education, as a means of integrating an immigrant population, in New York than in London. The area of regional planning was one in which the policy differences were at their greatest, but the differences in outcomes were probably significantly less, and such differences are mainly to be found in the suburbs.

NOTES

1   Figure is for the area that would be consolidated into New York City in 1898.
2   The population of Manhattan reached its historic high of 2.4 million in 1910.
3   Estimates are 50.0 percent foreign-born white and 2.4 percent black in 1880; 52.8 percent foreign-born white and 2.7 percent black in 1910 (Lampard, 1986, table 10).
4   By 1910 there were about 1.25 million Jews, at least a million of whom had immigrated from Russia and Poland since 1882 (Lowi, 1963, p. 53).
5   Extrapolating from Hammack's (1982, table 3–6) estimate, we can describe class structure in 1900 roughly as follows: 4 percent upper- and upper-middle-class white collar, 33 percent middle- and lower-class white collar, 23 percent skilled working class, 30 percent semi-skilled, and 10 percent unskilled labourers. Much of the work of the bottom strata was extremely insecure (or "casual"), since it was largely not unionized and was concentrated in garment manufacturing, construction, and port-related activities – all industries with great fluctuation in their demand for labor. Except for its very different ethnic composition, the character of the labor force was quite similar to that of London at this time.
6   It should be noted, however, that New York experienced much more urban competition and was much less a primate city than London. Thus, while the value of international cargoes handled in New York doubled between 1880 and 1910, the port's share of US foreign trade declined from 57 percent to 47 percent (Hammack, 1982, table 2–1).
7   In the decentralized US urban system, New York still accounted for about 25 percent of national personal income in 1910 (Lampard, 1986, table 5).

8 After the turn of the century there was also decentralization of space-intensive industries to new manufacturing districts in Queens (Newtown Creek and Long Island City), the South Bronx, and New Jersey (Newark, Jersey City, Hoboken, and Paterson).

9 Katznelson calls this dynamic separation of workplace from home the building of urban trenches in the American system. As we will see, these trenches are never really dislodged, even as the social combatants change in major ways later in the century.

10 Perhaps 85 percent of the entire region's economy and population lived in New York City during the first decade of the century. The city comprised 68 percent of the 17 county Standard Statistical Area, which extended far beyond the bounds of the regional economy at that time.

11 As Hammack shows, however, the social composition of the old neighborhood school boards was not terribly different from that of the new city-wide board; both were almost entirely in the hands of business leaders and professionals. The real winners in the power shift were to be the professional educators, who elaborated in the following decades a closed bureaucratic system nearly autonomous from control by any external political forces, whether mass or elite.

12 Until the twentieth century, municipal governments regulated land-use only to the extent that they mapped streets for improved areas and issued franchises to transportation and utility companies. Governmental intervention expanded in New York at the behest of the old merchant class, whose large department stores and fashionable lady shoppers on Fifth and Sixth Avenues were threatened by factory lofts and immigrant workers. Thus, the city became a national leader in 1916 when it enacted a zoning ordinance that loosely guided future development, mainly by protecting new residential and commercial areas from industrial uses. While zoning would be elaborated thereafter, it would remain largely isolated from any more general planning conceptions or administrative mechanisms until a brief foray into this domain in the 1960s.

13 The name derived from the floor plan of the building. In front and back these structures filled the entire lot width of 25 feet, thus permitting no side windows. But for about the 75-foot middle of their 100-foot length, the buildings were pinched in 5 feet on both sides, like a very fat dumbbell. The air shaft, 10 feet wide, between adjacent buildings provided ventilation to interior rooms.

14 Estimates by Shannon (1935) suggest that for each decade from 1851 to 1891 at least 83 percent of in-migrants to London came from the remainder of Britain.

15 The absence of intensive housing redevelopment in Inner London, of the form that took place in New York, reflects several factors: the relatively lower level of demand, in the absence of large flows of low-income immigrants; the complexities of land ownership in London, where the initial building process created a very fragmented pattern of long-term leaseholding; and the rapidity with which new housing was being built in nearby

suburbs. London also lacked the water barriers that limited much of New York's housing to Lower Manhattan. Cultural factors may also have played a part, particularly the apparent English aversion to apartment houses (i.e. tenements for the poor, "French flats" for the upper classes). The British upper classes also seemed less willing than the American to relocate their residential districts when faced with working-class encroachment.

16   Britain had strong, nationally organized political parties whose local organization had a negligible effect on the development of the national party. In this they contrasted sharply with parties in the US.

17   The weakness of London's government structure meant that most efforts to deal with urban problems were left either to the private sector or to national government. Exceptions before the late 1880s were in the areas of public health and building regulation, where local government had effective powers of detailed control, though no area planning powers.

18   Technically, the "region" or the "metropolitan area" is used here to mean the US Census Bureau's New York Standard Consolidated Area (SCA), which includes New York City and 12 counties in New York State and New Jersey.

19   The city's black population, which had occupied part of the midtown west side in 1900, was now ghettoized in Harlem and a small area in central Brooklyn.

20   For example, blue-collar manufacturing and gray-collar service workers comprised 50 to 60 percent of Manhattan's population in the 1930s (N. I. Fainstein and S. S. Fainstein, 1989a, table 4.2).

21   Tobier argues, persuasively, that the city maintained its economic position because there was so little new investment nationally in manufacturing during the Depression and then such extreme demand during the war. The relative inefficiency of the aging capital plant, therefore, did not hurt the local economy until the postwar period. By that time, former immigrants were getting higher wages, so exploitation of labor was no longer a sufficient comparative advantage to compensate for inadequate capitalization and high operating costs.

22   The New York City Planning Commission was established only in 1940 and was a very weak body until the collapse of Robert Moses' empire in the 1960s.

23   Had it not been for the weakness of the City of London, the region would have done even better. The collapse of the international finance system and the decline in world trade in the period after 1929, created in part by the inability of Britain to retain its leading position in the financial system, led to a stagnation of the City and a decline in its turnover. It was no longer as significant an engine of growth of London's economy as it had been before the war, or was to be from the 1960s onwards. Combined with the growth of manufacturing industry, this sharpened the contrast in economic structure of London between this period and those that preceded and followed it. Nonetheless, even the Central London economy continued

to expand on the basis of the national government and the associated concentration of company headquarters and related services.

24 In New York the main "suburban" development took place in the city boroughs of Brooklyn and the Bronx. What Americans call the suburbs, i.e. political jurisdictions beyond the boundaries of the city, did expand in the 1920s. Most of these followed railroad lines and were limited to relatively affluent residents.

25 Parts of this section are drawn from N. I. Fainstein and S. S. Fainstein, 1989b, pp. 45–85.

26 The unemployment rate for city residents stood at only 3.1 percent in 1968, lower than the US average (Temporary Commission, 1977, p. 19).

27 But the city's economy declined relative to the remainder of the region – from 65 percent of regional employment in 1953 to 54 percent in 1973 – as 1.2 million jobs were added in the suburbs while city employment remained steady (Sternlieb and Hughes, 1975, p. 116, ex. 10). And both the city and its region lagged considerably behind the nation as a whole in overall growth – increasing employment by 21 percent between 1953 and 1973, compared with 45 percent nationally (Sternlieb and Hughes, 1975, p. 111, ex. 6).

28 While the city's population remained unchanged at 7.9 million between 1950 and 1970, it comprised 61 percent of the metropolitan region at the beginning of the period and 49 percent at the end, mainly the result of white suburbanization and minority group in-migration (N. I. Fainstein and S. S. Fainstein, 1988, table 7.1).

29 In Manhattan the black population never expanded south from Harlem, in good part because long-standing black enclaves in midtown were removed through the urban renewal program in the 1950s and 1960s.

30 This and the following paragraph are drawn from N. I. Fainstein and S. S. Fainstein, 1988, pp. 80–1.

31 Exactly the opposite course was followed in the US, where opportunities for immigration were greatly increased, with important consequences for New York in the coming decades.

32 The road proposals in the Greater London Development Plan were responsible for 18,000 of the 23,000 objections lodged against the plan. A long-drawn-out public inquiry, from 1970 to 1972, and a switch by the Labour Party to support the protest groups for largely electoral reasons resulted in the ultimate defeat of the proposals.

3

Dynamics of the metropolitan economy

Nick Buck, Matthew Drennan, and Kenneth Newton

The long-term perspective of the previous chapter has highlighted a broad similarity both in the economic structures of London and New York and in the processes of economic restructuring operating there. In relation to the more recent global economic developments, outlined in chapter 1, each appears to be rather similarly placed, playing a quite distinctive role in relation to other areas within the two national economies. The hypothesis is that these global changes and that distinctive role together underlie the new social and economic divisions in London and New York, which are the subject of this book. This chapter examines in more detail how these global changes have affected the economies of the two cities since the 1970s, and how far they, combined with more specific factors, may have been responsible for a genuine transformation in the structure and performance of the two urban economies. In particular we are concerned with aspects of their emergent economic structure which are liable to affect the pattern of labor market opportunities and/or the way in which these are allocated (both subjects for the next chapter), and thus have implications for new social divisions in the cities.

One of the central themes of the chapter is the economic complexity of these two cities, which defy simple generalizations about their roles and economic performance. The various sectors have responded to different global processes, in different ways and at different times. Spatial units within the metropolitan regions have also changed in very different ways. The trajectories of Manhattan and Central London are different from each other, but are also distinct from the trajectories of the Bronx and Hackney, or from those of Fairfield county or Berkshire. In this chapter we have to focus both on the differences between the cities and on what they have in common which distinguishes them from other cities, while recognizing that two of the attributes they have in common are complexity and diversity.

The 1970s and 1980s have seen both marked decline and marked growth within the London and New York economies. In both cities there is abandonment in older industrial areas, or their conversion to residential uses, but also an explosion of office construction both in the center and in the suburbs, and a continued growth of new industrial premises on the periphery of the metropolitan area. The state as well as private capital has been heavily engaged in large redevelopment projects. Growth in some activities and decline in others has resulted in decisive shifts in the balance between industrial sectors, especially in their urban cores, and, as the next chapter will show, a corresponding shift in the range of job opportunities available to their labor forces. There have also been periods of years (in the 1970s) in which overall the two economies seemed locked into an irreversible decline, subsequent periods (in the mid-1980s) when a long-term revival seemed underway, only to be followed by renewed doubts as recession loomed (at the start of the 1990s).

To make sense of these changes, they need to be seen as the outcome of three interacting sets of factors: the structures which the cities inherited from their past, conditioning their response to external changes, and the economic advantages and disadvantages enjoyed by their different sectors; the fluctuating performance of their national economies; and, third, a number of general tendencies in the global economy of particular relevance to metropolitan economies. We shall start by outlining six of these global tendencies, before discussing the economic structures of London and New York, and their transformation during the 1970s and 1980s. In the light of this evidence the penultimate section of the chapter considers how the global processes, and others more specific to one or other city, have contributed to the observed changes.

SIX GLOBAL TENDENCIES IN METROPOLITAN ECONOMIES

It is still a matter of debate whether changes in the functioning of the world economy since the early 1970s represent a new economic order, and what the spatial implications of such a new order are (Lipietz, 1986; Scott and Storper, 1986; Piore and Sabel, 1984). Nevertheless, the literature on economic restructuring in advanced capitalist countries does point to six general tendencies which have been clearly evident since the ending of the long postwar boom after 1973. Some obviously have earlier origins, and the change of direction since 1973 should not be exaggerated. Taken together, however, these tendencies do appear to have had considerable significance for the course of change in metropolitan economies over this time-span.

The first of these tendencies involved a crisis in some of the core manufacturing industries which had been the leading growth sectors of the 1950s and 1960s. As the growth turned to stagnation in the mass consumer markets on which the long postwar boom was based, the scope for productivity growth based on increasing capital intensity in these core industries was also restricted. This led in turn to a breakdown of the industrial relations system combining high levels of trade unionization with relatively high wage growth, which had itself sustained the growth of consumer demand. Alongside this crisis in the old industrial order there has been a growing use of new, more flexible production systems, and an increasing product differentiation. The main spatial implication of these processes was to undermine areas dependent on the mass production industries of the interwar era – most strikingly the motor industry centers such as Birmingham, Coventry, and Detroit. The British economy as a whole has suffered on balance from these developments, with a continuing de-industrialization which has not been matched in severity in the United States.

A second tendency, which compounded these effects, has involved a new more disaggregated geography of production, leading to changes in the pattern of locational advantage. This tendency reflected new opportunities, afforded by communications improvements and international business organization, combined with increasing competitive pressures. Corporations sought to increase or maintain profits by finding cheaper production locations, particularly by separating components of the production system involving different types of labor demand, moving them to areas where the relevant labor was most readily and cheaply available. Often this involved shifts away from older industrial agglomerations with their combinations of high wages, unionized workers, and often congested or outdated production facilities. In Britain, for example, control functions tended to remain in the large cities, particularly London; research and development activities were located in attractive areas of Southern England where skilled technical and professional workers could readily be recruited; production processes using more skilled workers remained in core areas of metropolitan England; while routine assembly was shifted to the periphery (Massey, 1984). Very similar processes have been documented in the USA (Markusen, 1984). The relocation of production also crossed national boundaries, as corporations sought lower cost locations in Third World countries (Frobel, et al., 1980); however, the most substantial shifts were between advanced industrial countries, rather than between these and the periphery.

The impact of the delocalization of industry has been particularly severe in some areas, but its effect on the global cities such as London and New York was much more ambiguous. London was particularly hard hit by manufacturing counter-urbanization, but the more disaggregated geography of production was accompanied by some centralization of control functions, and in the recessions of the late 1970s and early 1980s London's economy was more resilient than that of other parts of Britain. In New York the impact of industrial decentralization was compounded through much of the 1970s by an economic crisis in the city which involved precipitate reductions in manufacturing employment, but manufacturing decline actually slowed during the national recession of the early 1980s.

Third, the increasing complexity of production processes and of corporate structures of control has led to a growing importance of intermediate or producer services, such as advertising, professional services, consultancy, computer services, cleaning, catering, and other support services. The growth of specialist firms providing these services has also allowed firms to contract out activities which they had previously undertaken for themselves, with potential scale economies, or economies in adjusting to uneven demands. Such producer services tended to be highly concentrated in larger cities, and in the US this has resulted in the emergence of a new urban hierarchy (Noyelle and Stanback, 1983). In Britain the relative weakness of regional cities as counter-magnets has meant that these services are disproportionately concentrated in London. This could be a somewhat mixed blessing, however, since these externalized services are liable to experience more marked fluctuations in employment than was likely when they were provided in-house.

The fourth tendency, in parallel with the third, has been a growth in the significance and the complexity of international financial systems. This is linked to the growing internationalization of production, with the consequent increasing financial flows to fund trade and investment, but it also reflects the growth of an international market in financial assets themselves. This market has become highly centralized, with the world divided between cities dominating continents and time zones. This has led some writers to distinguish a top tier of "global cities," preeminently New York, London, and Tokyo (Friedmann and Wolff, 1982; Sassen, 1991a). The defining feature is that important parts of the economies of these cities relate primarily to the international economy, rather than to their host nation's domestic economy. They are not of course immune to processes originating in the domestic economy. It is also important to stress that the global role of these cities is not new.. London, for example, played an even more important role in the international economy at the turn of the century than it does now, and this role had a commensurate effect on its own economy (King, 1990). The change has been the growth in the absolute scale of the international economy.

Fifth, the postwar period has seen a significant expansion in the role of states in economic management, and in the provision of social and collective services. National and local state institutions have become major employers in most capitalist societies, either directly or indirectly through subsidized private provision. This growth is most marked in the large cities, both because they stand at the top of service hierarchies and because they tend to contain the greatest concentration of client groups for state services. After the recession of the early 1970s, demands for these services continued to rise, but resources were constrained and the provision of services in large cities became particularly crisis-prone. States have also become involved in the economic problem of urban decline, as the social impact of recession in the 1970s and 1980s was spatially concentrated in inner cities.

State policy has thus come to have a major impact on the economic fortunes of the major cities, through social expenditures, and consequent employment in state services, through transfer payments to city residents, and through infrastructure investments and projects for urban regener-ation. In London the impact of the first of these was to mitigate the effects of decline in goods production industries, but this effect has been much less significant in the 1980s than in the 1970s. In New York, also, public-service employment growth has been important, but with its dependence on an uncertain local tax base it has tended to exaggerate fluctuations in other sectors – notably in the aftermath of the 1975 fiscal crisis when City employment was harshly cut back.

Finally, there have been changes in private consumption patterns in large cities. There has been a growth both in the numbers of professional, technical, or managerial workers in service industries and in their pur-chasing power. Two consequences have been an increasing demand for housing close to the city center, and the creation of a powerful new group of consumers for central city services, both public and private. Together with the growth of business travel and international tourism this has served to counteract, or even reverse, the decline in consumer services occasioned by declining city populations. During the 1980s the swing toward a more differentiated and specialized pattern of consump-tion, in place both of mass-produced goods and the use of durable goods for domestic self-provisioning of services (which had been emphasized by Gershuny, 1978), added further to the demand for marketed services. But even more fundamentally it restored the role of cities as specialist centers and arenas for spectacle and conspicuous consumption (Harvey, 1990).

These trends have not all been linked in one single process. Nevertheless, in combination they have introduced a new economic regime with distinctive implications for the large cities. However, these general tendencies have been mediated by the historic structures of different metropolitan areas. Consequently they have had such uneven impacts on these economies that there has been no simple decisive change in their economic fortunes. Instead there has been a complex pattern of both growth and decline in different sectors and in different periods. To elaborate this in relation to London and New York, we need to look in more detail at their economies.

THE ECONOMIC STRUCTURES OF LONDON AND NEW YORK

As we have already suggested, both New York and London are composed of multiple economies operating within the same space. While there are differences between the cities in the composition of these economies, reflecting differences in inherited industrial structures, and of national context, historically there do appear to have been four major components to each of their economies: first, the production and circulation of goods; second, financial and commercial services and the associated complex of higher-level corporate services; third, national administration and control functions, in both public and private sectors; and, finally, a concentration of higher-order consumer services, associated with fashion, entertainment, and culture. These economies have been subject to differing processes of growth and decline, to internal recomposition and to spatial restructuring. However, because they operate in the same territory, they are linked by competition with each other for land and labor.

The first component, the production and circulation of goods, originated in the role of these cities as the leading port of each nation, but has been reinforced by the agglomerative market effects of their size and wealth. In both cities this component has been subject to considerable spatial change and to a lengthy process of decline, discussed in the previous chapter. However, in both cases three major elements have been subject to rather different processes of change: a goods transportation and distribution sector, based around ports, airports, and road and railway networks, and with a substantial wholesaling sector involved in both domestic and international trade; an inner city manufacturing sector based on labor-intensive small scale production; and, finally, a large, more modern suburban manufacturing sector.

In London the closure of the up-river docks from the 1960s and the decline of related manufacturing and goods circulation in Inner London has removed a large part of the traditional core of inner city industry. There remains a limited concentration of clothing and furniture manufacture, food processing, and especially printing, but all of these are in decline and depend on either finding cheap sources of labor or supplying a localized Central London market. A rather different goods-based economy developed in Outer London and the surrounding Outer Metropolitan Area (OMA). This was based around electrical, electronic and mechanical engineering, vehicle manufacturing, and the mass production of consumer goods. There was also an active wholesaling and warehousing sector linked to the developing road networks and the airports. Manufacturing in the OMA has been subject to the processes of deindustrialization which have afflicted much of British manufacturing, but it remains relatively successful and includes much of the country's high-technology defense-related industry.

In New York the goods-related sector of the economy has as its core the port, the production of nondurable items (particularly such labor-intensive low-wage industries as apparel and leather goods, together with printing), and the distribution of goods (wholesale trade, warehousing, transportation by rail, truck, and water). As in London, this sector has become progressively smaller and weaker over the past 20 years. The rest of the region historically has had a concentration of goods production and distribution activities, but with a higher proportion of capital-intensive high-wage manufacturing industries (chemicals, pharmaceuticals, cosmetics, machinery, instruments, and metals) than in New York City. This is particularly concentrated in northeastern New Jersey, including areas around Newark and Jersey City which form part of the regional core. Goods production and distribution in this part of the region has not become absolutely smaller, but its growth has been feeble over the past 20 years.

The second component has been based around the financial and commercial services historically located in the central business districts, originating in the City of London and around Wall Street, but spreading outward to embrace a much wider central area, and with some tendency for parts to be decentralized to other areas of the city and the wider region. The sectoral composition of this component is very similar in London and New York, though there are some differences in the functions which the international elements perform in the world economy, with London having a dominant role in international currency and commodity trading, and insurance. It also has the larger concentration of foreign banks. New York, by contrast, is dominant in international corporate finance and stock exchange transactions (Vogel, 1988).

In both cities this sector contains two elements: the financial sectors, heavily engaged in the international economy, but also central to their domestic economies; and the complex of corporate services serving both these financial sectors and other sectors, within the cities, throughout the two nations, and, to an increasing degree, on an international scale. Both elements are characterized by nonroutine information-intensive activities for which agglomeration economies continue to be critical. In more detail, this component of the economy consists of commercial and investment banking, securities and commodities brokerages, insurance, real estate, advertising, publishing, accounting, business consulting, communications including media, legal services, computer software services, plus other services to business (also to governments and nonprofit organizations), such as air transportation and transportation services. The distinctions between various of these activities have tended to be eroded over the past 20 years, particularly as the cities have acted to maintain their competitive position via a deregulation of financial markets with the 1986 "Big Bang" in London and a series of changes between 1975 and 1988 in New York (Schwartz, 1989). These are quintessential central business district activities depending heavily on agglomeration economies. Much of their net growth in jobs over the past 20 years has actually occurred in outer areas where more routine functions are being located. But this is heavily dependent on the central areas where producer services have the dominant place in the employment structure.

The third economic component, national administration and control functions, is the one which differentiates the cities most strongly. In London it has been an important part of the economy, because of the presence of national government. This itself has been a significant employer, but it has also ensured that London has a near monopoly of the headquarters of major private and nonprofit organizations operating on a national scale, including the media, pressure groups, trade unions and employers' organizations, professional and cultural bodies. In addition London possesses a majority of the British headquarters of large industrial and commercial firms. In contrast New York houses very few federal government activities, and many of the nongovernment national organizations which are to be found in London are drawn to Washington, DC. New York's control functions depend much more on its economic than its political power, and it has contained a substantial overrepresentation of the headquarters of the largest industrial and retailing corporations of the nation. These have, however, been in substantial decline, except where firms are heavily involved in the international economy.

The fourth component consists of the higher-order consumer services. In both cities it is difficult to distinguish those parts of the consumer services which depend simply on local needs from those which constitute a separate component of the economic base, especially as the wealth of the metropolitan areas leads to the development of particularly strong local service sectors. However, in both cities particular services, such as hotels, restaurants, entertainment, museums, luxury retail shops, and air transport, clearly depend on tourism, both domestic and international. Moreover, the sheer concentration of consumer services has led to a qualitative differentiation of London and New York from other centers as the cultural capitals of their respective nations, and international centers of luxury and fashionable consumption.

In the remainder of this section we examine how these economic functions are reflected in the employment structures of the two cities, first comparing them at the level of the metropolitan region and the core city, and then examining the spatial structure in more detail. There are some difficulties in making direct comparisons between the employment structures of the two cities, given differences in employment data sources. However table 3.1 shows the main similarities and differences in terms of five broad industrial sectors for which reasonably close comparisons can be made. In overall scale the New York region (i.e. the CMSA) is about half as large again as the London metropolitan region, with approximately 8.2 million jobs, compared with about 5.6 million. The administratively bounded core areas, New York City and Greater London, are of approximately similar scale. However, there are areas in the rest of the New York region, particularly in northeastern New Jersey, which functionally belong to the core area, and these include at least another million jobs. For more precise comparisons we should ideally use a larger area than New York City to represent the core of the region.

In broad outline the industrial structures of the two metropolitan areas are quite similar. There are differences, however, with the first component activities of manufacturing and circulation accounting for around 26 percent of jobs in the New York region economy and around 30 percent in the London region. Manufacturing, in particular, is significantly more strongly represented in London than in New York. By contrast the New York share of the second component, financial and producer services, is significantly larger than that of London, particularly when comparison is made between the core areas.

The other two components cannot readily be identified in comparable employment data. There are particular problems in the different treat-

Table 3.1 The employment structures of London and New York (thousands)

	Greater London 1987	London region 1987	New York City 1988	New York region 1988
Manufacturing	482	985	367	1,178
% share	13.7	17.5	10.2	14.3
Transport and wholesale distribution	488	720	408	980
% share	13.9	12.8	11.3	12.0
Finance and producer services	753	1,021	994	1,684
% share	21.4	18.1	27.6	20.6
Private consumer services, construction, etc.	896	1,461	735	2,041
% share	25.5	25.9	20.4	24.9
Government, health, education, and social services	896	1,453	1,102	2,307
% share	25.5	25.8	30.6	28.2
Total employment	3,515	5,640	3,606	8,190

Source: UK Department of Employment, 1991; US Department of Labor, n.d.

ment of government and public-sector employment. In the US data government employees, including, for example, public school teachers, are grouped in one category, whereas in British data they are dispersed according to industrial function (e.g. education), leaving only a residual category of public administration. The only way to derive comparable figures is to group together government, health, education, and social services, whether in public or private sector. This produces the surprising result that, in spite of London's employment in central government ministries, the New York "public and social services" share is substantially higher, particularly in New York City. By implication, employment in public and social services for the local population must be very much higher in New York, although some of these will in fact be privately run.

By contrast, in the other category of "private" consumer services (e.g.

retailing, restaurants, and entertainments, together with construction and utilities) the Greater London share is significantly higher than that of New York City, though the difference is less substantial at regional level. Decentralization of these services appears to have gone substantially further in the New York region than in London.

The spatial structure of the London economy is shown in some detail in table 3.2. In spite of the decline over the previous two decades, manufacturing remains a significant sector in Outer London and the Outer Metropolitan Area – although no longer in the central area or the inner city. This suburban economy accounts for three-quarters of all manufacturing in the metropolitan region, with a heavy representation of engineering and related industries. In Central and Inner London combined manufacturing is now much smaller than the financial and producer services, but across the region as a whole it remains almost as large an employer. In fact this comparison rather understates the significance of producer services in Central and Inner London, where large elements of transport, wholesaling, miscellaneous services, and manufacturing are either part of the corporate service complex (e.g. company headquarters) or are directly dependent on it. For example, the largest manufacturing industry in this area consists of information-intensive printing and publishing – the national press, book and periodical publishing, and service printing for Central London organizations.

The financial and producer services sector itself is rather diverse. Agglomeration economies are vitally important for those parts of the sector involved with the financial markets, international business and company headquarters, which tend to be concentrated in the City and West End. Other elements, including back offices carrying out more routine functions, and establishments serving a more local and regional market, are dispersed among a series of subsidiary centers with lower rent levels. Thus the central area accounts for only about 44 percent of employment in the sector, though for 53 percent of that in financial services, and 62 percent of company headquarters. Inner London's share is likely to continue rising with the growth of office space in the redeveloped Docklands.

The private consumer services are generally distributed in proportion to population and disposable income. Hence most of the employment in this sector, especially in retailing, is to be found in Outer London and the OMA. But there is a disproportionate amount of consumer service activity in Central London, particularly in hotels, restaurants, and cultural services, reflecting the concentration of tourist spending in this area and its role as a specialist consumer center. There is a similar division in the public-service sector, with the bulk of employment

Table 3.2 Employment by industry: London region, 1987 (thousands)

	Central London	Inner London	Outer London	Greater London	Outer Metropolitan Area	London region
Agriculture	0.0	0.0	1.6	1.6	28.0	29.6
Energy and water	22.4	10.0	13.7	46.1	32.2	78.3
Chemicals and metals	5.9	8.8	32.0	46.7	63.8	110.5
Engineering	16.6	42.8	136.9	196.3	281.4	477.7
Other manufacturing	59.1	84.3	95.7	239.1	157.6	396.7
All manufacturing	**81.6**	**135.9**	**264.6**	**482.1**	**502.8**	**984.9**
Construction	14.6	50.4	71.9	137.2	98.1	235.3
Transport	103.3	73.7	139.3	316.3	127.1	443.4
Wholesale distribution	42.2	50.8	79.2	172.2	104.9	277.1
Insurance, banking, and finance	216.9	43.7	59.2	319.8	92.3	412.1
Professional and technical services	106.7	24.2	41.6	172.5	81.0	253.5
Other business services	127.2	52.0	81.7	260.9	94.8	355.7
Retail distribution	84.6	85.1	155.1	324.8	222.5	547.3
Hotels and catering	68.8	38.3	54.6	161.7	95.6	257.3
Leisure and recreation	46.6	39.1	32.8	118.5	38.4	156.9
Other personal services	23.8	40.1	41.9	105.8	51.0	156.8
Misc. services	41.8	76.1	83.0	200.0	114.1	315.0
Health and education	80.7	156.7	152.6	390.0	300.0	690.0
Public administration	116.7	80.6	107.6	304.9	142.7	447.6
All services	**1,059.3**	**760.4**	**1,028.6**	**2,848.3**	**1,464.4**	**4,312.7**
Total	**1,178.2**	**956.7**	**1,380.4**	**3,515.3**	**2,125.2**	**5,640.5**

Source: UK Department of Employment, 1991

involved in serving local populations and distributed more or less proportionately, but with a core of central government employment concentrated in Central London. The rest of Inner London also has a disproportionate share of public-service employment (amounting to 25 percent of all jobs in the area). This reflects a concentration of many of the client groups for public services, the large service demands of London as business center, and the historically high levels of expenditure of Labour-controlled Inner London boroughs.

In New York the spatial distribution of activities and its pattern of change bears a number of similarities to that in London. The regional core – New York City and the adjacent areas of New Jersey, including Newark and Jersey City – is a preponderantly service economy, attracting a net inflow of commuters from the rest of the region, but, as a result of strong processes of decentralization, now the site for barely half of the region's employment. In 1988 there were just under 10 million nonagricultural jobs in the entire New York Region, of which about 4.1 million were located in New York City and a further 1 million in the New Jersey part of the regional core.[1] Within the city, employment is highly concentrated in the borough of Manhattan (table 3.3). With almost 2.7 million jobs in 1987, Manhattan employment represented 65 percent of all city employment and 27 percent of all employment in the region – compared with only 8 percent of the total population of the region.

Table 3.3   Employment by industry, New York region, 1987 (thousands)

Industry	Manhattan	Rest of New York City	New York City	Rest of region	Total NY region
Manufacturing	220	177	397	946	1,343
Construction	51	93	144	333	477
Transport, communications and public utilities	118	124	242	333	575
Wholesale and retail trade	389	325	713	1,369	2,082
Finance, insurance, and real estate	519	88	607	477	1,084
Services	901	525	1,426	1,684	3,110
Government	478	119	597	727	1,324
Total	**2,676**	**1,451**	**4,126**	**5,869**	**9,995**

Note: These figures include self-employed as well as employees.
Source: US Department of Commerce, 1989

The composition of employment in Manhattan is markedly different both from the other four boroughs of New York City and from the rest of the region. The production and distribution of goods, construction, public utilities, and retail trade, with less than a third of total jobs, employ significantly lower proportions of workers in Manhattan than in other parts of the region. However, it has much higher proportions of employment than the other subregions in finance, insurance, and real estate, and in government, which together account for nearly 40 percent of the jobs in Manhattan. A finer industrial subdivision of government and of other services would heighten this contrast by revealing that the Manhattan jobs are concentrated in high-wage activities (legal services, business and professional services, etc.) while those in the rest of New York City, in particular, are predominantly in low-paying employment, including health services (mostly hospitals), social services, auto and other repair services. Thus, it is clear that Manhattan specializes in what Gottman called the "quaternary" sector or what others have called information industries or producer services.

Financial and business services are actually more heavily concentrated in Manhattan, which has 48 percent of regional employment in the sector, than in Central London (with 44 percent of its regional total). On the other hand these sectors are underrepresented in the other boroughs of New York City. The Bronx, Brooklyn, and Queens account for only 6 percent of regional employment in financial and business services; by contrast the ring of inner boroughs around Central London has 12 percent of the London region's jobs in this sector, despite a smaller share of its overall employment. Commercial banking, securities, advertising, legal services, accounting, and international activities are particularly concentrated in Manhattan because of their dependence on access to the financial markets and the network of communications, entertainment, and art-related organizations. Suburban-based corporate service firms tend to be associated with local or regional markets, including smaller businesses and household consumers, or with data processing and other back office functions. But corporate headquarters are also now often located in the suburbs, being less constrained than many producer service organizations by the need to be accessible to clients from all parts of the region and for frequent meetings with other corporate service firms. The more collegiate structure of many of these firms may also make it more difficult for them to decide on an alternative noncentral location (Schwartz, 1989).

Neither of the other subregions are as specialized as Manhattan, although the suburban ring contains a disproportionate share of jobs in goods production, construction, and retailing, while the rest of the core has a significant concentration of transport employment. For private services the spatial distribution is linked to that of population, with a modest tendency to concentration in Manhattan and, particularly, the other boroughs of New York City. Government employment – mostly state and local government as federal government is of minor and shrinking importance in the region – was also somewhat more concentrated in the city, with 48 percent of the regional employment against 43 percent of the population, reflecting the long tradition of a strong public sector in New York City.

Despit such differences of emphasis, these broad comparisons do point to considerable similarities in the overall structures of the two economies and in their spatial structures, reinforcing the expectation that they will have been changing in similar ways in response to the global tendencies discussed earlier.

TRANSFORMATION OF THE LONDON AND NEW YORK ECONOMIES

London

Analyses of the significance of past change in the London economy, and prognoses about its future, depend very much on the spatial scale and time period over which it is examined, and the elements of the economy on which attention is focused. If we start with the core area, Greater London, there has clearly been a substantial fall in total employment which began around 1960, and leveled off around 1983, with some very modest growth then up to 1988, reversed in the following two years. Over the earlier period London lost about 820,000 jobs, while since 1983 it has gained about 45,000 jobs for employees, plus some 150,000 extra self-employed. Detailed figures for the period since 1971 (in table 3.4) show that the modest "revival" in employment after the recession of the early 1980s still left employment well short of the level in 1981, halfway through the recession, let alone that of 1978. Nor, despite significant fluctuations in the rate of job loss, is there evidence of any period of acute decline in the city. The picture is one of chronic decline which has abated, rather than one of crisis and recovery.

By contrast, the Outer Metropolitan Area surrounding Greater London (the rest of the London Region as defined in this book) enjoyed significant growth up to the late 1970s, gaining 158,000 jobs between 1971 and 1978. This was not enough, however, to balance the losses occurring within Greater London, and the region as a whole had continuing declines in employment. The OMA subsequently lost jobs in the recession of the late 1970s and early 1980s. Since 1981 employment has grown by 216,000 jobs, or more than 10 percent, and it remains one of the strongest areas of the British economy, yielding a net growth for the region as a whole after 1984.

In functional terms these outer areas are clearly a part of the London economy, which has displayed some economic health over a long period. The perception of London as an economy in decline, which has dominated much British discussion, is a consequence of a focus on narrow administrative boundaries rather than this functional region – and is misleading as a basis for diagnosis of the structural

Table 3.4 Employment change in the London region, 1971–1989 (thousands)

	Greater London	Outer Metropolitan Area	London region
	Total employment		
1971	3,937	1,858	5,795
1978	3,663	2,016	5,679
1981	3,567	1,995	5,562
1984	3,463	2,050	5,513
1987	3,505	2,125	5,630
1989	3,481	2,211	5,692
Change			
1971–8	−274	+158	−116
1978–81	−140	−21	−161
1981–4	−104	+55	−49
1984–7	+42	+75	+117
1987–9	−24	+86	+62
	Manufacturing		
1971	1,049	707	1,756
1978	769	656	1,425
1981	681	582	1,263
1984	569	537	1,106
1987	482	503	985
1989	444	489	933
Change			
1971–8	−280	−51	−331
1978–81	−99	−75	−174
1981–4	−112	−45	−157
1984–7	−87	−34	−121
1987–9	−38	−14	−52

Table 3.4   Continued

	Finance and producer services		
	Greater London	Outer Metropolitan Area	London region
1971	520	131	651
1978	560	178	738
1981	568	185	753
1984	631	225	856
1987	753	268	1,021
1989	793	321	1,114
Change			
1971–8	+40	+47	+87
1978–81	+32	+19	+51
1981–4	+63	+40	+103
1984–7	+122	+43	+165
1987–9	+40	+53	+93

Note: There were changes in the industrial classification, and the way data were collected in 1981, so that figures before and after this year are not strictly comparable, particularly for finance and producer services. Two sets of figures are available for 1981; those shown are comparable with the later series, whereas the changes over the period 1978–81 are based on the earlier series.
Source: UK Department of Employment, 1991

changes which have been proceeding. Much of the recorded change for the narrower area reflects a process of decentralization – as a result of which the outer boundary of the metropolitan region is reaching progressively further out. By contrast with the crisis which afflicted New York in the 1970s, affecting all sectors of the economy, London's long-term pattern of chronic decline in the core may appear as a "natural trend for a mature fully built-up city, with shrinking numbers seen essentially as a consequence of the persistent and general demand for lower densities of occupation" (Gordon and Harloe, 1991).

The decline of Greater London employment was dominated by the job losses in manufacturing, where employment fell from around 1.4 million in the early 1960s to 0.4 million. In this sector there have been no signs of an upturn since 1984. A further 125,000 jobs were lost in the five years after this date. London manufacturing has declined much more rapidly than that of Britain as a whole (except in the first half of the last recession), and until the recession of the early 1980s was declining more rapidly than in any other major city in Britain.

To identify the processes of growth and decline in the London econ-

Table 3.5 London region employment change by major industry divisions (% change p.a.)

		Central London	Inner London	Outer London	Greater London	Outer Metropolitan Area	London region
All industries	1971–8	−1.39	−1.50	−0.24	−0.99	+1.22	−0.28
	1978–81	−0.33	−2.38	−0.98	−0.81	−0.33	−0.63
	1981–4	+0.88	−1.05	−1.21	−0.97	+0.92	−0.29
	1984–7	+0.00	+0.63	+0.58	+0.40	+1.22	+0.71
	1987–9	−3.00	−0.95	+0.45	−0.35	+2.00	+0.55
Manufacturing	1971–8	−4.55	−4.41	−3.21	−3.82	−1.03	−2.69
	1978–81	+1.24	−6.43	−4.09	−3.94	−3.54	−3.75
	1981–4	−1.33	−7.13	−5.65	−5.24	−2.64	−4.03
	1984–7	−11.02	−1.83	−4.32	−5.12	−2.08	−3.65
	1987–9	−6.80	−0.06	−4.65	−3.90	−1.35	−2.60
Other production industries	1971–8	−2.94	−2.95	−0.33	−1.89	−0.25	−1.26
	1978–81	−4.86	−2.10	−0.21	−1.76	+0.62	−0.77
	1981–4	−2.02	−5.03	−3.39	−3.72	−1.00	−2.53
	1984–7	+0.27	−1.97	−1.25	−1.20	−0.70	−0.97
	1987–9	−2.00	−6.06	−0.40	−2.10	−7.90	−5.00
Transport and wholesale distribution	1971–8	−2.41	−2.87	+0.89	−1.50	+2.39	−0.70
	1978–81	−1.66	−2.24	+0.24	−1.10	−2.65	−0.15
	1981–4	−3.40	−0.86	−0.97	−1.78	+2.70	−0.54
	1984–7	−4.98	−3.54	+1.32	−2.06	+0.41	−1.30
	1987–9	−7.05	−1.09	+1.10	−1.85	+5.85	+0.70

Financial and producer services	1971–8	−0.42	+3.99	+4.89	+1.08	+5.13	+1.90
	1978–81	+1.38	+4.02	+1.11	+1.78	+3.20	+2.12
	1981–4	+3.00	+3.89	+7.54	+4.16	+7.13	+4.89
	1984–7	+6.58	+6.47	+6.58	+6.56	+6.47	+6.54
	1987–9	+0.65	+5.85	+5.30	+2.60	+10.05	+4.55
Private consumer services	1971–8	−0.49	−0.25	+1.25	+0.23	+3.04	+1.08
	1978–81	−1.16	−0.54	+1.28	0.00	+1.99	+0.68
	1981–4	+3.42	+1.48	+1.56	+2.08	+3.91	+2.72
	1984–7	−0.38	+2.25	+2.79	+1.58	+2.53	+1.99
	1987–9	−1.40	−0.97	+2.35	+0.40	+5.40	+2.30
Public services	1971–8	+0.28	+1.45	+1.54	+1.15	+2.68	+1.66
	1978–81	−0.96	−2.74	−0.91	−1.58	−0.92	−1.34
	1981–4	+0.88	+0.33	−1.94	−0.38	−0.13	−0.19
	1984–7	−0.76	+1.33	+0.60	−0.47	+2.25	+1.13
	1987–9	−3.20	+1.91	+0.10	−0.25	−0.10	−0.20

Note: Inner London in this table refers to the area outside the Central Statistical Area.
Source: UK Department of Employment, 1991

omy requires a more disaggregated analysis, since particular sectors have experienced very different trends. Rates of employment change during the period since 1971 in each of the six major sectors are shown in table 3.5. Manufacturing and the transport and wholesaling sector constitute the first component identified in the previous section. Finance and producer services constitute the second component. The third component is largely contained within the public services, and the fourth contained within the private consumer services, though the last two are dominated by the local-population-serving elements. A residual category, other production industries, includes industries such as construction and public utilities. The table shows that three sectors, manufacturing, the other production industries, and transport and wholesale distribution, had experienced significant and quite consistent job losses through the 1970s and 1980s. Over the period between 1971 and 1989, manufacturing in the London region lost 700,000 jobs, the other production industries 115,000 jobs, and transport and wholesaling 40,000 jobs. The rates of manufacturing job loss have fluctuated between 2.5 percent and 4 percent p.a. though with a rapidly declining base the absolute job losses have become smaller. Trends in the period since 1984, when the region as a whole experienced a net growth in employment, suggest no significant mitigation of the decline in these sectors.

The three other sectors grew absolutely between 1971 and 1989, though there has been a decline in public-service employment since 1978. Finance, insurance, and other business-related services gained 460,000 jobs, the private consumer services gained almost 280,000 jobs, mainly in the OMA, whilst the public services finished the period with almost 200,000 more jobs, virtually all outside Greater London. In aggregate, then, the share of the goods production and circulation sector in Greater London employment fell from 45 percent in 1971 to 26 percent in 1989, whilst its share in the region as a whole fell from 46 percent to 29 percent. By contrast, the financial and producer services increased their share of Greater London employment from 13 percent to 23 percent. In the region as a whole their share increased from 11 percent in 1971 to 19 percent in 1989. Given that the former sector has experienced consistent declines while the latter has experienced consistent growth, one possible explanation for the bottoming-out of employment decline in London is simply that the industries of long-term decline no longer feature as prominently in the London economy. If these trends continued the city would be set for substantial growth in the 1990s.

A second part of the explanation, however, is that employment growth in financial and business services has accelerated markedly since about 1981. Between 1971 and 1981 the growth rate in this sector across the London region was 2 percent p.a., significantly slower than in the rest of the country. The sector gained 74,000 jobs between 1971 and 1981, but would have gained 165,000 growing at the national rate. Similarly, service industries as a whole grew by 50,000 between 1971 and 1981, but growing at national rates of growth they would have gained a further 390,000 jobs. Thus, a disproportionate share of the growing service industries was being located outside London, and there were significant processes of decentralization going on. However, between 1981 and 1989 growth in the finance and producer services in the London region was 5.5 percent p.a., close to the national growth rate.

The spatial pattern of change up to 1984 was dominated by particularly heavy job losses in Inner London, and a deteriorating situation in Outer London. While Central London suffered significant losses up to 1978, it experienced much lower losses in the next three years, and significant gains between 1981 and 1984. The OMA has consistently been the most successful part of the region. This pattern changed somewhat after 1984 with a notable revival in the fortunes of both Inner and Outer London, and a relatively poor performance in Central London. At the industry level this recent change in Central London reflected a combination of strong growth in the financial and producer services (growing 6.5 percent p.a.), with heavy manufacturing losses and losses in both public and private consumer services. By contrast, both these last sectors have enjoyed considerable growth in the rest of Inner and Outer London since 1984.

In the declining sectors the spatial pattern of job losses has generally been one of progressively lower rates of job loss the further from the center, and in the case of transport and wholesale distribution there have been significant employment gains in outer areas – reflecting the outward shift of wholesaling and goods handling activities. The pattern in the center has been more uneven, with significantly lower losses, or even gains in manufacturing between 1978 and 1984, which probably reflects the greater protection of company headquarter employment in the recession. Losses in transport, and more particularly wholesaling, have, however, been particularly heavy in the central area.

New York

In New York, as in London, the economic decline of one set of sectors, mainly associated with goods production and distribution, has for several decades proceeded alongside the economic rise of key sectors of service activity. These massive structural changes transcend the neat time-frames of national or international business cycles, and cannot be explained in terms of one or other specific crisis in the global or local economies. However, the performance of both the declining and the growing sectors in New York has shown a much greater volatility than that of their London counterparts, and during the past 20 years or so there is a clear division between an early period in which almost all parts of the New York economy fared relatively badly, and a later period in which that was reversed.

Precisely because of this sharp change of fortunes it is necessary to see the recent history of the New York economy in the context of this longer period, over which more meaningful comparisons can be made with structural changes in the London economy. In fact to describe, and then understand, the transformation of the New York economy it is necessary to begin with 1969. That was the last year of a long economic expansion in both New York and the United States, soon to be followed by what can only be described as a depression in New York.

In 1969 total employment in New York City had reached an all-time high of almost 3.8 million jobs. Subsequently, through two national recessions (1969–70 and 1973–5), restructuring of the local economy, and the city's celebrated fiscal crisis, employment in New York City declined in every single year up to 1977, an eight-year downturn which left employment under 3.2 million. After 1977, recovery began and there were significant gains in employment in almost every single year until 1989, when total employment stood at 3.6 million, still 200,000 below the 1969 peak.

Most of the employment losses in the city from 1969 to 1977 were in the production and distribution of goods, and headquarters activities in these same sectors. These traditional basic industries oriented to nonlocal markets are referred to here as the "old core" of the economy. From over 1.2 million jobs in 1969, this old core had shrunk to about 0.8 million jobs by 1977. Even in the subsequent period of expansion in total employment in New York, from 1977 to 1988, the old core continued to lose jobs (−211,000), albeit at a slower rate.

But all sectors of the New York City economy performed much worse through this crisis than in either the preceding or the following decade. In 1969 the "new core" or producer services and the related nonlocal consumer services had accounted for under 1.3 million jobs in New York City. During the long period of decline in total city employment, 1969 to 1977, employment in producer services also declined by about 77,000 while consumer services employment added only about 50,000 jobs. (This is in marked contrast to London, where neither sector experienced periods of actual contraction until the recession of the early 1990s). The two specific activities showing the sharpest reversals between the periods of growth and decline were government and the securities industry, both of which had specific problems, associated with the city's fiscal crisis and a check to the rapid growth of the stock market. But the pervasiveness of the slowdowns and downturns during this period indicates a more general problem of competitiveness, with the combination of physical and social deterioration plus high taxes, and a perceived shortage of suitable employees all impairing the city's image.[2]

The general revival after 1977 similarly implies some recovery of that competitiveness, as well as other more sector-specific factors. The structural shift in employment continued, however. In fact between 1977 and 1988 the new core expanded by 419,000 jobs, more than offsetting a continued, though slower, drop in employment within the old core industries. So in 1988 the new core of producer and nonlocal consumer services, with over 1.6 million jobs, was more than two and a half times the sixe of the old core of goods production and distribution activities.

While the balance of the region had moderate employment expansion during the period of massive and continuous losses in city employment (from 1969 to 1977), the gains were not large enough to offset the declines in the city. To compare the transformation of the city's economy with the rest of the region, it is most instructive to focus upon the full period, 1969 to 1988.[3]

In 1969 employment in the old economic core in New York City was over 1.2 million, or just slightly higher than old core employment in the rest of the region (see table 3.6). But over the next two decades the city lost almost half of those jobs (0.6 million), with every component industry suffering declines. Clearly these losses were not simply the result of shifts in old core employment to the periphery of the region, because the region excluding the city gained only 70,000 such jobs. The biggest city losses were in manufacturing, which includes headquarters (−459,000), and in wholesale trade (−78,000). Manufacturing employment declined in other parts of the region as well (−130,000). Only one sector in the rest of the region had job gains large enough to offset city losses, namely wholesale trade (196,000). So the loss of old core employment in the city, mainly manufacturing, has not been simply a reflection of dispersion within the region.

The new core of producer and consumer services was not insignificant in 1969, but for the entire region it was smaller than the old core activities of producing and moving goods (1.8 million jobs compared with 2.4 million in the old core). The new core jobs were highly concentrated in New York City (70 percent) in 1969, whereas the old core jobs were more evenly distributed (51 percent in the city, 49 percent in the rest of the region). But in the period to 1988, the new core had strong growth in the city (up 390,000 jobs or 31 percent) and phenomenal growth in the rest of the region (up 824,000 jobs or 157 percent).

Thus, by 1988 the structure of employment in the region was markedly

Table 3.6 Employment by broad groups, New York City and region, 1969 and 1988 (thousands)

Industry	Total region		New York City		Region ex city	
	1969	1988	1969	1988	1969	1988
Old core	2,437	1,903	1,238	634	1,199	1,269
New core	1,777	2,991	1,251	1,641	526	1,350
All other private	1,525	2,041	762	735	763	1,306
Government	962	1,255	547	596	415	659
Total employment	6,701	8,190	3,798	3,606	2,903	4,584
Population	15,422	17,103	7,859	7,317	7,563	9,786

	Employment change, 1969–88					
	Number	%	Number	%	Number	%
Old core	−534	−21.9	−604	−48.8	+70	+5.8
New core	+1,214	+68.3	+390	+31.2	+824	+156.7
All other private	+516	+33.8	−27	−3.5	+543	+71.2
Government	+293	+30.5	−49	+9.0	+244	+58.8
Total employment	+1,489	+22.2	−192	−5.1	+1,681	+57.9
Population	+1,681	+10.9	−542	−6.9	+2,223	+29.4

Note: The old core includes goods production and distribution activities; the new core includes producer services and other services with nonlocal markets; other private services, and government, serve the local market.
Source: US Department of Labor, n.d.

different from that of 1969. Both parts of the region showed a strong relative shift away from the old core activities of production and distribution of goods toward the new core activities of producer and consumer services. The share of New York City jobs in the old core fell from 33 percent in 1969 to 18 percent in 1988, while the city share in the new core rose from 33 percent in 1969 to 46 percent in 1988. Similarly, in the rest of the region, the share of employment in the old core fell from 41 percent in 1969 to 28 percent in 1988, while that in the new core rose from 18 percent in 1969 to almost 30 percent in 1988.

Over the past two decades there has been a marked decentralization of both population and employment within the region, although that in jobs has been the more dramatic, because overseas immigration kept the population of the core up. In 1969 New York City had 57 percent of the region's jobs and 51 percent of its population; by 1988 these proportions had fallen to 44 percent and 43 percent. The convergence in the city's share of population vis-à-vis employment over this period reflects a combination of two factors (to be discussed in chapter 4), namely the falling rate of employment among New York City residents and a possible decline in the inward flow of commuters from the suburbs.

Decentralization is evident in all sectors of employment, but most strikingly in old and new core industries. New York City's share of old core employment in the region fell from 51 percent in 1969 to 33 percent in 1988, but that in the new core also fell, from 70 percent to 55 percent. Other private-sector employment, in activities serving more local markets, also showed a strong shift to the suburbs, with the city's share falling from 50 percent to 36 percent, much greater than would be warranted by the population shift. This suggests that for local service activities, as well as for goods production and distribution, the costs of a more central location (money, time, and congestion costs) now exceeded the agglomeration benefits. Another factor as far as the local services are concerned must be the falling level of per capita personal incomes in the core relative to the rest of the region.[4] The main significance of this shift is simply that the size of the local market has fallen even faster than population changes would indicate. But it is also likely that among this poorer population in the core areas an increasing larger proportion now satisfy some of their local service needs from outside the formal economy.

New York City's declining share of regional employment over the past two decades is in large part a reflection of the fact that the economic crisis of 1969–77 was a crisis for the city economy rather than for the New York region as a whole. In this period employment in Manhattan suffered the most, declining by 2.1 percent per year. The rest of the city had an average annual rate of job decline of 1.6 percent, while the rest of the region actually had a net gain in employment of 1.2 percent p.a. (table 3.7). In the first five years of the recovery period which followed, between 1977 and 1982, there was a marked turnaround in Manhattan employment, which expanded at an average annual rate of 1.2 percent, while in the rest of the city jobs grew by only 0.3 percent per year. The rest of the region also showed some acceleration in its growth, however, and continued to display the strongest employment growth of the three subregions, amounting to 2.2 percent per year. This period was the source of a general perception that the turnaround in the New York City and regional economy has blessed both Manhattan and the suburbs outside the city with economic growth and prosperity but has skipped over the remainder of the city. In fact the other boroughs did show some recovery in this period, with a modest net growth in jobs, albeit on a smaller scale than in Manhattan. This difference was hardly surprising, however, given Manhattan's specialization in the growing producer services and the other four boroughs' greater involvement in the declining goods production and distribution sector.

Nevertheless, in the second phase of the recovery, from 1982 to 1987, growth in these other boroughs actually overtook that in Manhattan, with an annual growth rate of 1.7 percent as against 1.5 percent. Even faster employment growth in the rest of the region, outside the city, running at 3.4 percent per year, reflected a general pattern of job decentralization. This change of pattern represents no weakening of the Manhattan economy, which continues to be the driving engine of regional growth. Rather, as the rising level of office rents shows, it is a consequence of capacity constraints which began to bite as the prolonged recovery turned into a boom in Manhattan from the early 1980s onward, leading to spillover of employment expansion into the outer areas of the city, and particularly the suburban ring beyond.

COMPARING CHANGE IN LONDON AND NEW YORK

From the data considered in the previous two subsections it is possible to make some broad comparisons of the patterns of employment change in London and New York during the 1970s and 1980s. This period is long enough to be reasonably independent of the (different) timing of particular crises or booms in the two places, and represents a sort of long-term trend. In New York it includes two subperiods – the crisis, 1969–77, and the subsequent recovery, up to at least 1987, with a slowing and possible reversal thereafter. For London the break comes later, around 1983–4, is less sharp, taking the form more of a leveling-off than a real reversal, and lasts until mid-1989, with a fall now reported for 1989–90.

Over the period as a whole overall employment trends are more

Table 3.7 Total employment change, New York region (% change p.a.)

	Manhattan	Rest of New York City	New York City	Rest of region	Total New York region
1969–77	−2.1	−1.6	−1.9	+1.2	−0.3
1977–82	+1.2	+0.3	+0.9	+2.2	+1.6
1982–7	+1.5	+1.7	+1.6	+3.4	+2.7

Source: US Department of Commerce, 1989

favorable in New York than in London, however these areas are defined, and also clearly more favorable in the wider region than in the urban cores. In New York City there is a modest decline in total employment (5 percent between 1969 and 1988), while in Greater London the decline is somewhat greater (12 percent between 1971 and 1989). For the wider regions the differences are more marked (with growth of 22 percent in the New York region 1969–88, against a decline of 2 percent in the London metropolitan region 1971–89).

In sectoral terms the simplest distinction is between manufacturing and other employment. Manufacturing shows declines for both cities and for the two wider regions. For the two core areas rates of decline were very similar: in New York City manufacturing jobs fell by 55 percent between 1969 and 1988; in Greater London they fell by 58 percent between 1971 and 1989. In the wider region, however, the New York performance was much more favorable. In the London metropolitan region manufacturing jobs decreased by 47 percent between 1971 and 1989, with a decrease of 30 percent in the OMA: even in the South-East as a whole manufacturing jobs fell by about 37 percent over this period, and the national decline was 32 percent. In the New York metropolitan region manufacturing fell by 34 percent between 1969 and 1989; outside New York City the decline was only 14 percent, but this was still poor by comparison with a national decrease of just 2 percent.

A rather broader picture can be derived by combining all of the production- and/or goods-related industries (including construction, utilities, transport and wholesale distribution, as well as manufacturing), which exhibit job losses in one or both of the cities, and which have some distinctive labor market characteristics, including a predominance of male-typed jobs. In New York City employment in this group of activities shrank by 29 percent between 1969 and 1985, compared with 33 percent in Greater London between 1971 and 1988 – that is, at much the same rate; in the tri-state region as a whole, however, most of the parts except for manufacturing showed an increase between 1970 and 1986 and the net loss was only 9 percent, as against 45 percent for the London region between 1971 and 1988.

In the remaining service industries the general pattern has been one of employment growth in both places. In the London region as a whole this amounted to 29 percent between 1971 and 1989, as against 37 percent in the tri-state New York region between 1970 and 1986. The difference in rates of employment change is clearly less than in the declining sectors. In the two core areas the gap was even narrower, with a growth of 14 percent in employment within New York City between 1970 and 1986, and the same increase in Greater London between 1971 and 1989. Considering the substantial decline in London population over this period, the similarity with New York in service growth rates is particularly striking.

At this rather broad level it appears, then, that the difference in employment trends between London and New York over the past two decades is principally a reflection of the faster contraction of the declining sectors in London, notably a faster rate of loss of manufacturing employment, especially when outer parts of the regions are compared. The difference was not, however, as great as that between national trends in the two countries. In the case of the two core areas it is likely that the rather similar rates of long-term decline, particularly in manufacturing, are basically determined by common constraints on the availability of space – or industry's ability to compete for it – which would be required to support a constant level of employment, given the labor-saving character of technological change. In the outer areas of the two regions, on the other hand, the divergent performance of manufacturing needs to be explained rather in terms of national economic success or failure in this sector, notably the incidence of de-industrialization in the United Kingdom economy.

PROCESSES OF GROWTH AND DECLINE

We began this chapter by considering a number of global processes which have shaped the changes in the world economy and in large cities such as London and New York. In this final section we review the evidence presented above on the changes occurring in London and New York, to explore how far they are to be understood in terms of those processes. We would stress that the explanation of the change involves not only the individual processes themselves, but also the way they have combined in large dense cities. Change has in many cases taken forms which are familiar from much longer periods of their histories: the dispersal of routine activities; decline and decentralization arising from high costs and intense competition for land, and in some cases labor; and the spawning of new activities within the economic complex at their center. Technological change has also been instrumental in facilitating and accelerating some of these changes.

The two economies have certainly experienced the effects of the first two global processes, the slow growth or decline in manufacturing and related employment experienced in most capitalist societies, and its shift toward lower cost regions, but in both cases these sectors have declined more rapidly than would be expected on this basis alone, particularly in their core areas. The cities had both a concentration of less efficient firms, and intense competition for land leading to space shortages and rising costs.

In Britain the problems of these sectors at the national level were probably more severe – between 1978 and 1987 manufacturing employment declined by 30 percent, and this is one major factor in London's decline, particularly in the outer areas. However, the pattern of manufacturing employment change has been rather different from the national pattern both in timing and in having place-specific causes, at least in core urban areas. The analysis in Buck et al. (1986) showed that differential job losses in manufacturing (i.e. after deducting changes expected on the basis of a uniform change at the national rate) were negatively related to national change itself, that is, that London lost relatively more when national employment was growing, and was relatively insulated from the impacts of national recessions. This was related to the arguments which Fothergill and Gudgin (1982) advanced, that manufacturing decline in the conurbation resulted from the increasing space demands of industry and the difficulties of making new space available there, compared to undeveloped areas. The problems of London were thus in part a consequence of constraints on growth in the London environment at a time when industry was becoming more demanding of space, rather than of any intrinsic weakness of London manufacturing. However, it was also clear that there are sectors of London's manufacturing which are weak, and unable to compete under London conditions, particularly in relation to wage levels. London wages remained distinctly higher than average and even now the wages of manual workers in manufacturing in London are around 10 percent above the national average, and have been rising more rapidly. This in part reflects the competition for labor from other sectors. There is some contrast here with New York, which has been a rather low-wage manufacturing area.

In London manufacturing has also suffered from competition for space from other activities, increasing costs of land in the area. This has included competition from goods circulation activities. There is evidence that warehousing and storage have tended to gain at the expense of industrial uses. This has raised problems of absolute shortage of space in more congested parts of the city, and of rising rents. It is in the outer areas where new industrial building could take place that the decline has been least, but even here rents are relatively high by British standards. These cost pressures have probably been less intense in the outer areas of New York, in part because of less restrictive planning regulations.

The dynamics of wages and rents in both cities have a very selective effect on industry, providing some niches for low-wage or labor-intensive manufacturing, though this is much more significant in New York, where there are a number of ethnically segregated subsectors. In London the bulk of manufacturing now consists of high-wage, high-value-added industries, tied to London headquarters, to the agglomeration economies of the M4 corridor, or to airport communications. Similarly in New York most manufacturing is now to be found in the suburban ring, and is of a very different character from that in New York City.

In both cities long-term changes in communications systems have accelerated the decline of goods production and circulation in the core areas. For example, in the USA the construction of the interstate highway system beginning in the 1950s along with the falling real price of motor fuel (until 1973) combined to reduce the real cost of moving goods and people into New York. Simultaneously, rising rents, congestion, and outmoded industrial space was increasing the real cost of producing and storing goods in New York City. Consequently, manufacturing and wholesale trade firms realized that they could serve the New York market without being in New York. The interstate highway system greatly increased the radius of "overnight delivery" locations for apparel, printing, food processing, and other manufacturing operations serving the New York market. And the increased radius extended deeply into low-wage nonunion areas of the southern states. The advent of jet air freight (plus trade liberalization) extended the radius of almost overnight delivery locations to the Far East and Europe.

The almost complete replacement of break-bulk ocean cargo by containerization plus the substitution of intercontinental jet travel for passenger ships led to both a precipitous decline in port employment, and shifts in its location in both cities. The economic impact was not only upon dock jobs but also upon railroads. For example, in New York City jobs in water transportation and railroads dropped from more than 100,000 in 1958 to 62,000 by 1969 and to under 18,000 in 1988. The collapse of port activity had an adverse impact on trucking and wholesale trade employment in the city as well, which totaled 350,000 jobs in 1969 but by 1988 was down to 250,000. Equivalent changes have occurred in London, as port activity has moved out of the city.

Central to growth of the two cities have been the third and fourth of the global processes outlined above, the growth of the international financial system and the growth of producer services. London and New York, as well as Tokyo, have emerged at the top of a new layer of world cities, with a growing concentration of specialist commercial and financial activities, and multinational corporate headquarters. Through the 1980s this trio has gathered an increasing share of international financial activities, and this has been a major factor behind employment growth. There has been increasing need for banks, and other financial institutions, to be represented in these cities, and for international corporations to have their headquarters there, and particularly in the few square miles of Manhattan or Central London. In both cities, but particularly in London, there has been government-inspired institutional reform with the aim of enhancing the role of the financial center. In particular, the so-called "Big Bang" of October 1986 involved a substantial deregulation of the City of London, and led at least in the short term to an expansion of activity, and a significant increase in the degree of concentration in City firms. There has also been a substantial increase in employment in foreign-owned banks and finance houses, which gained 20,000 jobs between 1984 and 1987. The impact of the slump following the stock market crash of October 1987 has been rather uneven; the securities and banking sector in New York City had lost 33,000 jobs by 1990 but other producer services were growing strongly (Drennan, 1991); in London a slowdown in growth in the central area was counterbalanced by continuing growth elsewhere until the credit boom was halted in 1990.

The expansion of financial and producer service firms in the large nodal cities is because of the very high value added from agglomeration in these sectors, far higher than that for manufacturing, wholesaling, or corporate headquarters. The central common characteristic of producer service firms is that they are information intensive. Their information inputs and outputs are complex, nonroutine, and quite often external to the firm.

Technological change in transportation, communication, and computers has worked to strengthen and enhance the core of the new economic city. In the US in particular the expanded use and declining real cost of jet air travel in the past three decades has greatly expanded the competitive reach of the producer service firms in New York. They grew to be large because they were in the largest market. Their size was an asset in aggressively expanding their client base in other US metropolitan areas. The jet air travel which enables attorneys, investment bankers, and accountants from large New York firms to easily serve clients in distant cities also enables corporate executives of headquarters which departed New York to come to New York easily to confer with attorneys, investment bankers, and accountants. Interviews with headquarters which have moved out of New York revealed that none of them changed their commercial bank, their investment bank, their law, accounting, or advertising firm as a result of their move. In short, they continued to use producer service firms located in New York.

Computer and communication technology has enabled the head office of the bank, securities firm, or insurance company to effectively control a far larger and more dispersed volume of transactions from their city headquarters than was possible in the past. But this same technology has eliminated or shifted out of the two cities tens of thousands of routine clerical jobs. In securities, life insurance, and commercial banking it has greatly reduced the armies of clerks required to handle an increasing volume of transactions. Computers and telecommunication advances have made the back office functions separable in space from the front office. Just as in the case of the manufacturing and goods circulation sectors, productivity increases, cost pressures in metropolitan areas, and the possibilities for decentralization and dispersal are leading to job losses. In New York, at the peak of the 1960s bull market in 1969, securities industry employment was at an historical high of 105,000. By 1977 rationalization and computerization had cut securities industry employment by 33 percent while daily trading volume was 150 percent higher. For similar reasons, life insurance industry employment in New York has been falling continuously for 30 years, declining from 103,000 jobs in 1958 to 63,000 jobs by 1988.

The improvement of communications, particularly in US jet air travel, has also made corporate headquarters less tied to downtown locations. The count of corporate headquarters in New York has diminished markedly in the past two decades or more, and in addition the numbers of employees at head and branch offices of manufacturing and mining corporations in the city have been decimated. There were 86,000 such employees in 1969 and only 33,000 in 1988. The count of *Fortune* 500 headquarters in the city fell from 128 in 1965 to 48 in 1988, although much of this change reflected moves to other parts of the region, which now have as many headquarters as New York City, 54 in 1987 compared with 16 in 1958 (Schwartz, 1989). In London, however, the rate of loss of these headquarters has been much slower, with a decline from 312 of the top 500 headquarters in Greater London in 1971 to 260 in 1986, partly compensated by a growth from 28 to 57 in the OMA. Thus, London has kept its concentration of corporate headquarters while that in New York has been sharply diminished. The obvious explanation is the continuing primacy of London within the British urban hierarchy. There are no British metropolitan areas with an equivalent role to those of Chicago or Los Angeles.

New York's role in managing production has become significantly more specialized over the 20 years since Stephen Hymer first speculated about the coming of a few world cities where the management and control of worldwide production would be centralized. While London and New York both fit this mold, the division of labor is, as Adam Smith noted, limited by the extent of the market. With the United States economy roughly four times larger than the United Kingdom economy, it is to be expected that New York would be more specialized in its role, becoming distinctively an international control center with limited involvement in the control of domestic production, while London still combines the two roles. At the same time as New York has lost major industrial retailing and transportation headquarters to the suburbs and to other US metropolitan areas, it has reinforced its preeminent position as the headquarters site of the nation's largest banks, diversified financial corporations, service corporations, life insurance companies, and US multinational corporations. What is distinctive now about large US multinational corporations with New York headquarters is the high share of their total revenues earned outside the United States. All of this suggests that the specialities of New York are financial and service headquarters plus the most internationally oriented large US corporations. While London remains the dominant center for both national and international business, its position is liable to change substantially within the context of the Single European Market. A range of alternative locations are now becoming available for headquarters, as well as for corporate services, exposing London to more direct competition, and the risk of periodic crises, which previously only New York faced.

Thus, in examining the relative dispersal of jobs, both in goods-related and services-related industries, it is important to focus on the kinds of jobs being dispersed and the kinds of jobs staying put. In any industry (or, indeed, in any enterprise with operations at two or more locations) cost pressures push the more routine activities with low value added to lower cost locations. The cost pressures arising from high land values and thus high rents in cities like New York and London are a necessary condition for the dispersal of routine work. But the sufficient conditions are transportation technology (in the case of goods production and distribution) and communication technology (in the case of financial and other producer services). Modern computer and communication technology enables the head office of a large bank or insurance company to maintain effective control over high-volume operations whether they be located in the same building or at a distant site. For example, in the case of banking in New York, the city enjoyed a large gain in employment (+41,000) between 1969 and 1982. Thereafter, in the frenetic expansion of Wall Street, banking employment in New York City was unchanged through 1987. Yet, data on the expansion of existing and newly arrived foreign banks in New York (which are included in the employment statistics) indicated that they added nearly 20,000 banking jobs in the city. Those gains must have been offset by shrinkage of domestic banks' employment in New York. That probably reflects the shifting of back office bank functions to locations outside the city.

As in London, one of the largest manufacturing industries in New York is printing and publishing. It shrank from 126,000 jobs in 1969 to 88,000 in 1988, with almost all of the losses concentrated in the period of the city's depression, 1969–77. Technological change has facilitated the separation of printing from publishing. New York City has been losing printing jobs to other locations (and to automation), but it continues as the premier center for publishing in the United States. Thus, the stability since 1977 in the statistics on printing and publishing employment probably reflects large losses in printing jobs offset by large gains in publishing jobs.

In the case of London we have noted that the financial and producer services sector was growing more slowly than in the country as a whole. This reflects the effects of the costs of London location, particularly very high rents and relatively high labor costs – though the decline of London manufacturing has itself reduced somewhat the demand for business services. There has been considerable relocation of offices from London, particularly affecting back offices, but including whole offices in such sectors as industrial company headquarters and insurance. A significant amount of this decentralization has been into the OMA, but in this area also the cost pressures are rising, and there has been a development of provincial office centers, such as Bristol, and a movement of back offices to older industrial areas.

More than in New York, decentralization in this sector has involved all parts of the metropolitan region, including the inner city, though gains have been greatest in Outer London and the OMA. However, over much of the period the growth rate in all these areas is greater than in Central London. This also reflects the difficulties of adding central office space at an equivalent rate, given the constraints of the planning system. Much larger increases in office floorspace have occurred in the areas beyond Central London than in Central London itself, and its share of the region's floorspace fell from 60 percent to 48 percent between 1967 and 1985. There is currently a considerable level of investment in offices in Inner London, particularly in the redevelopment of Docklands, but also in areas on the fringes of the central area.

The growth of private-sector consumption in large cities, identified as the sixth global process above, as well as the more faltering growth of public services, the fifth tendency, have certainly also been major contributory factors in change in the cities. New York and London are becoming increasingly important as centers of nonroutine consumption. Whereas supermarkets and cinemas, department stores and furniture shops can easily be decentralized to suburban shopping centers and malls, the more highly specialized retail outlets are still concentrated in the central cities. The more expensive and specialized the commodity the more it relies on a critical mass of wealthy consumers – often the employees of and visitors to the complex of corporate services in the central cities. Consequently the economies of London and New York are increasingly dependent upon tourists, commuters, and residents who spend money in the specialist, nonroutine leisure and luxury markets.

In spite of growing demands for these consumer services, both public and private, job gains have been rather small in the central and inner areas. Some of this reflects the absolute or relative decline in population, but it also reflects cost pressures encouraging decentralization, as well as, in the case of public services, constraints on government expenditure. In London this has been particularly important for local government and local health authorities. The requirement for public services has been boosted in both cities by their "global" role, by changing population composition, and by rising social divisions. The actual pattern of change in local government employment, however, has also reflected an interaction between the political preferences of city governments, and resource constraints involving central or state governmental pressure on inner city authorities, in particular, for economies. These resource problems have been most marked in London during the 1980s, while in New York severe cuts after the 1975 fiscal crisis were followed by significant growth before further budgetary problems at the start of the 1990s. Both public services and private consumer services face significant cost problems in the cities. In London they are placed under particular pressure by the high relative wage rates, which are essentially generated by the demands of private finance and the producer services sector, and which cannot be matched in organizations operating national salary scales. Even where there is not direct competition for the same type of labor, the higher private-sector wages have driven up London house prices and made recruitment and retention of relatively lower paid service sector workers – such as teachers or nurses – increasingly difficult. A consequence is perceived to be a deterioration in the quality of service, which weakens London's competitive position for other activities. Similar cost pressures are also leading central government to seek to move routine departmental functions out of London. In the late 1980s London was thus becoming more predominantly a private-sector economy.

CONCLUSION

This chapter has described a transformation of the economies of London and New York, which has involved a decline of their goods production and circulation sectors in the core areas, and a growth of the complex of financial and corporate services in which the cities have long been specialized. Both metropolitan areas have also seen a relative and absolute growth of employment in their outer areas, and an extension of the area which falls within their orbit. There have been differences in the timing and in the rates of change in different sectors, in the influence of national contexts, and in the role that the cities play in those contexts. However, in broad outline the processes of change, and the factors that lay behind them, have been similar. New York and London share two main characteristics: their role as core cities in the global financial system and the fact of being very large cities with consequences for the locational advantage and spatial redistribution of economic activities.

Later chapters will consider the implications of this pattern of economic structure and change for different segments of the population, but we need to finish by considering what the economic prospects for the cities are. The processes of change have radically altered the employment structure, so that in contrast to the situation 20 years ago, the growing sectors are now much larger than the declining sectors. In this sense, an aggregate projection would suggest substantial future growth. However, we have also stressed that even these growing sectors have been decentralizing activities, and that there are considerable cost pressures, born of intense competition for land and labor, which will accelerate this decentralization. These pressures will also increase the difficulties of other sectors, and this may increase some of the problems of the basic functioning of the cities, for example if public services continue to deteriorate. These cities are also now more dependent on a single sector than they were in the past, though London's economy has a supplementary form of support in the presence of national government and its associated activities. A significant decline in activity in the international financial system, or a competitive loss to other cities specializing in the complex of finance and corporate services, could now pose as severe a threat for the two cities as the decline of manufacturing and goods circulation did in the past.

NOTES

1   These figures, in contrast to those shown in table 3.1, include self-employed workers.
2   Quante, 1976, cited in Lampard, 1986.
3   It would be preferable to include with New York City the contiguous old, urbanized, industrial counties of northeastern New Jersey which have shared with New York City a marked shrinkage in their industrial base. However, to continue the analysis based upon detailed industry groups requires a cruder geographical dichotomy between New York City and the rest of the region.

4   Data in Hughes and Sternlieb, 1989, on total personal income and population indicate that average personal incomes in the core areas fell from 80 percent of the regional mean in 1970 to 72 percent in 1986.

4

Restructuring the urban labor markets

Ian Gordon and Saskia Sassen

INTRODUCTION

The urban labor markets of London, New York, and their hinterlands
arc crucial links between the restructuring of economic activity, discussed
in the previous chapter, and the distributional outcomes for different
groups, to be described in the following chapters. And labor market
processes have been critical to the implementation of the new patterns
of activity represented by the ascendance of producer services and the
decline of goods production and transportation. As a first approxi-
mation, the distributional effects might simply be "read off" from the
account of sectoral employment changes, given a knowledge of the types
of job on which particular groups have depended. And, indeed, it would
be no surprise to find that the massive shift in the employment base of
each city from manufacturing and goods handling jobs to finance and
producer services has benefited educationally qualified, predominantly
white workers of both sexes at the expense of men from established
working-class communities, even if there has also been some growth of
low-wage service jobs requiring few if any qualifications. But such a
deterministic reading can be very misleading in obscuring the fluidity of
labor markets in these two cities characterized by high rates of job
turnover and occupational or spatial mobility. Thus, it is very likely
that employment changes in any particular sector, occupational group,
or area within the metropolitan region will produce a ripple of mobility,
eventually affecting all or most of the other sublabor markets in the
region and many outside as well. In this situation which segments of
the labor force actually gain or lose depends not simply on which jobs

are growing or declining but on other factors conditioning *their* access to those sets of jobs. Similarly, in important respects, such as trends in unemployment, the migrational linkages mean that the New York and London labor markets are always going to reflect to some degree developments originating elsewhere in their respective national economies. Indeed in the New York case, where renewed international immigration was a key factor in the city's labor market during the 1980s (though not really in London), labor market developments outside the US may also have a significant impact in the city. For London high unemployment occasioned by job losses in the more industrial regions of the UK has been a stimulant to (more modest) inflows of migrants seeking work in the city.

To understand how various groups in the urban population have been affected by the restructuring of economic activity, we have therefore to look more closely at how the London and New York labor markets function, and at how this has been changing over the past decade or so. Two key characteristics of the two cities' labor markets now, as a century ago, are the fluidity and openness already referred to, which influence the types of activity prospering there, and the labor market experiences of their residents. But an equally important factor is that the complex of labor markets in and around the cities are *structured*, with particular sets of jobs having attached to them distinctive combinations of rewards, security, and conditions of access. Hence the process of labor market restructuring is not simply a matter of growth and decline in particular sorts of job, and consequential matches or mismatches with changes in the labor supply. It also involves a renegotiation of the conditions under which these jobs are available.

More concretely the way in which these metropolitan labor markets function reflects a variety of factors, including their large size and density, the particular industrial and occupational mix of their employment base, the overall level of tightness or slack in labor demand, and the presence and characteristics of immigrant groups.

Size and density particularly affect a key characteristic of different segments of the labor market, namely the stability or instability of employment. In respect of each group of jobs employers have a fundamental decision to make about what duration of employment relation to plan for, since this has implications for how much it is worth investing in recruitment, training, and personnel functions. From the worker's side, too, this factor has fundamental implications for security and conditions of employment, the possibility of occupational advancement, and for access to (this and future) jobs. They, too, have decisions to make, about accepting particular job offers, and (where the employment is not entirely casualized) about quitting, or retaining, an unsatisfactory job. However, in metropolitan labor markets where there are very many employers of the same kinds of labor, the incentive to invest in a long-term relationship is less, for both employers and workers, than in a smaller or more concentrated labor market, since the costs of turnover are lower (cf. Scott, 1988a). Surplus or discontented workers find other jobs more readily within the metropolitan region than they would elsewhere, while employers have less need to hang on to such workers when they have access to a large labor pool within which to find replacements.

The recent transformation of the two cities' economies may have modified this pattern. In New York City in particular the expansion of the various informal economies, together with lower rates of participation in the officially recorded labor force, points to the existence of alternatives to staying in the formal labor pool. These developments also raise a question about whether a growing segmentation along racial, ethnic, and gender lines has impeded the fluidity of movement between the labor markets of growing and declining industries, or whether exclusion from stable employment is based on long-established processes of discrimination (N. I. Fainstein, 1987).

These structural changes have, however, not reduced the tendency toward shorter-term employment relationships in both London and New York[1] which has been compounded by the market characteristics of many important industries in the two cities. Fashion-oriented industries such as the garment trade, private consumer services, (historically) in trades associated with the port, and (currently) in the more speculative finance houses, have in both cities been characterized by establishments operating in competitive and unstable markets. Turnover rates in those activities are much higher than in large establishments and monopolistic, bureaucratized organizations, and one of the attractions of London and New York to these industries is the ease with which, in their fluid labor markets, employment levels can be rapidly adjusted. High rates of turnover also have implications for labor supply, adding to the attractions of the cities for speculative migrants, particularly minorities who find it difficult gaining access to more closed sectors of employment, and young single workers for whom job security may be a lower priority. The availability of such types of labor in turn has further implications for employers' strategies.

This is an important set of tendencies, as evident a century ago, in the casualized labor market of working-class London (Stedman Jones, 1971) and the exploitation of cheap immigrant labor in New York, as it is today. But the actual structure of the labor markets has always been more complex and changeable than can simply be explained by agglomeration economies and the "natural selection" of activities and groups of workers. Both cities have recently emerged from a period in which their labor markets exhibited what may be an uncharacteristic stability. From roughly the 1920s to the 1960s, during the fordist era of mass production but before extensive development of the vertical division of business functions, the peculiar labor market factors noted above seem to have played a lesser role in the economic development of the two cities. In London the late arrival, in the early decades of this century, of substantial factory employment, unionization of the docks, and the development of bureaucratized public-service employers put an end to the casual labor market and most of its associated social problems. In New York, from the time of the First World War, mass immigration was greatly reduced and then ended, only to recommence in 1965. In the intervening period there developed in New York a more homogeneous, organized working class with an employment base in manufacturing, transport, and public services. Though New York was worse hit by the Depression than London, in both cities there was a core of employment for manual and nonmanual workers tied to the strength of the cities' overseas trade, dominant roles in finance (and, in London's case, government), and the mass consumer markets of their regions, with only limited competitive pressures in any of these activities. All of this has changed in the past 15 to 20 years.

ADJUSTMENT TO EMPLOYMENT CHANGES

As the previous chapter has shown, London and New York have experienced massive shifts in the composition of employment since 1973, particularly in the urban cores. However, whereas in the New York metropolitan region this has been accompanied by substantial employment growth, in the London region there has been no significant change in the overall level of employment. The broad outlines of this structural change – involving a shift from goods handling and production into service employment, particularly in producer services – represent a much accelerated version of changes in the respective national economies. In the UK, with a modest overall growth in employment, this shift has been led by a continuing contraction in manufacturing jobs; in the US, however, where overall employment has grown by a third since 1973, manufacturing employment has shown only cyclical fluctuations during this period. The national labor market context for change in the cities has thus been significantly different, with no British counterpart to the American "employment growth machine." This remained true even in the recovery phase from 1983, when all of the UK employment growth was either in part-time jobs or self-employment, whereas in the US full-time employees grew just about as fast as total employment.

The achievement of large-scale employment growth in the US reflects not only a remarkable dynamism in the economy but also the availability of an elastic labor supply, in the form of immigrants from poorer nations. In the US immigrants accounted for 22 percent of labor force growth in the 1980s and they are expected to account for 25 percent in the 1990s. This marks a second major difference in the national labor market context. While in the 1960s the US was reopening its doors to immigrants irrespective of country of origin, the UK was closing off the admission of economic migrants, on a basis which discriminated against those from the cheap labor countries of the Third World. The divergence in national immigration policies has especially marked implications for the two global cities, since London has always been the principal destination for migrants to the UK, while New York is now jointly with Los Angeles the main US reception area for immigrant workers. The potential importance of the presence or absence of a large immigrant labor force in the cities extends to a range of issues such as the level of wages in the lower part of the labor market, and its implications for the cost of living and competitiveness of local activities, and for patterns of segmentation and opportunities of advancement for indigenous workers. Also, because of the concentration of new migrants in inner city areas, the different significance of immigration in the two cities has contributed to a notable contrast in the spatial pattern of change in labor supply. There has been a marked decentralization of the established population (or at least of its white majority) from both London and New York into the outer rings of the metropolitan region, and in the former case well beyond, to the margins of the Greater South-East, 70–100 miles out from the center (Hall, 1989). Overseas immigration to New York City more or less counterbalanced this out-migration from the mid-1970s on, whereas in London immigration, largely of service-class workers, has been insufficient to do so, except in the brief "Big Bang" period of the mid-1980s, when foreign firms had new opportunities to compete in the City markets.

London

The previous chapter has shown that within a total employment figure for the London region which has shown little net change since the early 1970s, the following trends have been evident:

1 There has been a considerable fall in manufacturing employment, with lesser falls in other production industries and transport/whole-

saling, balanced by a large growth in producer services, and less rapid increases in private consumer services and public services. In total the first three sectors declined from 2,735,000 jobs in 1971 (47 percent of the total) to 2,325,000 in 1978 (41 percent) and 1,789,000 (31 percent) in 1988.

2   There has also been a substantial outward shift in the balance of employment, with the number of jobs in Greater London falling by 430,000 (11 percent) between 1971 and 1988 while those in the surrounding Outer Metropolitan Area increased by 377,000 (21 percent). Until 1981 there was also a clear outward shift in the balance of employment *within* London, although even the Outer London ring has consistently lost jobs, and net growth has occurred in the core Central London area only since 1981.

3   Since 1983 there has been a turnaround in employment, with the loss of 338,000 jobs in the region as a whole during the previous 12 years being virtually made good by 5 years of consistent employment increases. This shift in employment trends has been equally evident in both Greater London and the OMA, with the largest single component in each case being an acceleration in the growth of producer services; in Greater London, particularly, this has been backed up by the much reduced base of employment in the declining manufacturing sector. The pace of restructuring of employment in terms of changes in the relative shares of employment within the declining (production and transport) sectors and the expanding (producer and consumer service) sector has scarcely altered during this time.

The expanding sectors of employment differ from the contracting sectors in several important respects. In particular they have a much lower proportion of male jobs and fewer jobs open to workers lacking formal qualifications (except in private consumer services: see table 4.1). These growing sectors are short of the skilled and supervisory manual jobs on which males lacking school-level qualifications have traditionally relied to provide more secure and reasonably paid jobs. Labour Force Survey data show that 20 to 30 percent of the jobs in the three con- tracting sectors (i.e. manufacturing, construction/utilities, and transport/storage) fall into this category, as against 3 to 8 percent in the expanding sectors (i.e. consumer, producer, and public services).

Shifts in occupational mix within particular sectors have amplified the changes in occupational demand arising from the altered sectoral composition of employment, notably by adding to the growth of admin- istrative, technical, and professional jobs and accelerating the decline of manual jobs. In the case of clerical jobs, however, a general reduction

Table 4.1 Employment characteristics of expanding and contracting sectors in the London region

Sectors	Percentage of female workers	Percentage of workers without qualifications
Contracting		
Manufacturing	29.5	24.8
Other production	15.5	24.3
Transport storage	25.5	27.5
Expanding		
Private consumer service	53.7	24.5
Producer services	43.8	10.3
Public services	62.9	17.2
Total	42.2	21.1

Source: unpublished data from the 1985 Labour Force Survey

in their share of employment within many sectors, exacerbated by the dispersal of back office functions from London, neutralized the growth which might have been expected from the growing importance of producer services.

At the aggregate level fluctuations in employment within the region have very largely been absorbed by migration and/or changes in commuting, with only a limited residual effect on unemployment or participation rates, which are more strongly affected by national labor market developments (Gordon, 1988). Indeed in the late 1980s there was clearly a considerable growth in commuting into Central London. In any case for Greater London the downward trend in employment has been substantially offset by a continuing reduction in labor supply, as people move to the OMA and beyond, primarily for housing and environmental reasons, but with subsequent changes in their place of work. So changes in employment trends have had only weak effects on unemployment or participation within Greater London, and no evident effect on population levels there, although they appear to have affected population growth in the surrounding OMA. As far as London itself is concerned, the major adjustment seems to have been in the balance of commuting flows. However, the same openness which diffuses the effects of changes in London employment over a much wider region also exposes the city to rising unemployment when there are heavy job losses elsewhere in the country. Thus, *national* recession between 1979 and 1983, hardly apparent in London's own employment trends, brought soaring unemployment in the city as migration and commuting patterns adjusted (Buck et al., 1986). And recovery in the national economy brought London unemployment down after 1986, although even in 1989 the rate among residents of Greater London was 7.7 percent, according to the Labour Force Survey.

At the level of the London region as a whole (i.e. including the OMA as well as Greater London) much of this picture still stands, although since the regional labor market is less open, the leakage of employment changes into migration and commuting across its borders is rather less. Over this area some part of the responsibility for rising unemployment from 1979 to 1985 would have to be laid at the door of a temporary shift from employment growth to decline in the OMA. But for the region as a whole (as for London alone) persistent employment decline up to 1983 was borne without raising unemployment above the national level. Some hidden unemployment, in the form of those "discouraged" from participation, undoubtedly exists among married women in London, as elsewhere, although female participation rates remain notably high in London and the strong pressure of demand for females is reflected in a high proportion of full-time jobs. Among single males in Inner London there is some unexplained inactivity[2] which may reflect involvement in unofficial forms of work, but in contrast to New York experience this involves only 3 percent or so of the city's labor force.

For spatial shifts in the balance of demand *within* the region, the evidence indicates even more strongly that the predominant effect has been on the balance of commuting, although again much of the general impact of employment decentralization has simply been offset by an independent process of population decentralization. Changes in relative levels of unemployment within the region (always higher in the inner areas) have primarily reflected the residential distribution of the groups most disadvantaged in labor market competition, whose relative unemployment rate worsened as general unemployment rose. Even after unemployment leveled off in the mid-1980s, the gap between unemployment rates in Inner London and those in the outer metropolitan ring continued to widen, through to 1988. This probably reflects mainly the reversal of population decline in the inner areas, but also seems to reflect an increasing marginalization of groups of inner city workers during the period of sustained high unemployment.

In relation to the large sectoral shifts in the balance of employment, an obvious question to ask is what has happened to the former workers in the declining sectors. Evidence from the Office of Population Censuses and Surveys' Longitudinal Study linking a sample of individuals' records from the 1971 and 1981 Censuses, however, indicates that the adjustment has been achieved essentially through lower rates of recruitment into the declining industries (both from other sectors and from the inactive) rather than higher rates of exit. One consequence is that, while 1981 unemployment rates tended to be higher amongst those who had worked in declining sectors in 1971 (e.g. 11 percent among sea/port transport workers and 9.5 percent in the fastest declining manufacturing sector, against 2 percent in producer services and 3.5 percent in public services), the differences were small in relation to the intersectoral shifts in employment, and partially a reflection of other factors, as indicated by a high (7.5 percent) unemployment rate for those who had worked in private consumer services in 1971. Overall the 1981 unemployment rate for those employed in the London region in 1971 was 5.4 percent for those previously working in the declining sectors (manufacturing, construction/utilities, and transport/storage) against 4.7 percent for those from the growth sectors (personal, producer, and public services). The crucial, and more difficult, question about sectoral adjustment thus concerns what has happened to those who would previously have been expected to enter the declining sectors – notably males with minimal or no formal educational qualifications, two-thirds of whom were still to be found in the declining sectors in 1985, according to the Labour Force Survey. Their numbers are actually falling as more younger workers leave school with a qualification – but for those who remain the principal alternative employment has been the unstable and (for them particularly) low-paying private consumer services, in which one in six of them work; and unemployment, which is the outcome for one in ten.

The shift in employment toward sectors which employ a higher proportion of females has apparently been occurring faster in London than elsewhere in the country, because of the more rapid de-industrialization here. But there are limits to this feminization of employment. Demand for female labor has always been relatively strong in London, which consequently has one of the highest participation rates for married females anywhere in the country, and wage levels closer to those for males than elsewhere. Migration patterns for married couples are largely determined by employment opportunities for men not women, while, with a much diminished stock of private rented accommodation and high rents, single women find migrating to London difficult. And with lower wages than males, and possible family constraints, long-distance commuting into the London area is a much less attractive option for women (who comprise only a quarter of inward commuters). Hence, it is scarcely surprising that employment forecasts predict a growing problem in meeting the demand for female labor.

In fact the shift towards females in the overall balance of employment since the early 1970s has been less marked than might have been expected, for two reasons. In manufacturing some of the fastest declines in employment (both absolutely and relative to other parts of the country) have been in low-productive/low-wage sectors employing a higher than average proportion of females – notably in the clothing trades. And the occupational shift toward high-status nonmanual jobs, still dominated by males, has more than compensated for the shift away from the other male stronghold, in skilled manual occupations. Also the vertical division of labor within both manufacturing and services has tended to retain a higher proportion of male jobs in London, while back offices and routine assembly activities with more low-status work for women have been dispersed, or lost, to other areas.

New York

In many respects the pattern of change of employment opportunities in New York has paralleled that outlined for London, although the New York metropolitan region (unlike London) has seen a substantial net growth in employment, amounting to some 1.7 million jobs between 1970 and 1986 (in the tri-state region), or about 20 percent. Within this overall growth the main features have been as follows:

1   There has been a substantial fall in manufacturing employment, with lesser falls in transport/public utilities and government employment. There was growth in almost all other sectors, with the largest absolute growth occurring in "other services" and the highest rate of growth in FIRE and other producer services. In the tri-state region production industries and transport/wholesaling declined from 3,728,000 jobs in 1970 (41 percent of the total) to 3,470,000 (32 percent) in 1986. This represents a substantial shift from manual to nonmanual activities, but one proceeding less rapidly than in the London region, where the former group declined much faster.

2   As in the London region, there has been a substantial outward shift in the balance of employment, with the number of jobs in the core of the tri-state region (including a million jobs in the Newark area as well as the 4 million in New York City) falling by 155,000 (3 percent) between 1970 and 1986, while those in the suburban ring increased by 1,882,000 (49 percent). As in London, the outward shift in the balance of employment has proceeded at a similar rate in the predominantly manual and nonmanual sectors of employment. Until the late 1970s there was also evidence of decentralization within the regional core, with employment falling fastest in Manhattan.

3   The 1970–86 period divides into two phases. Between 1970 and 1977 there was a modest decline in regional jobs, but from 1977 to

1986 there was consistent growth, amounting to over 1.6 million additional jobs. All parts of the region then showed employment growth, including Manhattan, where there was a significant net job gain, but during the 1980s the acceleration was most marked in the suburban ring. In financial and business services this does not reflect job decentralization but, rather, new jobs being created in the suburbs.

Alongside these changes in the balance and location of employment there have been two important changes in population location, and thus in labor supply. On the one hand, there has been a large-scale out-migration from New York City, mostly of whites going to the suburban rings of the metropolitan region. This has reduced the white population of the city by about 1.5 million since the early 1970s, a substantially faster rate of population decentralization than that from Greater London during this period, though not very different from that occurring there before the 1974 oil price crisis. On the other hand (see chapter 6), overseas immigration added an almost equal number of blacks, Latinos, and Asians to the New York population. These migrants were economically motivated, although their rate of arrival in New York City was not so much less in the period of employment decline from 1970 to 1977 than it was in the succeeding decade of growth.

The white outflow may have been as related to the "flight" from higher taxes and racial tensions in the city, as to its poor economic performance relative to the regional hinterland. Nevertheless, Census reports show that during the 1970s there was only a modest growth of commuting into New York City, indicating that the great majority of those moving out also found a job outside the city. Despite further growth since 1980, New York has maintained a lower share of commuters in its workforce than most major US cities (Ehrenhalt, 1984). In contrast to London, where population and employment dispersal more or less canceled each other out, in New York overseas immigration prevented labor supply from falling as fast as demand during the period of employment decline, thus pushing up unemployment. This, at a time of rapidly rising US unemployment in the late 1970s, resulted in the New York unemployment rate rising to considerably above the national level, remaining at about 9 percent well into the 1980s. So rising NYC unemployment was not reversed until substantially after the 1977 turnaround in the city's economic trends, and not until the late 1980s did city unemployment fall significantly below the national average, with its first sharp drop, to 5.7 percent, coming in 1987. More recently, since 1989 there have been renewed increases as growth in the city slowed, with unemployment reaching 7 percent in 1991. As in London, these trends are not simply a reflection of employment changes in New York but are affected by national developments also. The impact of local employment changes on New York unemployment levels is, however, considerably stronger than appears to be the case in London.

An important question is whether employment growth in New York has been essentially independent of the new influx of overseas immigrants. It could well be that by lowering the real wage in the market for low-skilled labor, migrants have actually served to boost employment in those labor-intensive activities which could not otherwise have survived in the city; or that an elastic supply of labor for consumer and support services has maintained the city's competitive position in core activities by moderating cost of living increases. Chapter 6 will show that the new migrants of Hispanic and Asian origin have taken a rather wide range of jobs. Nevertheless, one in three, and more in the former group, has gone into manufactuirng employment. Between 1970 and 1980 these new migrants absorbed about a third of the jobs vacated by the out-migration of native-born whites and the upward mobility of native-born blacks and whites. This "replacement" effect was concentrated particularly in manufacturing, retailing, personal services, wholesaling, and, to a lesser extent, in transport. In manufacturing it has been accompanied by a sharp fall in relative wages. In 1970 the average hourly wage in manufacturing production was 101.2 percent of the national figure; by 1982 it was only 87.6 percent. By contrast London manufacturing wages remain the highest in Britain, and the fastest rates of employment decline there have been occurring in the lowest paying industries, which find it especially hard to recruit staff.

In New York underemployment, in the form of low economic activity and withdrawal from the labor force, amongst both men and women, probably accounts for a larger share of the employment shortfall than does open unemployment. Participation rates in the city have been falling behind US levels for the past 20 years, and at about 55 percent are now well below the national average of almost 70 percent. In this respect there is a sharp contrast with London, where participation rates have remained amongst the highest in the country, with very few males or unmarried women apart from students outside the labor force.

Two aspects of this comparison require explanation: first, the much higher level of nonemployment in New York; and second, why this should take the form of nonparticipation rather than formal unemployment. Part of the explanation for the first factor may be the much more acute character of New York's employment crisis between 1969 and 1976, when the rate of employment contraction, especially in male-typed production jobs, must have resulted in many more forced exits from the declining sectors than occurred in London, where "natural wastage" predominated. The evidence in chapter 6 also points to the entry of new types of worker into surviving jobs (including both white-collar and downgraded production jobs), specifically new immigrants. It is unclear how far mass inmigration of groups willing to work for low wages in manual jobs has been responsible for the rise in unemployment and inactivity among Afro-Americans, but it must have been a factor. With a high proportion of those new nonmanual jobs which are open to the less qualified being female-typed, underqualified black males in particular have been squeezed into a sharply declining segment of the labor market. Thus, the higher level of unemployment and inactivity in New York City may be a product of additional labor supply, particularly at the bottom end of the labor market, occasioned by immigration, combined with a stronger ethnic segmentation of the labor market.

To explain why so many of those lacking jobs should be outside the labor force in New York City, not just unemployed, other factors would have to be taken into account, including the alternatives which are available. On the one hand, this involves the comparative incentives which the two unemployment benefit systems provide for remaining available for employment, which are probably stronger in the British case. On the other hand, it involves the possibility of other forms of remunerative activity in the criminal and informal economies, both of which appear substantially larger in New York than in London. Increased fertility rates among young minority women have also probably contributed to low labor force participation rates in the city, although the participation rates for female heads of household in New York are actually higher than in other parts of the country.

Shifts in the mix of employment in New York have had similar immediate implications to those noted for London. The growing sectors and occupations have generally been characterized by a higher proportion of female jobs and both higher entry requirements with fewer skilled or supervisory manual positions and a higher proportion of low-skilled jobs. For example, in FIRE half of all jobs are clerical, mostly not very well paid, and about a fifth are professional, mostly very well paid; in contrast to this bipolar pattern, retail and catering contain mostly low-skill, low-pay jobs, while professional services contain mostly high-skill, high-pay jobs.

In New York, as in London, a key feature of the labor market is that the share of jobs available for people lacking any formal qualification (specifically, in this context, high school graduation) has been shrinking. The growth of low-level service- and/or informal-sector jobs, in some cases linked to the availability of immigrant labor, has only partly compensated for the loss of these jobs in manufacturing and transport. Although even in FIRE about one in six jobs are held by the unqualified, this is only half the proportion in manufacturing. The position is made worse because in New York (in contrast to London) the number of adults lacking qualifications has almost certainly been growing significantly, rather than declining. There are two reasons for this. First is the lower level of educational attainment amongst the foreign-, and Puerto Rico-, born (around 40 percent of the city's adult population), about half of whom have not completed high school. The second is that in New York City high school drop-out rates have risen throughout the 1980s, and college completion rates have fallen among blacks and Hispanics. According to the 1980 Census, 22 percent of jobs in New York City were held by people without high school qualifications, close to the national average. However, in New York City 40 percent of the population fell into this category, against 30 percent nationally (Chall, 1985). This suggests that the educationally unqualified are heavily represented amongst the unemployed and those working in the informal and criminal economies (including the labor-intensive crack industry), accounting for a large part of the low participation rates in the city.

URBAN LABOR MARKET RESTRUCTURING

The changes in the functioning of the London and New York labor markets occurring since the early 1970s have several possible origins. The most evident are the long-term shifts in the occupational and industrial balance of employment, which directly affect the mix of job characteristics, including earnings levels and employment stability, and the careers available to local workers. These changing trends in the character of labor demand predate the oil price crises of the 1970s but their effects have been cumulative, and magnified by other developments in the labor market over this period. On the demand side these include the new flexibility which employers have sought under the pressure of international competition, unstable product markets, and a weakening of political support for public-sector programs. On the supply side a key factor common to the two cities has been the persistence of high unemployment over a decade (or more, in New York), which has strengthened the bargaining position of employers, and the insecurity or marginalization of the most disadvantaged groups in the labor market. In New York but not in London a factor of equal importance has been the rapid growth of a new immigrant population since the late 1960s, occupying distinct positions in the labor market. In combination these major developments on the two sides of the labor market, all of which have operated most strongly in the urban cores, imply, on the one hand, a growing destabilization of employment, with increasing casualization and/or informalization of jobs, and, on the other hand, an increasing polarization of employment opportunities, with new forms of social divisions. However, the extent to which these outcomes have in fact materialized needs to be examined in relation to possible countervailing forces in the two cities.

In London the shift in the occupational and industrial mix of employment has indeed produced a polarization of jobs in terms of earnings levels. Table 4.2 shows that the three growth sectors of employment exhibit higher proportions of jobs in *both* the highest and lowest hourly earnings brackets than is the case with the three sectors whose employment has been declining. This pattern reflects the substantial proportion of jobs for educationally highly qualified workers, particularly in producer services, as well as the very low hourly earnings received by workers lacking any formal qualification. In growth sectors 44 percent

Table 4.2 Hourly pay and turnover rates for expanding and contracting sectors in London

| Sector | % workers with hourly pay: | | | | Percentage workers changing firm during year |
	<2.72	2.72–4.48	4.48–7.39 (£)	>7.39	
Contracting					
Manufacturing	18.3	41.5	30.0	10.2	10.9
Other production	16.1	36.8	36.8	10.3	8.4
Transport/storage	16.6	44.9	25.4	13.0	9.1
Expanding					
Private consumer services	48.3	30.1	14.2	7.5	14.7
Producer services	8.6	37.2	36.2	17.9	12.3
Public services	21.5	34.7	28.6	15.8	9.6
Total	22.0	37.0	28.0	13.0	10.8
of which:					
3 contracting sectors	17.4	41.8	29.5	11.1	. .
3 expanding sectors	24.6	34.3	27.2	14.0	. .

Sources: Greater London Living Standards Survey (GLC area *only*), 1987–8 unpublished data; and 1985 Labour Force Survey (GLC and OMA together)

of this latter group of workers had hourly earnings in the lowest category identified in table 4.2. However, in the contracting sectors only 18 percent of unqualified workers had such low earnings, the same proportion as for all qualified workers. Many of these low-paid workers are employed in private consumer services. This is the only one of the expanding sectors to offer a proportion of opportunities for unqualified workers comparable to those of the three declining sectors. However, pay in private consumer services is depressed by more competitive market conditions, small firm sizes, relatively short employment durations, and a preponderance of "female" jobs.

Occupational shifts within industries, with growing proportions of administrative, technical, and professional staff, and falling shares of manual workers, have also contributed toward earnings polarization. In this case, however, the polarization is concentrated in the upper tail of the earnings distribution, whereas intersectoral shifts in employment have enlarged both tails at the expense of the middle. The polarizing tendency in earnings levels has been accentuated by changes in the relative earnings of the major occupational groups, although again these changes have primarily affected the upper end of the income distributions. In particular, the rapid growth of administrative, technical, and professional workers, especially in producer services, has been accompanied by a substantial enhancement of their earnings. The most conspicuous examples have occurred in the City of London, where substantial skill shortages in the expanding financial services were compounded by the increasing internationalization and openness in the relevant labor market. These factors caused a leveling up of salaries for top London-based dealers and managers to those offered in other global financial centres, including New York (Thrift et al., 1987). Thus, a gap in the earnings distribution has been opening up below the top 5–10 percent of the London workforce.[3]

The second important consequence of the long-term sectoral shift in London employment has been a change in the division of the labor market between more and less stable jobs. Of the three expanding sectors, only public services display rates of turnover close to those in the three declining sectors (see table 4.2). Private consumer services, including activities such as retailing and catering, have rates of turnover almost half as high again as typical jobs in the declining sectors – a fact of particular significance to the formally unqualified workers, who increasingly have to rely on these jobs. But even the producer service sector, including such traditionally secure employers as the banks and insurance companies, was by the mid-1980s experiencing turnover rates well in excess of those in manufacturing (or public services). For a time this phenomenon reflected the strength of labor demand in financial services, as firms scrambled to recruit scarce skills in the period around "Big Bang," but, as subsequent redundancies have indicated, this event almost certainly marked a once-for-all shift away from the very secure employment conditions which oligopolistic market structures had previously afforded in the City. (In that respect this part of the London labor market may have moved closer to its New York counterpart.) However, while this change has produced individual casualties, instability in employment conditions for qualified workers in producer services lacks much of the significance which it has for the less qualified. At the individual level, analyses of the determinants of earnings indicate that careers which include multiple jobs within a particular occupation (reflecting what has been called a "guild" labor market) can prove as positive a work history as having a series of occupations for one employer – avoiding the stigma often attached to the multiple occupation/multiple employer careers of those without strong occupational identities (Gordon, 1991a). For professional or managerial jobs in a competitive sector it is hard to prevent workers acquiring skills and experience with transferable value. This is very unlikely to occur in many other types of unstable jobs. Nevertheless it is an important fact that, since growth in public services was checked in the early 1980s, employment expansion in London has been dependent on sectors with relatively high turnover rates, since this increases the importance of the external labor market, and the value of the particular pools of labor to which it provides access in London.

One factor which has, in contrast, depressed turnover rates in London over the past decade has been the high level of unemployment, which has made workers much more reluctant voluntarily to quit their jobs. At the same time, however, the pressures of recession and the existence of a slack labor market have encouraged employers to seek more "flexibility" in employment conditions and in sourcing services. One important instance has been the restructuring of the "Fleet Street" national newspaper industry on new sites in Docklands, and elsewhere, where it has been able, despite prolonged and even violent resistance in some instances, to introduce new technology, multi-skilling, and lower manning levels, and to remove union control over labor supply and working practices. However, now that a substantially new workforce is in place, this restructuring may not in the longer term have increased turnover rates or instability at the firm level, since a feature of the traditional system was short-term hiring from a pool controlled by labor unions – the last important case of this kind (following the loss of the port employment) among London's manual workers.

A second significant instance of the new flexibility is the drive to "contract out" public services to private firms, pioneered by Wands-

worth, a Conservative Inner London borough, and then actively promoted by legislation which requires competitive tendering for a range
of local government tasks. The cost-cutting rationale for these initiatives
(which also had political/ideological functions) in typically labor-intensive manual tasks depended largely on the intensification of work and
the use of cheaper and more flexible sources of unorganized labor.

Another facet of labor market change in London during the 1980s
was a sharp growth in the number of self-employed workers. These
increased by almost a half between 1981 and 1989. By the latter date
they accounted for a sixth of male jobs in the city – although only about
5 percent of female jobs. Rapid growth has also occurred in temporary,
casual, or fixed-term appointments. However, all of these latter groups
remain limited in size, accounting for only some 7 percent of the London
workforce in1989, and greatly outnumbered by those in nominally
permanent but practically short-lived employment relationships.

Earnings polarization is also a clear feature of economic change in
New York City, associated with the growing importance of service
employment. Cross-sectional comparisons of US metropolitan areas have
shown that high levels of service employment are associated with greater
inequality in male earnings, primarily due to the effect of producer
service employment on the highest bands of earnings (Nelson and Lorence, 1985, p. 115). In New York City FIRE is clearly the highest paying
sector, with an annual average pay in 1987 of $43,964, twice the city
average and well ahead of its nearest rival industries. This was despite
the fact that no more than 25 percent of the labor force in the FIRE
industries were in the professional and managerial category, 49 percent
being clerical and 13 percent service, production, and maintenance
workers.[4] And Bureau of Labor Statistics data on median earnings of
office workers show that for many of these categories rates were actually
lower in services than in manufacturing, transport, or utilities. The
implication is that (as in London) high average earnings in financial and
business services largely reflect the very high salaries achieved by a small
minority of professionals in the industry. Indeed Sheets, Nord, and
Phelps (1987) indicate, from an analysis across metropolitan areas, that
the corporate service sector (of which FIRE is a significant part) was
also responsible for the highest proportion of full-time jobs paying
poverty level wages (37 percent). Its only rival in this respect was
retailing, which in addition contained a *very* high proportion of poverty
level part-time jobs. The prominence of these two sectors in New York
City contributes to an overall assessment that 21 percent of workers
there are "underemployed," in the sense of having poverty level annual
earnings: this is at the high end of the range for the 100 largest Standard
Metropolitan Statistical Areas (Sheets et al., 1987, p. 162).

Alongside this change in the city's employment structure there have been major shifts in the composition of its labor supply, with a large growth in the share of Afro-Americans, Puerto Ricans, and immigrant minorities in the city's resident labor force. These two trends largely account for the "ethnic succession" detailed in chapter 6. This succession of minority workers to niches in the labor market previously occupied by whites suggests that continuing inequalities in the labor market and growing underemployment cannot really be ascribed to a "jobs mismatch." However, this may not signify any more fundamental opening-up of the opportunity structure to nonwhite minorities, as suggested, for example, by Kasarda (1985). This is because, while some of these groups have gained greater access to professional, managerial, and administrative jobs, most of these jobs are in government, particularly local government, while private-sector management and the key corporate service jobs remain largely the preserve of whites. Secondly, nonwhite minorities continue to earn significantly less than whites in the same occupational segments, although this white advantage, while very pronounced among men, is slight among women, partly because of the industries and occupations that all women tend to be concentrated in. The pattern clearly remains one of a highly segmented labor market in which race, as well as class and gender, determines competitive success.

This picture is elaborated in Melendez's (1990) detailed analysis of 1980 Census data for New York City in terms of core and periphery industries and the primary and secondary occupational segments. Almost all core sector employment among Afro-Americans was in local government, with fewer than 19 percent of Afro-American men and 3 percent of women in private-sector core industries. Puerto Ricans and other Hispanics had only slightly higher shares of private-sector core industry employment. The distribution of workers by occupational segment shows that half of white men were in the upper tier of the primary occupational segment compared with 30 percent in the case of Afro-Americans, Puerto Ricans, and other Hispanics. But only one-sixth of these white men, compared with almost all of the Afro-Americans, were in government jobs. This confirms data presented by Brint (1991) which show the concentration of those Afro-Americans in professional occupations within the social services and their slight representation in corporate services. Melendez's analysis also shows that Hispanic men were concentrated in the secondary occupational segment and Hispanic women in the lowest tier of the primary occupational segment.

Melendez's study also found significant earnings differentials between whites and minority workers in the same occupational segments. White men are overrepresented in professional, technical, and control occupations. Observed earnings of minority men in white-collar jobs were similar to those of white men in crafts, the second tier of white-collar jobs. And observed earnings of minority men in these occupations were similar to those of white men in the next lowest occupation segment. In the case of women he found similar patterns but with a much smaller advantage for white women than for white men, perhaps because the women were less able to achieve labor market closure. Significantly he found that whites obtained over 30 percent higher returns on education than did Afro-Americans and Hispanics – effectively paralleling evidence for London that the possession of formal qualifications does less to reduce the chances of unemployment for Afro-Caribbeans and South Asians than for whites. Though there were great variations between different groups, Melendez's findings lend further support to the view that labor market outcomes reflect uneven processes of competition for available opportunities rather than any simple allocation on the basis of the human capital required.

From this perspective any explanation of the growing problem of underemployment in New York City in terms of an inability to adapt to the increasingly skill-intensive nature of its job structure – the so-called "mismatch thesis" – must be seen as too simplistic (N. I. Fainstein, 1987). The significant change is not that low-skill jobs are no longer being created but that many fewer of these offer stable employment prospects, the opportunity for occupational advancement, and a reasonable incentive to develop the personal skills required to compete for primary-sector jobs.

INFORMAL EMPLOYMENT

The extreme case of this pressure toward "flexibility" in employment relations is the growth of the so-called "informal sector." This has been defined in various ways, for different purposes. In labor market terms the salient aspect of "informality" is employers' avoidance of state-regulated employment conditions, in regard to health and safety, minimum wages, and work permits, etc. This can allow a lowering of the costs of employing labor, and also of space costs, by operating out of basements, homes, and other spaces not approved for commercial or industrial uses.

The incentive for firms to evade such regulations, and their capacity to do so, vary according to the sectors and locations involved. Pressures to reduce labor costs are greatest in labor-intensive and highly competitive industries with limited profit margins. Some of these activities have been squeezed out of London and New York as rents and wages are pushed up by higher bidders. Those remaining are strongly linked to local demand, as in the case of building, consumer services such as catering, retail, and cleaning, and the high fashion end of the garment trade.

Some of these local demands have risen as a consequence of the "globalization" of London and New York (Sassen, 1991a). One example is the sharp growth in demand for small-scale renovation, woodwork, painting, etc. associated with residential and commercial gentrification. Polarization in the income and consumption structures has also affected the organization of work and the types of job being created, especially in private consumer services. At one extreme, gentrification and growth of the high-income workforce has increased demands for customized goods and personal service on a more labor-intensive and small-scale basis than was characteristic of middle-class, suburban, "fordist" development (Sassen, 1988). The Yuppy life style, with its specialist boutiques, delicatessens, and hired maintenance staff, depends to a large extent on the availability of a local supply of low-wage workers. At the other extreme, the growing mass of poor and underemployed people, with more limited mobility and storage capacities than the middle mass, have consumption needs which are better met by small local manufacturing and retail establishments (often reliant on family labor and falling below minimum safety and health standards) than by large-scale standardized factories and stores. And throughout the consumption spectrum, pressure to operate for longer hours, including nights, weekends, and holidays, is being met more economically through part-time work than costly overtime payments, especially where little in the way of skills or training is involved.[5] Such part-time work is not necessarily either unstable or unregulated, but is generally lower paid and more readily escapes formalization.

Firms' opportunities to escape control are greatest where establishments are small, labor-intensive, and/or mobile, and when the labor force is transitory and/or part-time but drawn from a relatively closed community of groups marginalized from the mainstream labor market. It is principally this last factor, rather than cultural traits or specific skills, which links the informal sector to immigrant communities and indigenous minorities.

There is a much more substantial informal sector in New York than in London. In New York the informal sector has been shown to be important in various aspects of construction, in auto-repairs, "gypsy" cabs, home-based personal services in low-income areas, in the clothing trade, and in some other manufactures (such as furniture, electronics, and toys) competing with Third World production (Sassen, 1989). Many of the services just listed are also undertaken "informally" in London, and comparative studies have shown very similar immigrant sweatshop operations within the garment trade in the two cities (Morokvasic et al., 1988). But the scale, particularly of manufacturing operations, is almost certainly much smaller in London – because of the considerably lower level of recent immigration from the Third World, the smaller scale of the clothing industry compared with New York, and the lower proportion of the working-age population falling outside the official labor force. Comparisons of the 1981 Population and Employment Censuses for London suggest that around 2 percent of workers might then have been outside the formal sector (mostly in service activities), to which might be added a lesser number from among those claiming to be inactive (Gordon, 1991b). However, in both cities the boundaries of the informal sector are hard to establish. Informality is not necessarily associated with the employment of undocumented immigrants. There are informal operations that employ citizens. Nor is informality the same as criminality. Thus, many informal operations are not clandestine, and are even above ground, as in the case of unionized garment sweatshops in New York City.

In fact, the strictly unregulated sector of the labor market is only the tip of an iceberg of poorly or barely regulated employment, in which minimum wage and other provisions are commonly breached and conditions are generally poor. What is distinctive about this part of the labor market is not simply its low pay and low entry requirements. Indeed in many cases pay and skill levels can be higher than in the fully regulated economy (Portes et al., 1989). Rather, they are characterized by competitiveness and instability, coupled with a dependence on particularistic local relationships. The spread of such conditions has proceeded in parallel with the growing high order activities of these cities.

CONCLUSION

At the end of the 1980s the labor markets of these two cities had much in common. Within each city, as in the two nations as a whole, there is now an emergent employment structure which is strongly differentiated in terms of rewards, the permanence of the employment relation, and conditions of access to the jobs for workers from different class, race, gender, and educational backgrounds. Highly unequal outcomes have resulted from employment restructuring. These are further exaggerated, particularly in relation to unemployment, when there is slack in the wider labor market, as was the case in both countries during the early 1980s (and is again in the early 1990s). The competitive metropolitan context encourages greater instability in employment relations than in the two national economies as a whole, and this tendency has been reinforced by rapid de-industrialization and the enhancement of the two cities' role as global control centers. These processes have had two polarizing effects on the labor market. Employment growth has occurred at both the top and (to a lesser extent) the bottom end of the earnings distribution, while in the period of rapid growth of financial and business services during the 1980s scarcity pushed the topmost salaries even higher. Even more fundamental, however, has been the loss of a core of manual jobs offering both security and the chance of occupational advancement to formally unqualified individuals from the cities' working class. The new employment structure continues to offer job opportunities to the unqualified, but preponderantly within unstable sectors of employment, presenting recurring risks of unemployment and economic marginalization.

New York's experience differs from that of London in three main respects: the acute economic crisis preceding its 1976–87 boom in employment; the large-scale immigration from the Third World; and its growing proportion of working-age people who are outside the formal labor force. A further contextual factor is that, while racial discrimination clearly operates in both cities' labor markets, in New York its victims comprise about half of the labor force as against a sixth in London. Together these differences point to, and help explain, the much more severe impact of restructuring processes on the lower part of the New York labor market. In London there has been a growing "underclass," if one defines this in Runciman's (1990) sense of a group "unable to participate in the labour market at all," but these remain a very small minority, generally lacking the distinct cultural attitudes often attributed by analysts such as Murray (1990) to an "underclass" (cf. Heath, 1991), and substantially outnumbered by those who *do* participate in the labor market, albeit on an interrupted, insecure, and unsatisfactory basis. In New York, however, the potential members of such an "underclass" apear substantially more numerous, and more independent of the mainstream labor market, and the associated social and regulatory controls. Contrary to the notion, advanced by Murray (1984), for example, that welfare dependency is the problem, this could partly reflect the fact that fewer of those involved in New York City can actually "depend" on welfare! In neither city is it clear, contrary to the thesis advanced by Kasarda (1985) and Wilson (1987), that exclusion from the formal labor market is mainly the product of job mismatch.

NOTES

1   Turnover rates in London employment are significantly higher than in most other areas of Britain and Scott (1988a) shows a similar differential between manufacturing in New York City and in its hinterland.

2   According to unpublished 1989 Labour Force Survey data.

3   According to the New Earnings Survey, for full-time adult men in Greater London the ratio of upper decile to median weekly earnings increased from 168 percent in 1979 to 199 percent in 1990; the comparable national ratios were 156 percent and 181 percent; because *most* of London workforce (if not the lower quartile) had faster earnings increases than workers elsewhere, the upper decile in London as a ratio of the *national* median actually moved up from 186 percent to 247 percent over this period.

4   According to unpublished data from New York State Department of Labor occupational surveys for 1984–6.

5   In recent years about 40 percent of registered openings in New York City have been for part-timers; these are heavily concentrated in service occupations, with very few openings for part-time factory work. For example, in 1987 60 percent of the openings were part-time in the case of professional, technical, and managerial occupations, and also of clerical jobs, as against 1 percent of the jobs in benchwork, or in machining (New York State Department of Labor, 1988).

5

Poverty and income inequality

John Logan, Peter Taylor-Gooby, and Monika Reuter

Previous chapters have documented the rapid restructuring of the economies of London and New York and the changing social mix of the cities' populations. These changes raise pressing questions about patterns of inequality in the two cities. In the early 1980s civic boosters assumed that if the cities could successfully manage the transition from a manufacturing to a service-based economy, general prosperity would result. Governing regimes in both places developed strategies to encourage rapid transformation (see chapter 8). It quickly became apparent, however, that growth in property development and advanced services did not improve the situation of the bottom quartile of the population. This chapter examines in detail the impacts of economic change on income differences within the two cities; broader issues relating to the changing patterns of social stratification are discussed in chapter 9.

The New York economy has been transformed with massive losses in the industrial sector. Since manufacturing served earlier in the century as the basis for the absorption of working-class immigrants, many have argued that its precipitous decline has reduced opportunities and led to an equally rapid increase in poverty and income inequality (Tobier, 1984; Sassen-Koob, 1984). Even during the peak of 1980s economic growth, the city's poverty rate stabilized at a level substantially above that of the preceding decade (Rosenberg, 1989). A newspaper columnist (Hentoff, 1989) recently compared current conditions to those of the nineteenth century:

> When Charles Dickens first came to New York in 1842; he was shocked to see so much that was cruel and hideous in the way certain people were allowed by the city to live here. But today,

again, the contrasts between prosperous New York and poverty-stricken New York are startling, indeed frightening.

Moreover, although it gained in total population in the 1980s, New York City lost residents to its suburban ring with a high degree of selectivity: out-migrants have been disproportionately white and middle class, while the streams of new migrants into the city have been disproportionately poor and composed of racial and ethnic minorities (Frey and Speare, 1988).

In London the loss of manufacturing jobs proceeded even more rapidly (see chapter 4). The expansion in service-sector jobs was most marked in the recovery from the recession of the early 1980s, but, as in New York, the benefits of this growth were unequally distributed. There was a substantial decline in population within the entire region. London lost over a quarter of its inner city population between 1964 and 1982, and a twentieth of the population of its Outer Metropolitan Area, although the population of both inner and outer areas stabilized between 1983 to 1987 and even showed a slight increase (London Research Centre, 1989a). As in New York, the irony of simultaneously expanding deprivation and affluence became quickly evident. A report on Townsend's 1986 survey of Londoners' Living Standards (LLS) points out that the evidence of severe deprivation – disabled and elderly people too poor to heat their homes, unemployed people sleeping rough in winter – precisely parallels the concerns that led to Booth's London study a hundred years earlier (Townsend et al., 1987). A recent observer wrote:

> If Thomas Barnado were to return to London today, no doubt he would be impressed by the advances and technology of the eighties. However, he would also have a sense of *déjà vu*. Beneath the veneer of our civilisation there is a great deal that has not changed since the time he began his work ... in the mid-nineteenth century. (O'Mahony, 1988: xi)

By contrast, as in New York, the desirable areas attract the super-rich: "London combines pockets of Britain's greatest wealth with some of its worst unemployment – and within walking distance of each other" (Kellner, 1989).

PATTERNS OF INEQUALITY

The simplest and most general indicators of welfare and inequality are the level and distribution of real income. The available evidence indicates a substantial increase in income inequality in both cities. For New York, the pattern appears roughly comparable to changes in other US cities, while income inequality in London has deteriorated relative to other British cities. At the same time, inequalities between ethnic groups and between different spatial areas have become more marked in both.

Table 5.1 shows the pattern of inequality in gross household incomes for both cities, measured by the ratio of the first and third quartiles (the 25th and 75th percentage points of the distribution). In London in the late 1970s, inequalities in gross incomes were less marked than those in New York. As the recession of the early 1980s deepened, however, inequalities became substantially greater for London, and the trend to inequality continues to include the latest available data (for 1988) despite the economic recovery and the fall in unemployment from the mid-1980s. Hence, while initially inequality in New York considerably

Table 5.1 Inequalities in household income in London and New York, 1977–1988

(a) Ratio of incomes of top and bottom quartile

	1977–80	1980	1983	1986	1987	1988
London	2.77	2.85	3.44	3.68	3.86	4.37
New York	3.47	3.50	3.73	3.81	NA	NA

(b) Percentage changes in real household income

	1977 80	1980–3	1983–6	1986–8
Lowest decile				
London	+12.2	+1	−8.6	−13.7
New York	−5.4	−7.1	−1.2	NA
Lowest quartile				
London	+5.0	−12.7	+4.0	−3.7
New York	−1.0	−5.0	+10	NA
Highest Quartile				
London	+8.3	+5.1	+11.2	+14.3
New York	0	+3	+15	NA
Highest Decile				
London	+12.1	+6.5	+19.3	+8.4
New York	+2	+6	+16	NA

Note: Quartiles for New York are based on third and eighth decile means. Statistics are adjusted for inflation by the Consumer Price Index and the Retail Price Index.
Sources: Stegman, 1988; UK Department of Employment and Central Statistical Office, 1977, 1980, 1983, 1986 (rev.), and 1988

exceeded that in London, the situations have almost converged (Buck, 1990). The lowest income groups in London have fared particularly badly: the ratio of the income of the lowest quartile to the median has fallen from 54 percent in 1980 to 39 percent in 1988, and that of the lowest decile from 30 percent to 20 percent – a striking drop in the relative living standards of the poor. The statistics for New York show a more gradual pattern of change. There is some indication that inequality there was more directly linked to the impact of the recession of the early 1980s, and that the income gap may have ceased to grow broader.

The difference between the New York and London patterns is due to changes at both ends of the income scale, as section (b) of table 5.1 indicates. Not only have the better-off grown wealthy more rapidly in London than in New York, the worse-off have grown poorer at a much faster rate. As of this writing, data showing the impact of the 1990–2 recession in both cities on income are not yet available. The likely effect, however, is continued worsening of the bottom combined with stagnation or decline at the top.

The degree of inequality in New York does not seem to be remarkably greater than that in other American cities. The Gini coefficient is a measure of the extent to which income distribution deviates from the straight-line relationship of perfect equality. A coefficient calculated from the Annual Housing Surveys of the US Census Bureau for New York City increased from 0.43 to 0.46 between 1976 and 1983. The mean coefficient for cities with over 100,000 population was somewhat lower at 0.41. In Britain the pattern is rather different. Incomes in other conurbations tend to be substantially lower than in London (Buck, 1991a, tables 4–8). However, inequality increased rather more rapidly over the period within London than it did outside it. The inter-quartile ratio in Britain's other major conurbations shifted from 2.86 in 1977 to 3.71 in 1988, compared with a shift from 2.77 to 4.37 in London. It is noticeable that, although inequalities become more marked everywhere during and after the 1980–3 recession, the situation in London deteriorated much more rapidly than elsewhere.

Table 5.1 also shows the striking advantage of the highest income groups. Section (b) of the table shows changes in real incomes for groups at various levels in the income distribution. In both London and New York the higher groups made gains in real income throughout the 1980s. This is particularly true after the end of the 1980–3 recession. Lower-income groups fared less well. In New York the lower quartile sustained real losses in the early 1980s which were retrieved only toward the end of the period. The lowest decile faced real income losses over the whole period. For London the lower quartile retrieved some of its losses in the mid-1980s only again to face further deterioration in real household incomes. The lowest decile experienced an accelerating decline in income – a stark increase in the misery of the poorest. Better-off groups are predominantly dependent on earned income for their living standards, whereas the poor rely almost entirely on state benefits. These statistics give a preliminary indication that economic restructuring has led to a sharper concentration of high incomes at the top end in London, and that the decline in state benefits relative to earned income has been more rapid in London than in New York.

The New York housing study also gives data on the impact of income inequalities among ethnic minorities. Table 5.2 shows the pattern of changes. White and black people experienced real losses in the late 1970s which were restored in the 1980s. The losses experienced by Hispanic people and other groups (mainly Asian) were larger and less easily made up. There is some suggestive evidence from the survey that the pressure of falling living standards led to an increase in participation in paid employment among those hardest hit by it. The average number of wage-earners per household increased from 0.89 to 0.98 among black people in the period 1976–83, from 0.84 to 0.91 among Hispanic people, and remained at 1.13 among people in white households. The average number of workers in households in the top 20 percent of the income distribution actually fell.

Equivalent data showing changing patterns over time for London are not conveniently available. British black minorities are heavily concentrated in London, especially in the inner city. In 1982 12 percent of the white population of Britain lived in Greater London, as against 49 percent of the population of West Indian origin (two-thirds of them in the inner city), 34 percent of the population of Asian origin (half in the

Table 5.2   Changes in real household income for different racial groups (percentages), New York

	1977–80	*1980–83*	*1983–6*
White	−2	+10	+11
Black	−2	+7	+14
Puerto Rican	NA	−4	+8
Others	−14	−6	+16
All	−2	−1	+19

Note: "Others" are mainly Asian and Native American. All figures are adjusted for inflation by the Consumer Price Index.
Source: Stegman, 1988

inner city), and two-thirds of the Bangladeshi population (95 percent in the inner city: C. Brown, 1984, p. 61). The black minorities in London tend to get lower wages and face higher levels of unemployment than does the white population, but the gap is not as wide as in other regions, particularly the East Midlands and the North-West. Average full-time earnings for black people are about 8 percent lower than those of white people in London, as against 15 percent nationally (Bhat et al., 1988, p. 65). Analysis of the 1985 to 1987 Labor Force Surveys shows that unemployment among ethnic minorities in Greater London was 16 percent as against 9 percent for white people (*UK Department of Employment*, 1988b, table 12). There is some evidence that black people fare disproportionately worse in the labor market in times of recession. It thus seems likely that ethnic minorities will have experienced worse deprivation than the rest of the population in the early 1980s, and that this will have been translated into household incomes. The effect of this on labor force participation in London is unclear, since pressure to increase incomes may be offset by decreased job opportunities.

EXPLANATIONS OF INEQUALITY

In an authoritative paper on explanations of inequality, Buck (1991a) identifies six themes which are interlinked in explanation. These are: changes in state benefits compared with labor market earnings; the different rate of growth of earnings for different occupational groups; changes in household composition; changes in the level of unemployment; increased rates of participation in paid work by married women; and the changing balance of manufacturing and service-sector employment.

Evidence can be found to point to the importance of all six factors in Britain and in London. Thus the basic means-tested benefit (supplementary benefit/income support rates) fell behind the increase in prices by 1 percent betwen 1979 and 1987, whereas per capita disposable income forged ahead by 14 percent (Hills, 1987); top decile earnings for men rose from 160 percent to 173 percent of the median between 1976 and 1986, and for women from 166 percent to 170 percent, whereas the bottom deciles shifted from 68 to 66 percent and 60 percent to 65 percent, respectively. (*UK Department of Employment*, 1976, 1986). The proportion of households outside the labor market increased – thus the proportion with a retired head rose from 18 percent to 24 percent between 1979 and 1986 and the proportion with a head "unoccupied" (that is, a student, long-term unemployed, or a house-spouse) rose from 10 percent to 13 percent (*UK Department of Employment and Central Statistical Office*, 1980, 1987).

The growth of unemployment, the increase in jobs performed by married women (mainly in the service sector), and the restructuring of the labor market have already been discussed in previous chapters. The problem is how to analyze the relative importance of each factor. Buck applies a method which involves reweighing data from the official Labour Force Surveys for 1979 and 1985 to analyze the effect of each factor taken separately. His work demonstrates that a rather different pattern of causes of inequality is at work among the various income groups. For the bottom three deciles, where the lion's share (some 70 percent in 1985/6, according to the LLS survey) of household incomes comes from state benefits, the main reason why incomes fall behind the median is the lack of growth in these benefits. In the next two deciles the most important factor is rising unemployment, coupled with the increase in numbers of one-parent families. At the top real incomes rise because people suffer relatively little from unemployment and because managerial, professional, and technical grade salaries have risen rapidly.

The evidence in table 5.1 suggests that the inadequacy of state benefits to sustain living standards among the poorest has become more marked in the mid- and especially the late 1980s. On the other hand, the restructuring of the labor market to create more service-sector jobs, especially in the financial sector, has particularly benefited those groups who are already relatively well-off.

THE IMPACT OF INEQUALITY ON THE POOR

Inequality is an abstraction. Poor people rarely have a very good sense of just how their own situation compares with the whole population. More concretely, though, they experience the discrepancy between their own resources and what it costs to live decently. For the nonpoor it is harder to grasp the reality of the social situation.

The impact of inequality on the poor and the implications for social polarization have excited considerable attention in London (for example, Dahrendorf, 1987; Murray, 1990). The most striking evidence of destitution is to be found in the reemergence of beggars and homeless people in large numbers (see chapter 7). This highly visible face of poverty, including large numbers of young unemployed people denied benefits by changes in social security regulations, has attracted considerable media attention. For example, the *Guardian* (1988) reports "five years ago it was unusual to be accosted and asked for money on a walk round the centre, but now it is almost inevitable and the supplicants are younger." The Advisory Centre for Squatters estimated that there were over 30,000 young squatters in London by the mid-1980s (O'Mahony, 1988, p. 14). A survey carried out by the Salvation Army in July 1989 found over 75,000 people sleeping rough on one night in the city.

The less publicly visible face of homelessness is the treatment of those who are accepted as qualifying for rehousing under legislation that excludes almost all single people and families without dependent children, and who thus generate official statistics. The number accepted more than doubled between 1978 and 1988 to about 30,000 – equivalent to over 1 per cent of the households resident in the area. The main reasons for this increase are the cuts in social housing expenditure – amounting to an £11 billion reduction in planned spending between 1979 and 1989 – and competition with better-off people for available housing, in which the poor inevitably lose out. The shortage of adequate property for rehousing is indicated by the increased use of temporary accommodation. In 1978 less than 15 percent of the homeless were placed in temporary dwellings. By 1988 the proportion had risen to over 80 percent, the biggest single group of them in cheap bed-and-breakfast hotels specializing in homeless people, which provide unsatisfactory housing for families with children (London Housing Unit, 1989, pp. 60, 61). A disproportionate number of the households accepted as homeless in 1988 were female-headed. Black people were also heavily overrepresented. Forty per cent of acceptances were for ethnic minorities, who account for less than a tenth of all households (London Housing Unit, 1989, pp. 52–4). Over half of households accepted as homeless had previously lived with friends or relatives.

In New York, as in London and many other cities, increasing poverty coincided with sharp cutbacks in the construction of low-income housing (see chapter 7). Further, the private housing market has operated to replace large blocks of cheap housing in single-room occupancy hotels with renovations or new construction at high rents (Swanstrom, 1989). Large numbers of homeless persons, including increasing numbers of families with children, have appeared on the streets of New York. Welfare hotels have been filled to capacity, and emergency shelters have been established throughout the city, often meeting resistance from angry neighbors. In August 1988 there were about 5,100 families in emergency housing (including 6,900 adults and 10,800 children). About half of these families leave emergency housing within two to three months; the remainder could expect an average duration of one to two years.

One study of the origins of homeless people in New York (New York City Human Resources Administration, 1989, p. 6) found a similar pattern to that of homeless people in London. About a quarter were families headed by young mothers or pregnant women. Another 18 percent were families who had never had a place of their own. Many of these had previously lived with friends or relatives: estimates of doubled-up housing in New York City range from 100,000 to 300,000 units. Another 19 percent had been evicted or left their own homes due to problems in paying their rent.

The evidence by official definitions

Less visible than the homeless, but much greater in numbers, are the persons who live below the poverty line, but out of the public eye. In the United States the federal Bureau of Labor Statistics determines income levels for households of various sizes in each metropolitan area that are used to mark the poverty line, based on the cost of living. For New York City there have been increases that can be described only as shocking in the proportions of persons who are below this level. In 1970 the proportion of persons living below the official poverty line was 14.6 percent. This increased to 18.5 percent in 1977, 20.9 percent in 1980, and 23.9 percent in 1985, falling slightly to 23.2 percent in 1987 (Rosenberg, 1989, p. 57). Nearly one in four persons was in poverty in 1990.

Poverty in New York disproportionately affects children, families headed by unmarried women, and the nonwhite racial groups. The poverty rate in 1987 was 37.5 percent for children under 18 years of age. The number of families headed by an unmarried woman increased by about a third between 1975 and 1986 and the percentage of these families who lived in poverty rose from 47 percent to 67 percent over that period (Barbanel, 1989a). The current poverty rate is 33.8 percent for black and 41.6% for Hispanic people (Levine, 1989). Even Asians, who are often stereotyped as the successful immigrant group, are over-represented among the poor, with a poverty rate of about 30 percent (Howe, 1989). The risk factors are cumulative. For example, the poverty rate among Puerto Rican women under the age of 25 in female-headed renter households is 73 percent, making poverty the norm for such persons (Stegman, 1988).

The concentration of poverty among nonwhite and among female-headed households in New York is striking. Households in the lowest fifth of the income distribution in 1983 were roughly twice as likely to be female-headed as male-headed. The chances of being included in the poorest fifth of households were about 1 in 7 for white, about 1 in 4 black, and about 1 in 3 for Hispanic people. Of renter households receiving public assistance, over 80 percent are nonwhite and over 80 percent female-headed.

For London, estimates based on the government's means-tested benefit standard and using official figures indicate that about a third of a million people lived below the means-test level in 1983 (Townsend et al., 1987, p. 47). Another 600,000 received means-tested benefits and a further 900,000 lived at the margins of poverty. Taken together, these figures indicate that some 28 percent of the 6.4 million population of Greater London live in poverty. The percentage for London thus exceeds New York's, although differences in measurement techniques might account for the dissimilarity. The greater availability of publicly provided services, especially health and housing, in London than in New York undoubtedly lessens somewhat the burden of poverty for most poor London households as compared to their New York counterparts.[1]

Poverty in London is concentrated among nonwhite and female-headed households, but the extent of the concentration is nothing like as great as in New York. In the LLS survey, for example, over two-thirds of the individuals reporting problems in managing financially were white, and only one-fifth black or Asian people. Forty percent were in couple households, as against 12 percent in households based on a lone female. Black people were only twice as likely to report difficulties in managing financially as were white people (although there are concentrations of much higher rates of deprivation, for example among the Bangladeshi community in Tower Hamlets). Single-parent households were roughly three times as likely to say that they found it hard to manage. A key difference is that no ethnic minority in London contains anything like the concentration of single-parent households which exists among Hispanic and black people in New York. Thus, the factors which lead to risk of falling into poverty do not overlap to the same extent in London as they do in New York.

The politicization of poverty in New York

Poverty in its intersection with age and gender and its overlap with race and ethnicity has become well-established in New York. Social divisions are taken for granted in public discourse as permanent features of the metropolis. They are also highly politicized, as people debate the role of public agencies: what are these agencies achieving, and what should be expected from them?

In a commentary on the current social situation, Paul Goldberger (1989), the architecture critic of the *New York Times*, asserted that there is no longer a collective conscience in New York:

> Human anguish is surely more visible on the streets of New York than ever before. But the illness that affects the cityscape is not only a matter of human suffering. In a broader sense, the city is

only rarely these days a place of hope or promise or glory. It is not merely that it is harsh and dirty, for New York and most other American cities have always been harsh and dirty. It is that it has become so indifferent to the very idea of the public realm, to the notion that the city is a collective, a shared place, a place that is in the most literal sense common.

In New York the expanding army on the streets and the attempts by police and social security officials to drive them elsewhere are the most obvious aspect of poverty. The withdrawal from the notion of the city as a shared "common ground" seems to correspond to the extent to which poverty is concentrated among identifiable social groups, not to the scale of the problem. So far this sense of a radical departure, an abandonment of the civic sphere, does not appear in London, despite the evidence of growing misery for the poor, and the fact that inequality in London seems to be increasing more rapidly than in New York in the late 1980s.

The crucial reason for this difference in attitude seemingly resides in the greater ethnic homogeneity of the London population. Whereas New York's poor see themselves as suffering from racial and ethnic discrimination, and are identified by the better-off as dissimilar in color and ethnicity, these perceived divisions exist to a far lesser extent in London.

Spatial aspects of poverty

In both London and New York there is a clear spatial pattern to inequality. The main concentration of disadvantage in London lies in three adjacent inner city boroughs just to the north and east of the City of London – Islington, Hackney, and Tower Hamlets. Containing about a quarter of the population of Inner London, these boroughs (especially the latter two) have all experienced gentrification; thus wealth and poverty are further concentrated within them. All three have high levels of overcrowding, renting, lack of access to a car, and unemployment. Other boroughs also have high levels of deprivation, particularly the Lambeth/Brixton area, located in southeast Inner London and home to the main concentration of Afro-Caribbean settlement, and Newham in the East End, but the concentration of deprivation here is not as acute as in the cluster identified.

The most severe concentration of deprivation in New York lies in the Harlem/South Bronx area, which is of a comparable size at about two-thirds of a million inhabitants. However, there are substantial differences in degree in the spatial concentration of poverty in New York, corresponding to the evidence already discussed about the more marked concentration of poverty among particular racial groups and family types. In 1986 a clear majority of households in the Harlem/Bronx area had incomes below the poverty line, and two-thirds had incomes below $12,500 a year. Ninety percent of the population is black or Hispanic, as against less than a quarter black or Asian in the London zone of highest deprivation. Half of the households with children have only one parent as against one in eight in London. Moreover, whereas the London high-poverty boroughs contain important pockets of gentrification, except in a few parts of Brooklyn New York has no parallel to this, and the homogeneity of impoverished black areas remains largely unbroken.

The impact of state policies

New policies for state welfare have had important consequences for the poor. The public sector has reduced its role in provision of public assistance, especially in New York. The actual value of welfare payments in New York declined by about one-third between 1978 and 1988 (New York City Human Resources Administration, 1989, pp. 2–3). Further, the number of recipients also declined, by 6 percent between 1970 and 1982 (Tobier, 1984, table 6), and by about 10 percent more from 1983 to 1988 (Levine, 1989).

Evidence from the Annual Housing Survey shows how these changes have affected poor people in New York. We focus on households where the head is under 65 years of age, since older people dependent on social security receive automatic cost of living increases whereas families receiving aid to families with dependent children (AFDC) do not. Older poor households received more than three-quarters of their incomes from public programs in both years, whereas the proportion for younger households was smaller.

The data show that assistance for larger households declined markedly over the period. For households with three or more members the level of average public assistance declined by over a third, taking both welfare and unemployment benefits into account. For smaller households, the value of such benefits increased substantially.These changes are consistent with the observation that state-determined aid to the AFDC program was cut by some 25 percent nationwide over the period (P. Passell, 1989). At the same time, the proportion of all household income received from public assistance increased from about half to about three-fifths, indicating an increased reliance on the state benefits which were themselves declining in value.

The data also show marked differences between the different ethnic groups. White households officially categorized as poor received on average less than half as much of their total income from public sources as did black and Hispanic households. This may be because they are more reluctant to apply for public assistance, or because they are better able to gain support from other sources. This disparity in level of support, taken together with the overrepresentation of nonwhite people among the poor, helps to explain why public assistance policies in New York have such strong racial overtones. This makes a powerful contribution to the politicization of poverty in New York which was discussed earlier.

In London the pattern is somewhat different. Except for school-leavers, program eligibility is not restricted by age and family status, as is the case in the United States. In general, the safety-net of welfare benefits for the mass of the population had not been cut back in relation to prices until the changes in last-resort assistance in 1988. Even before 1988, however, the living standards of the poor did not keep pace with the real increase in living standards of the better-off. Rights to welfare benefits are generally stronger in London than in New York, and racial issues in poor relief have not emerged to the same extent. There are, however, three major changes in state policy that affect the pattern of social inequalities.

First, the welfare safety-net has been withdrawn from some social groups – most strikingly for unemployed school-leavers. Since 1988, if they reject the government's Youth Training Scheme, they are denied benefits. This is a major cause of the sharp increase in begging and homelessness among this group and has had an especially significant impact on London, where such youth are disproportionately concentrated. Second, changes to benefits introduced in 1988 resulted in real cuts for some groups. For example, the new rates cut the value of payments to a childless couple by over 5 percent in real terms (UK House of Commons, 1990). Again, the incidence of this demographic category is higher in London. Third, other aspects of welfare have been cut sharply. The most important cut is in council house provision, with attendant policies of substantial real rent increases, cuts in rent benefits, and the subsidized sale of existing stock to better-off tenants. Real rents have increased on average by a factor of three in the decade from 1979, and London's public housing plans have been cut by £11 billion (London Housing Unit, 1989, p. 13). This policy of housing cuts has made a major contribution to the increase in numbers of homeless families in London.

The poor receiving state benefits in London have grown in numbers, mainly because of trends in unemployment up to the mid-1980s. In New York, despite increases in the numbers of poor people, more stringent means-tests have caused the proportion who receive welfare benefits to fall. Coupled with the decline in the real value of benefit for all but smaller and older households, this implies an absolute increase in the misery of the poor in New York. The evidence quoted in table 5.1 indicates that this is also true for the very poorest groups in London.

The social implications of widening inequality

Social change has major implications for people's views about the world they live in. One way to assess the impact of changes in the public-service infrastructure of the city on public perceptions is through surveys of public opinion. The most recent surveys of New Yorkers reveal a mood of deepening discouragement. A CBS/*New York Times* poll conducted in June 1989 found that a majority do not expect the city to be a better place in which to live during the coming decade, the most pessimistic result since CBS/NYT polling began in 1977 (Barbanel, 1989b). Further, a majority agreed that race relations are "generally bad." The subsequent election of a black politician as mayor might be taken as a sign of change. Yet a majority of both white and black people stated that neither a white nor a black mayor would be likely to be effective against drugs, crime, or homelessness.

A *Time* magazine poll found that 59 percent of New Yorkers would, if given the choice, move somewhere else, and 72 percent indicated that the city had become a tougher place in which to live (Attinger, 1990, pp. 39, 41).

To examine the development of people's ideas we turn to the Annual Housing Surveys from 1976 to 1983. These included questions about the adequacy of public schools, police protection, public transportation, and health care facilities. White people gave slightly *higher* ratings to police protection and health care facilities in 1983 than they had in 1976. For all other groups, the proportion of "adequate" ratings declined. For example, adequate ratings for police declined from about 79 percent to about 71 percent among Hispanic people. Adequate ratings for health care facilities declined a surprising 15 points among Asian people, from 94 percent to below 79 percent, perhaps because this group now contains a greater proportion of more highly educated people who are more inclined to be critical of unsatisfactory provision.

On public schools and public transportation there is consensus among all groups: judgments of the adequacy of services declined sharply from 1976 to 1983 – down about 7 points for schools, and also 7 points for transportation. Similarly, a telephone poll conducted for CBS News and the *New York Times* in 1985 on public services in New York showed a high level of dissatisfaction with emergency services, public schools, and hospital provision; markedly higher among black and Hispanic people.

Once again, our findings show a deterioration in the public sector. Not only have direct transfer payments been reduced for those groups most heavily dependent on them, but the public infrastructure of collective services is also perceived to be failing these same residents. As in the data on poverty, there are socially significant racial/ethnic differences in these processes.

For London there is a broadly similar pattern of growing concern with public services, becoming more sharply focused towards the end of the 1980s, as the changes in London's local government discussed elsewhere in this book began to have an impact in reducing the level of provision. Various rounds of the annual British Social Attitudes survey provide evidence that Londoners are more dissatisfied with services and with the dailh experience of avoidable pollution than are people who live elsewhere (Jowell et al., 1984 –). The 1984 report showed that 25 percent of interviewees in the Greater London area were very dissatisfied with the National Health Service, as against 18 percent nationally. In the 1986 survey only 24 percent of Londoners reported that council estates were pleasant places to live, as against 36 percent elsewhere. Information on dissatisfaction among ethnic groups which is precisely comparable with New York data is not available. The Townsend Survey, however, did show that Asians and blacks reported considerably higher levels of housing dissatisfaction and fear of crime than did whites.

SOCIAL AND RACIAL POLARIZATION

New York City appears from the evidence presented so far to be a racially polarized city, and perhaps the most characteristic aspect of the "new patterns of inequality" in this case is the tendency toward hostility and fear between white, black, and Hispanic people. The CBS/*New York Times* poll provides further documentation on this point. Less than half of the respondents reported having spent an evening with a friend of another race in the previous three to four months. Neighborhoods are highly segregated by race and ethnic background, and the highest level of intergroup contact is in the workplace. But here contacts are rarely on the basis of equality. Only 25 percent of black people reported having a black supervisor, and only 20 percent of Hispanic people reported an Hispanic supervisor; many interracial contacts are therefore hierarchical. Less than a quarter of any group, including white people, reported that any one of the five people at work that they are most friendly with is of another race.

The survey also revealed that a plurality of all groups believe that there is discrimination against minorities. For example, the largest number of black, Hispanic, and white people believe that minorities are hired as tokens rather than because companies are really looking for qualified minority members. A majority of black and Hispanic people report that new York City police "often" engage in brutality against members of both minorities. Among white people, nearly half of those revealing an opinion agreed with this assessment. There is even a plurality of white respondents who report that the city government pays too little attention to minorities, and that the courts are "too hard" on minorities.

In London there is also evidence of racial discrimination, although the problem is not so serious as in New York. A quarter of Afro-Caribbean and a tenth of Asian people in the capital reported experience of racial discrimination in a 1982 survey (C. Brown, 1984, p. 218). Members of ethnic minorities were roughly twice as likely to say that they had been victims of assault. About half stated that the position of ethnic minorities had got worse in the last five years. A study by the Metropolitan Police showed that West Indian and Asian people were about twice as likely to be the victims of assaults and that Asian people were nearly four times as likely to suffer robbery as white Londoners (UK Home Office, 1983, table 8). Racially motivated assaults on black people in Tower Hamlets that were serious enough to be reported numbered over 250 in 1989, roughly one for every 200 black people in the population (Crampton, 1990). A major study by the Policy Studies Institute confirmed deep-seated racist attitudes in London police officers, and that young black people tend to view the police with a greater degree of mistrust than do young white people (D. Smith et al., 1983).

In New York a series of widely publicized cases both reflected and exacerbated racial tension. The death of a black man chased by a group of whites onto a busy highway (Howard Beach), the killing of another black man who entered a white neighborhood to purchase a used car (Bensonhurst), and the rape and nearly fatal beating of a white investment banker (the Central Park jogger) preoccupied New York's press and local television stations for months. The trials of the alleged perpetrators of these crimes prompted a series of protests and demonstrations by blacks, and some white counter-demonstrations, that deepened divisions and attracted further publicity. In one journalist's view, "any suggestion of violence across racial lines is enough to push a story onto the front page" (Cose, 1989). Is the press exaggerating interracial violence? Or is it merely responding to a public concern over racial issues?

Sociologists commenting on these cases emphasize the provincial and self-protective character of neighborhoods such as Howard Beach and Bensonhurst, or the sense of exposure to danger in more affluent white neighborhoods of Manhattan (see, for example, Kornblum and Beshers, 1988). Our view is that New York City is becoming more precarious for all people, but especially those in the lower half of the system. Growing inequality overall, and displacements in the occupational structure, heighten insecurity and fear for the future. Public resources have not been brought to bear in proportion to the problems that people experience, and in some respects they have been pulled back. Even the Dinkins administration, elected by a minority-based coalition, has responded to the public safety question primarily by enlarging the police force rather than by attempting to address its social causes.

The major focus of public concern about racial issues in London has been the riots in 1981 and 1985, which culminated in the killing of a police officer by black youths. Much of the media response to these events served to decontextualize racial violence by laying the responsibility at the door of outside "extremists" and "agitators." This approach is summed up in a *Daily Express* story on November 8, 1985, which claimed that:

> the thugs who murdered policeman Keith Blakelock in the Tottenham riots acted on orders of crazed left-wing extremists. Street-fighting experts trained in Moscow and Libya were behind Britain's worst violence . . . they include men from Jamaica, Barbados and Nigeria. (Quoted in Solomos, 1989, p. 168)

Such an account not only separates analysis of riots from the social conditions which are their context, it also enables the media to blame politically active black people in general for the events. Solomos discusses the media treatment of figures like Bernie Grant (formerly Labour Leader of Haringey Council, now an MP), termed a "High Priest of Race Hate" by Douglas Hurd, the then Home Secretary. Thus, the problem of urban disorder is analyzed in such a way that its solution does not require the mitigation of the inequalities suffered by black people in London or of the injustices of racism: rather, the appropriate solution is to pay less attention to demands made by black politicians.

Both London and New York have experienced a social and racial polarization, closely linked to income inequality but complicated by the politicization of ethnic relations, which in New York spills over directly into discussion of the social welfare system, whose most disadvantaged clients are largely members of ethnic minorities. The extent of racism seems greater in New York, corresponding to the greater concentration of poverty among black and Hispanic people.

The experience of social polarization

Journalistic accounts, ethnographic work, popular fiction, and survey research all depict the social implications of the widening gulf between rich and poor. While, as discussed in the final chapter of this volume, a simple duality offers an inadequate description of social life in London and New York, the vision of cities divided sharply between rich and poor has become embedded in both popular and scholarly consciousness. Consequently much of the literature concentrates on the top and bottom of the social hierarchies. Although an exclusive focus on the extremes distorts an accurate characterization of urban society in the two cities, examination of this material does allow us to understand the quality of life at the top and bottom.

A number of studies of the life style and social consciousness of the poor in London have been carried out. Harrison's *Inside the Inner City* (1985) paints a grim picture of the bleak world of hand-to-mouth existence inhabited by those on benefits. The Campaign Against Poverty's *Decade of Despair* (1989) provides more recent accounts of the misery of poverty. For example, Joan, a basic rate pensioner, writes in this volume:

> When you are poor, you have to be extra good at managing, extra good at self-discipline, extra good at economising, extra good at managing without and extra good at dealing with constant crisis, stress and frustration. Few of us are extra good. The rich aren't.

A descriptive account of an Inner London housing estate, based entirely on discursive interviews, shows how complex the pattern of everyday life is among people whose one factor in common is that they are not well-off. The council caretaker describes it as "the rubbish of the local authority, that's who lives here if you want my honest opinion ... but there's still nice parts" (Parker, 1983, p. 11). The term most commonly used to describe the estate by those who live there is "mixed."

The range of interviews includes women under effective curfew through fear of street violence, residents who cannot use part of their dwellings because the local authority's standards of maintenance are grossly inadequate, people with criminal records for shop-lifting and domestic violence, and single parents whose children are under threat of removal by the social services department for suspicion of child-battering, but also couples whose life is concerned to establish and maintain "respectability" against the threat of the disreputable life around them and those who describe themselves as "deep down happy" with a "nice home." Under this variety there is an underlying impression of the insecurity of life, of the continual effort required to avoid trouble and violence, to maintain personal standards, to raise children, and to sustain a precarious standard of living. The difference between the poor and the better-off is essentially to do with the experience of chronic insecurity in every aspect of life – access to paid work, housing, and the confidence with which one can deal with officials and walk the streets in one's own neighborhood.

A 1991 account of homelessness in New York, which chronicles its increase after a brief period of mitigation, describes the process by which those seeking emergency shelter must wait most of the day for placement only to start the process over the next day:

> On a recent night, a city office in Brooklyn where homeless families come to be placed in shelters was crowded with more than a dozen families, among them Kristy Morales and her 4-month-old daughter, Stephanie, who had come in at 5 P.M.
>
> By midnight, Mrs. Morales was near tears, rocking her daughter, whispering over and over: "I'm sorry, I'm so sorry." She was not taken to a shelter to put her baby to sleep until 4 A.M. (Morgan, 1991)

At the other end of the spectrum, the lives of the new rich received primary attention in the popular rather than scholarly media. One British study, however, examines attitudes to career and life style among a small group of young highly paid financial sector professionals (Pahl, 1989). Two findings stand out. First, the "new rich" tend to gain "the high salaries they want" at the "expense of the leisure time in which to enjoy them," because work absorbs so much of their energy. Second, the awareness of their own arduous labor reinforces a structure of attitudes in which "most felt they worked hard and long and deserved a high reward" (Pahl, 1989, p. 22). This generalizes into a "£k culture," in which moral worth is judged by the number of noughts on the salary check. The corollary is that the poor merit their poverty and are despised for it.

Many scholars consider that a best-selling novel of the period, Tom Wolfe's *The Bonfire of the Vanities*, captured the lives of the 1980s' wealthy better than any social science tome. Its protagonist, bond trader Sherman McCoy, characterized as a "master of the universe," inhabited a million-dollar Park Avenue apartment. Viewing Manhattan from the Triboro Bridge, he thought

> of the millions, from all over the globe, who yearned to be on that island, in those towers, in those narrow streets! There it was, the Rome, the Paris, the London of the twentieth century, the city of ambition, the dense magnetic rock, the irresistible destination of

all those who insist on being *where things are happening* – and
he was among the victors! (Wolfe, 1987, p. 77)

Wolfe's portrayal is, of course, fictional, and Pahl's work is based
on a small and unrepresentative sample. Their representations, however, are consistent with the evidence of larger scale structured
questionnaire attitude surveys. Townsend's 1985–6 survey asked its
representative sample of 2,703 individuals a series of questions on
their attitudes to poverty and welfare. A striking feature is the division
between better- and worse-off. Those who see themselves as in poverty
are over twice as likely to see poverty in terms of a lack of basic
citizenship rights enjoyed by the mass of the population as are those
who see themselves as well above the poverty line. Similarly the self-
rated poor are three times as likely to support redistributive government
policies as are the well-off (Taylor-Gooby, 1989, p. 10). In New York
region, as surveys between 1972/4 and 1984/6 show, attitudes to welfare
spending have fluctuated, with professional workers having markedly
more polarized (liberal versus conservative) views than the population
as a whole in 1972/4, becoming far more conservative in 1977/80, and
rather more liberal again in 1984/6 (Brint, 1991, table 6.3, p. 168). In
both cities, therefore, inequalities in living standards are accompanied
by polarization in social attitudes, although the gap in attitudes does
not seem to be accompanied by a corresponding politicization of poverty
policy.

CONCLUSION

Income inequalities in both New York and London have grown more
marked in recent years. The motor of change in both cases is to be
found in changes in employment patterns, in demographic structure,
and in government policies. On the one hand, occupational restructuring, the decline of the manufacturing sector, and a decline in job
prospects in traditional industries in the inner city, and the expansion
of the new financial and technical service sectors have destroyed many
stable working-class jobs, but provided highly paid employment which
boosts the real income of the expanding groups of well-off people.
On the other, policies which cut back the availability of welfare
benefits for the poor and choke off public investment in services
which benefit the least well-off, most importantly, social housing,
contribute to a real increase in relative and absolute poverty at the
bottom of the income distribution. In both London and New York
inequality grew more marked after the end of the recession of the early

1980s, despite revival in parts of the cities' economies, the stabilization of population decline, and the improvement in unemployment rates. To mix the metaphors, the city "turned the corner" for some, but others were left behind. In 1990, with both cities once again characterized by economic decline, the situation of the well-to-do has become precarious and of the poor even more hopeless.

There are three main differences between the two cities. First, the rate of growth in inequality in London is greater, becoming especially marked in the mid- and late 1980s. This was due in part to cuts in welfare spending and housing provision, but also to the improvement in incomes at the top end. Second, despite the large gap between rich and poor, the degree of social polarization associated with inequality in London is lower than in New York. There appear to be two reasons for this: on the one hand, levels of welfare provision in London, as a consequence of a larger public sector, are still higher and more securely established for many groups of poor people, despite the cuts of the 1980s; on the other, poverty in New York is firmly linked with racial, social, and spatial factors, being overwhelmingly concentrated among black and Hispanic people, among single parents, and in large areas of the city in which poverty is so widespread as to be the norm. In London there are clear racial, social, and spatial correlates of poverty, but the strength of association between these factors and poverty is much less marked.

The dissimilarity in degree of polarization leads to the third difference. Social inequality has become politicized in New York along racial and ethnic lines but not yet in London, except in relation to the highly visible social problem of the growing number of young destitute street beggars. In New York the question of whether the winners from economic change should be prepared to pay taxes to finance help for the losers, from whom they are separated by color, culture, life style, and area of residence, or whether a harsher degree of repression should be used to make life more comfortable for themselves, is very much an open one. In London social circumstances have not forced the city to address the question yet, despite the incidence of inequality, poverty, and home-lessness. In both cities the question of whether economic revival is to be accompanied by deliberate action to regenerate the city as a "common ground" for the whole community – indeed whether the idea of com-munity has any relevance to the modern city-dweller – is becoming increasingly urgent.

NOTE

1   A thorough study of poverty in London based on a questionnaire survey carried out in 1985–6 directed by Peter Townsend indicates that the figures quoted above may be substantial underestimates of the extent of human misery caused by inadequate incomes, because the official poverty level is itself too low (Townsend, 1989). This study produced an empirically based measure of deprivation which combined individual experience along the dimensions of diet, clothing, housing, home facilities, environment, location, working conditions, rights in employment, participation in the community, recreation, and education. This then related deprivation to household income. The analysis used statistical techniques to establish an income threshold below which the risk of multiple deprivation markedly increased for a given type of household, an approach analogous to that employed in Townsend's previous national study of poverty (1979). The research shows that the poverty threshold lies between one-and-a-half and one-and-two-thirds the government's level of means-tested assistance. Moreover, since access to housing, education, and other public services has deteriorated over the 1980s, as these services face financial stringency, the growth in deprivation is not fully revealed by data on cash income. Townsend's analysis, if applied to New York, would undoubtedly provide similar findings.

6

Migrants, minorities, and the ethnic division of labor

Malcolm Cross and Roger Waldinger

Immigration has been a constant in London as in New York. But in the past several decades the flows of people converging on these world cities have changed in dramatic and important ways. Both cities have gained a substantial non-European-origin population base: New York, first through the internal migration of African-Americans and Puerto Ricans, and, subsequently, through foreign immigration from the Third World; London, through the influx of workers recruited from England's former colonies.

That both cities should be transformed by long-distance migration is testimony to their changing relationship to the world economy. As the cities' economies have become increasingly international in focus, movements of population have paralleled the movement of capital and goods. But while the demography of London and New York is characterized by growing minority populations, their prospects are unclear. In both cities goods-producing activities that provided a staging ground for earlier groups of immigrants are a sadly declining enterprise. And the new sources of economic dynamism found in symbolic manipulation and information processing appear to offer few opportunities to minority residents. Thus, the debate about minorities in New York and London turns around a single question: what is the fit between the postindustrial metropolis and its non-European population base?

This is the question we seek to answer in this chapter. The argument we develop is simple: the common understandings of this relationship mistake demographic descriptors for underlying sociological categories. The term "minority" may provide a convenient rubric for grouping Londoners or New Yorkers of non-European origin, but it obscures important, and in some cases growing, differences within highly differentiated groups. These varied populations occupy different positions in the economy and the ecology of the postindustrial city. Those contrasting positions in turn expose groups to disparate opportunities and constraints, promoting possibly diverging interests.

Our emphasis on differentiation *within* the populations of non-European origin is linked to another theme: namely the consequences of broader population shifts. Both cities, we shall show, have seen a steady outflow of whites from job and housing markets; white exodus has produced vacancies into which non-European New Yorkers and Londoners have advanced – though, once again, along many different roads.

We explore these issues by first describing the evolving ethnic demography of the two cities, with a particular emphasis on immigration. We then discuss the new ethnic division of labor, the housing market, education, and politics.

POPULATION TRENDS AND CHANGING ETHNIC PATTERNS

New York

The demographic transformation of New York can be divided into two phases. The first, which began with the end of the Second World War and lasted to the end of the 1960s, involved the exodus of the city's white population and the massive inmigration of displaced black agricultural workers from the South and of Puerto Ricans uprooted by that island's modernization. The second phase, beginning in the 1970s, marked by initial population decline, led to a shift in migration flows in and out of the city. While white New Yorkers accelerated their departure to greener pastures in the suburbs and beyond, native black and Puerto Rican migration to New York withered. Instead of moving to New York, native blacks and Puerto Ricans joined the outward flow.

While New York no longer retained its native population, it once again became a mecca for the new immigrants arriving after the liberalization of US immigration laws in 1965. The arrival of the new immigrants is the driving force of demographic and ethnic change in New York – today and for the foreseeable future. We first briefly describe the characteristics of the new immigration to the United States, then focus on those immigrants moving to New York.

The new immigration to the United States began with the passage of the Hart–Cellar Act in 1965, which abolished the old country-of-origins quotas, affirmed family connections as the principal basis for admission to permanent residence in the United States, and increased the total numbers of immigrants to be admitted to the country (Reimers, 1985). Despite a number of changes, this system has essentially remained in place to this day. The major, entirely unanticipated consequence of the Hart–Cellar Act was a dramatic increase in immigration from Asia, which has become the largest regional source of legal immigrants. While arrivals from Europe have fallen off sharply over the past 20 years, immigration from the Caribbean and Latin America has also been on the upswing. The size of the legal immigration flow has also increased. Between 1966 and 1970 an average of about 374,000 newcomers entered the country each year; between 1982 and 1986, by contrast, annual inflows averaged approximately 574,000.[1]

In addition to the legal immigrant flow have come substantial numbers of undocumented immigrants – people who either cross the borders illegally, or enter the US legally but extend their residence beyond their

Table 6.1 Immigration, United States and New York City, 1966–1987 (thousands)

	United States	New York City	NYC as percentage of US
1966	323.0	61.2	18.9
1967	362.0	66.0	18.2
1968	454.4	75.4	16.6
1969	358.6	67.9	18.9
1970	373.3	74.6	20.0
1971	370.5	71.4	19.3
1972	384.7	76.0	19.8
1973	400.1	76.6	19.1
1974	394.9	73.2	18.5
1975	386.2	73.6	19.1
1976	500.5	90.7	18.1
1977	462.3	76.6	16.6
1978	601.4	88.0	14.6
1979	460.3	82.4	17.9
1980	560.6	NA	NA
1981	596.6	NA	NA
1982	594.1	85.0	14.3
1983	559.8	75.0	13.4
1984	543.9	87.4	16.1
1985	570.0	85.4	15.0
1986	601.7	89.8	14.9
1987	601.5	92.3	15.3

Sources: US Department of Commerce 1966–1979, 1982; Immigration and Naturalization Service, Public Use Tapes

legally permitted stay. Just how many undocumented immigrants have been living in the United States has been a matter of controversy for over two decades. However, there is now a consensus among experts that the number of illegal immigrants lies within the three to four million range.

As in the past, the new immigrants have overwhelmingly settled in cities and no city has captured as large a share of the new immigrant population as New York. Between 1966 and 1979 New York absorbed over 1 million legal immigrants; the 1980 Census recorded 1.67 million foreign-born New Yorkers, of whom 928,000 had arrived after 1965. Data gaps, due to the virtual collapse of record-keeping procedures in the Immigration and Naturalization Service, afflict the record for 1980 and 1981, but the figures available for the years since 1982 indicate a steadily rising immigrant flow.

As in the country at large, an indeterminate number of undocumented or illegal immigrants can be added to the legal immigrant population base. In 1980 the Census counted 210,000 undocumented immigrants in the New York standard metropolitan statistical area (SMSA) (J. Passell, 1985). If the city's share of the New York SMSA's undocumented population is the same as its share of the new immigrant population overall, this would produce a total of 188,000 undocumented immigrants counted in the 1980 Census. Some undocumented immigrants were undoubtedly missed in the Census counts: but it seems implausible, given the immigrants' characteristics, and, in particular, their high level of employment, that the undercount for the undocumented could exceed the 20 percent undercount for black males – the group most severely missed in Census enumerations (J. Passell et al., 1982). Even if the undocumented were undercounted by half, the undocumented population would barely total 380,000.

New York differs from other principal immigrant-receiving areas in several important respects, as data for metropolitan areas from the 1980 Census shows. First, leading immigrant-receiving areas vary in the diversity of their new immigrant populations. Of the five main receiving areas, three are dominated by a single origin group: Mexicans in Los Angeles and Chicago and Cubans in Miami comprise, 47, 32, and 59 percent respectively of 1965–80 immigrants in those areas. By contrast, San Francisco is diverse, with the largest group, Filipinos, making up 19 percent of the new immigrant population. New York's new immigrants are even more heterogeneous, with no group accounting for more than 10 percent of the newcomers.[2]

Second, those groups that dominate the other major immigrant entrepôts have a greatly reduced profile in New York. There were barely 7,000 Mexican residents living in New York City as of 1980; Filipinos and Cubans were more numerous but still comprised only 2 percent and 2.5 percent respectively of the 1965–80 newcomers residing in New York. In New York the most important source countries have been the Dominican Republic, followed by Colombia and Ecuador, with substantial numbers from the rest of the Caribbean. Less than 2 percent of the Asian immigrants resident in New York as of 1980 were from Vietnam; almost a third were from China; Indians, Koreans, and Filipinos accounted for 10 percent each.[3]

Immigration patterns since 1980 have been remarkably stable. Newcomers from the Caribbean are the largest single component, accounting for about 40 percent of the annual inflow, with Dominicans consistently the largest single national grouping. Close to 25 percent of the post-1980 immigrants have come from Asia, with China providing the most numerous, but by no means dominant, contingent of Asian newcomers.[4]

The consequence of immigration has been to both accelerate and transform the postwar pattern of demographic change. Although small samples make intercensual population estimates subject to error, consistent findings from different surveys using differing sample bases provide strong grounds for the following generalizations.

- First, New York's population decline decisively turned around during the 1980s. In 1987 the city had 245,000 more people than it did in 1980. Furthermore, almost all of the population gained by the New York region was concentrated in New York City, representing a dramatic reversal of a more than 50-year-old trend.
- Second, despite net population gains, the white, non-Hispanic share of the city's population continued to decline. Although it seems likely that the economic boom of the 1980s may have reduced the imbalance between out- and in-migration flows, this change was too modest to offset the impact of low birth rates and high mortality rates. Hence, the white share of the population appears to have fallen just below the 50 percent mark.
- Third, the immigrant presence has continued to be strongly felt, more so than at any time since the 1920s. Not only has the foreign-born proportion of adult New Yorkers increased since 1980, but the immigrant population has shifted decisively to newcomers who arrived after the liberalization of the immigration laws. Today's most common source area, the Caribbean, is itself extraordinarily variegated, culturally, linguistically, and ethnically. And the three most important Caribbean source countries, the Dominican Republic, Jamaica, and Haiti, each represent distinct cultural systems.

Consequently the "minority" population, now the numerical majority, is far more diverse than before. High rates of immigration have made Hispanics, rather than blacks, the larger of New York's minority groups, while also diminishing the relative weight of Puerto Ricans among this expanding Hispanic population. And large foreign inflows from Asia have produced high rates of growth for this group as well, albeit on a relatively small population base.

The new immigrants have engaged in a type of "leapfrog migration," bypassing the previously established migrant or immigrant concentrations and moving instead into previously white areas of decent housing quality. The neighborhoods that had sheltered the previous wave of migrants – blacks and Puerto Ricans – have received little or no immigrant inflows. Instead the high immigrant-receiving neighborhoods have been those that had previously been homes to a mainly white population. This pattern of replacement has also had implications for the housing quality to which the immigrants have gained access. With one exception – Manhattan's Lower East Side, onto which its old Chinatown enclave spilled over – all of the immigrant-receiving areas possess housing that had been built for middle-class, not poor or even working-class, residents. Though this housing stock is obsolete by the standards of today, by historical standards it nonetheless provides decent accommodation, and much better than is to be found in the traditional areas.

What accounts for the newcomers' distinctive patterns? One factor leading to leapfrog migration is that the old ghetto areas no longer provide much shelter. These areas, Central and East Harlem, Williamsburgh, the South Bronx, have suffered a wave of abandonment that has robbed them of their supply of cheap rental space. In other cases, as on Manhattan's West Side, urban renewal and gentrification have turned the areas over to higher paying users. The precise characteristics of the housing stock have been a factor as well. Public or publicly assisted housing, which grew substantially up until the 1980s, houses almost 10 percent of New York's population. But the bureaucratic procedures by which entry into this stock are regulated combined, in the 1980s, with a housing shortage that has produced long waiting lists to virtually freeze immigrants out of the public sector. Native blacks, only 18 percent of the city's population, comprise 55 percent of the residents of public housing; Puerto Ricans, who make up about 14 percent of the city's population, account for another 29 percent. By contrast, immigrants make up less than 7 percent of the public housing population; instead, they have found access in areas where private owners hold the bulk of the housing stock.[5]

While homeowners have always been a minority in New York, with its dense stock of multi-family dwellings, there are important ethnic variations. In contrast to London, Caribbean immigrants in New York show a strong propensity toward homeownership. Having settled in areas with ample stocks of modest homes in which owners could often rent out one or two apartments, a third of all black immigrants reported owning their own homes as of 1980, more than any other nonwhite group. By contrast only 12 percent of the native Hispanic population lived in their own homes. More recent data, from a large 1987 sample, show that this same pattern is still in place.[6]

Thus, New York is now a "majority minority" city, but one that is most unlike the other large, older cities of the United States. The impact of immigration is what makes the import of New York's transition to "majority minority" status different. In contrast to Chicago or Detroit, New York's minority population is extraordinarily heterogeneous. That diversity makes it unlikely that the dichotomy inherent in the "minority/majority" distinction will capture much of the variation in economic position, political orientation, and social integration that actually characterized "minority" New Yorkers.

London

Just as in New York, migrants from abroad have also converged on Greater London. Though the size of the London-bound migration stream has been considerable, the numbers have never approached the levels reached in New York. Consequently London's ethnic demography has changed more gradually than New York's and persons who could claim recent migrant origin account for a smaller proportion of its population.

Postwar migration to Great Britain is often considered a seamless process, but in fact it falls into two distinct phases. The first resembles the internal migration from the rural south of the United States to its manufacturing heartlands. This phase involved movement from the colonial "south" in the Caribbean to the "mother country" of Britain in response to demands for unskilled labor power that arose in the years after 1945. Approximately 1.1 million people from the West Indian territories made this journey to British cities in search of work. This process was all but complete by the Commonwealth Immigration Act of 1962.

A second phase, much more characteristic of migrant labor flows into the rest of northern Europe, started in the late 1950s and ran on until 1973. Whereas migrants to Germany or France mainly came from the European periphery (e.g. Turkey or Yugoslavia), these migrant workers to Britain came from the Indian subcontinent to work in the manufacturing industries of the South East, Midlands, and North of England. In 1974 this population was supplemented by a sizeable influx of Ugandan Asians who were fleeing the repression of Idi Amin.

The total size of the populations which result from these processes of migration is notoriously difficult to estimate. The British Census did not include an "ethnic" question until 1991, leaving researchers no recourse but to make estimates based on increasingly erroneous projections from birthplace data. Insofar as a consensus exists among analysts, most estimates suggest a population of visible minorities numbering approximately 3.5 million, most of whom come from Commonwealth (or former Commonwealth) countries (S. Smith, 1989). National surveys provide results that fall within reasonably close range of this estimate, but also point to the distinctive age structure of the minority population. Thus, it is estimated that 7.5 percent of the total population of Great Britain under 16 could be classified as "ethnic minority," 4.6 percent of those of working age, and only 0.8 percent of those of retirement age (UK Department of Employment, 1988a). These figures imply a steady increase in the proportion of the total population that is ethnic minority, even without future immigration.

Whatever the national origins of the migrants, economic considerations provided the main motivation for the move to Great Britain in the first place. As a result, these populations mainly live in the main industrial centers. Angus Stuart (1989) calculates, using the Longitudinal Sample from the 1971 and 1981 Censuses, that 60 percent of Asians and nearly three-quarters of Afro-Caribbeans are found in the four main conurbations. This concentration makes the geographic distribution of the minority population very different from that of whites. Of the "white" population who are of working age and economically active, 11.5 percent live in Greater London and 9.2 percent in the traditional industrial heartland of the West Midlands. By contrast 46 percent of ethnic minorities live in Greater London and 15 percent in the West Midlands. Workers of recent migrant origin are approximately six times as likely as others to live in these two industrial centers (UK Department of Employment, 1988a).

We have very little reliable evidence on whether this pattern has changed much in recent years but differential processes of out-migration and a differential age-structure, with its consequent effects on fertility, would suggest further concentration. Data from the Census, however, suggests that in 1981 the pattern of internal migration for Afro-Caribbeans was rather different from the two main Asian groups and the majority of the population. Afro-Caribbeans are less likely to migrate internally, whereas all Asian groups have an internal migration rate over the 1971–81 decade approximately the same as that of the majority population.

Within Greater London ethnic minorities constitute a higher proportion of the total population than in the country as a whole. According to the official estimate, ethnic minorities make up 14 percent of Greater London's residents; this population is divided almost equally into those of Asian origin, those of African/Caribbean ancestry, and a mixed group composed of many others. At first sight the concentration of minorities in London is far less pronounced than in New York. But this disparity is partially an effect of differences in city demarcations. The ethnic minority population falls into two categories: an archetypal "inner city" sector and one that is located near zones of recent suburban growth. Estimates for 1996, for example, show that 14 boroughs in Greater London will by then have ethnic minority populations of approximately 20 percent or more. Generally Afro-Caribbeans dominate in the inner city boroughs (Hackney, Hammersmith, Haringey, Islington, Lambeth, Lewisham, Southwark, and Wandsworth) whereas South Asians cluster in the outer boroughs (Brent, Ealing, Hounslow, and Waltham Forest). Two boroughs, the adjacent inner boroughs of Tower Hamlets and Newham, which lie to the east of the City of London, do not conform to this pattern: here South Asians (mostly Bengalis) outnumber Afro-Caribbeans by two to one. In addition, substantial numbers of Afro-Caribbeans live in the northwestern borough of Brent, although in quite separate parts of the borough from the majority Asian population. Notwithstanding these exceptional cases, there is a striking degree of spatial separation between the major ethnic segments of London's minority populations, as shown in table 6.2.

A corollary of this pattern is that a far higher proportion of London's Afro-Caribbean population is physically located in the "inner city." Two-thirds of this group reside in the 14 boroughs that make up the inner area, compared with one-third of London's Asians.

As in New York, the effects of labor market change in Greater London interact with the extent of broader population change. Twenty-two percent of the whites living in Greater London in 1971 were living outside the area in 1981 – a rate of out-migration that was almost three times the rate of ethnic minorities. But out-migration rates varied

Table 6.2 Estimated ethnic minority population in Greater London, 1986 (as percent of the total population)

	Afro-Caribbean	Asian
Inner city	10.4	5.4
Outer city	3.2	6.6

Source: London Research Centre, 1989b

considerably among ethnic minority groups as well, with those of Indian origin twice as likely to migrate out of Greater London as Afro-Caribbeans.[7]

Ethnic differentiation in Greater London is not merely a spatial phenomenon; it is also reflected in patterns of collective consumption. Most importantly, the two major groups comprising the city's visible minorities occupy different structural positions in the housing market. Nearly 60 percent of Asian householders are in owner-occupation, a figure which puts their rate of owner-occupancy above that for the native white population; by contrast, only a third of Afro-Caribbeans are in a similar tenure state. Of course, ownership of private housing does not necessarily mean better housing; in particular, data on Asian households in private accommodation reveal a high proportion suffering from very severe overcrowding. Nonetheless, the dramatic rise in London housing values is creating new social divisions within the ethnic minority population. Homeownership generates wealth which is unrelated to earnings, and to the extent that it correlates with ethnic origin it will increasingly divide groups economically. In the long run it is probable that this will be reflected in patterns of political support.

Household *type* also differs markedly. All ethnic minority groups possess few pensioners, which is a reflection of their recent migrant origin, but a third of Afro-Caribbean households are either single individuals or single parents. For Asians, this is very rare, with only 7 percent falling into these categories (London Research Centre 1989a, p. 12).

Accommodation provided by local housing authorities has traditionally been an important source of housing for Londoners; even now, after a decade of public-sector housing sales to the private market, almost a third of households in the city are provided in this way (or by nonprofit housing associations). The type of households served by public housing, however, is strongly correlated with ethnic category. Thus, nearly 40 percent of white UK households in local authority housing are pensioners, while the most commonly occurring household in this tenure among Afro-Caribbeans is that with a single adult. By contrast, two-thirds of Asian households in the public sector are families with two or more adults.

This review suggests two major generalizations about the incorporation of postwar migrants from the "New Commonwealth" into Greater London. First, the populations are not proportionately as large as in New York, although they are certainly larger than the figures in the previous section suggest. Underestimation is partly the result of under-enumeration and partly the consequence of an inadequate statistical base that precludes the possibility of estimating the smaller minority communities (e.g. Chinese, Arabs, etc.). These other groups probably add another third to the proportion of visible minorities in the city as a whole.

Second, the two largest groups (those from the Caribbean and from South Asia) settled in different parts of the city, although the latter grouping is itself divided into an "inner city" (largely Bengali) population and a much larger "outer city" segment (mainly Hindu, Sikh, and Muslim). The differential distribution of ethnic minorities is not simply true in settlement terms but also dynamically; that is, over time the differences are widening as London comes to have two main areas of ethnic minority concentration.

Finally, the main ethnic minority groups in London occupy different "social space." The housing arena exemplifies these disparate social locations, with Asians concentrated in areas of owner-occupation and Afro-Caribbeans more likely to be in public housing. These variations result, in part, from other differences in the two populations, with family type being the most important. The variations in housing status also produce distinct patterns of social tensions. For Afro-Caribbean households, the key problems lie with their location in declining inner city housing estates, where they lack the equity needed to exchange this housing for anything better. Asian families, by contrast, experience pressure to find private housing of an adequate size and quality and tend to suffer from poor facilities and overcrowding. An added tension is the corrosive effects of racial harassment, which is more common on housing estates and may be part of the reason why Asian households are keen to enjoy the greater flexibility of the private sector.

THE NEW ETHNIC DIVISION OF LABOR

Thus, the ethnic make-up of London and New York is very different from what it was three or four decades ago. But, as we have seen in earlier chapters, this same period witnessed a major economic transformation. The goods-producing and transporting sectors went into irreversible decline, replaced by growth in service jobs, which often required higher levels of formal training.

How have ethnic minorities fared in this new economic environment? The conventional wisdom suggests that manufacturing to services transition has been a disaster, removing low-skill jobs that in the American context, at least, historically provided a staging ground for newcomers who entered the labor market at the bottom and gradually moved up. But the emphasis on the skills mismatch is incompatible with the immigrant phenomenon itself: if there are no jobs for the low-skilled, why do we find a growing immigrant presence in the labor market?

The key to understanding the labor market role of ethnic minorities, we argue, lies on the supply side. Compositional change, resulting from the disproportionate outflow of whites from both metropolises, has produced "replacement demand," offsetting the impact of manufacturing decline. Once vacancies emerged, however, groups responded in very different ways, yielding a new ethnic division of labor in which ethnic minorities have sorted themselves into very different economic niches.

New York

· In New York, as table 6.3 shows, the demographic shifts of the 1970s created the conditions for replacement demand. Table 6.3 shows the number of jobs held by eight different ethnic groups in New York City in 1970 and 1980. The table also indicates how many jobs each group would have been expected to lose had it declined by the same percentage as total employment in New York City – this is given in column 3; how many jobs the group actually lost (column 4); and then what the difference was between expected and actual employment loss (columns 5 and 6). We observe that the biggest job losers over the course of the 1970s, both quantitatively and qualitatively, were whites. The total job loss of native and foreign-born whites together was almost twice as great as the total job loss for all New Yorkers. By contrast the employment picture among the non-European origin immigrant groups shows significant job growth, especially among Asians and blacks.

This disproportional white outflow had two consequences of note. First, because the net outflow of whites was disproportional to the decline of the total economy, ample vacancies were created for replacements who, under the conditions of population change, would inevitably be nonwhite. Second, white job loss meant not only more jobs, but also better jobs for nonwhites. If we assume that employers preferred whites, if only in part on the basis of prejudice, any decline in the size of the preferred group would allow all other groups to move up the hiring queue.

Support for this argument comes from an analysis of data from the 1970 and 1980 Censuses, in which we focus on five key categories of employment: three industry sectors – manufacturing, advanced services, and the government; and two occupational categories, high-status white collar (professional and managerial) and low-status white collar. These data show that native whites lost substantially in four of the five categories and gained only a small fraction of the new jobs generated in the white-collar category. Moreover, white losses in the

Table 6.3 Changes in employment for ethnic groups, New York City, 1970–1980

Ethnic group	Employment		Job change			
	1970	1980	Expected[a]	Actual	Actual − Expected	A−E as % 1970 emp.
White						
Native	1,785,200	1,382,980	−155,939	−402,220	−246,281	−13.8
Foreign	417,400	315,520	−36,460	−101,880	−65,420	−15.7
Black						
Native	462,700	440,180	−40,417	−22,520	17,897	3.9
Foreign	55,500	170,320	−4,848	114,820	119,668	215.6
Asian						
Native	8,000	10,460	−699	2,460	3,159	39.5
Foreign	31,200	108,740	−2,725	77,540	80,265	257.3
Hispanic						
Native	242,000	232,640	−21,139	−9,360	11,799	4.9
Foreign	132,700	205,520	−11,591	72,820	84,411	63.6

[a]The expected change is equal to the change in employment for all New York City residents.
Source: 1970, 1980: Census of Population, Public Use Microdata Sample

low white-collar, manufacturing, and public sectors were disproportionately great relative to the net decline, thus creating substantial opportunities for nonwhite replacement. In contrast to whites, native blacks gained in advanced services overall (finance, insurance, real estate, professional and business services) and in both high white-collar (professional and managerial) occupations and in low white-collar (sales and clerical) occupations. Substantial losses, however, occurred in manufacturing. Although both foreign Asians and foreign Hispanics gained jobs in all five categories, their experience diverged in significant respects. Most importantly Asians increased their representation in both white-collar categories and in the advanced services, while Hispanic representation in low white-collar jobs and in advanced services declined.

While compositional changes in New York's labor force thus created ample opportunities for nonwhite workers, the process of ethnic succession was hardly uniform. As evidence, consider the public sector: in

1980 the employer of one-third of all native blacks, it employed only 8.5 percent of foreign Asians and 7.8 percent of foreign blacks. Or look at a stronghold of immigrant employment – manufacturing, with a third of foreign Hispanics, almost a quarter of foreign Asians, but a smaller proportion of native blacks than either of these.

These examples hint at the development of a new ethnic division of labor in which non-European origin groups have succeeded whites by establishing distinctive niches within the economy. Though on average New York's ethnic groups worked in less segregated industries in 1980 than in 1970, the succession of groups was not orderly and the pattern of industrial differentiation extends across white and non-European origin groups. Thus, by 1980, native blacks were more segregated from native whites than were foreign blacks; furthermore, segregation had increased in the first case but declined in the second. In both 1970 and 1980 native and foreign-born workers in every group were considerably segregated from one another. Finally, distance between particular non-European origin groups, for example between foreign Hispanics and native blacks, was often greater than the distance from whites.

London

At the start of the 1980s ethnic minorities in London found themselves concentrated in industrial sectors undergoing major decline. For example, males of Afro-Caribbean origin were mainly employed in mechanical engineering, vehicle repair, and transport, reflecting the maintenance of patterns laid down in the early years of migration and reproduced among the children of settlers (C. Brown, 1984). Asian men were also overrepresented in both nonmetal manufacturing industries, metal manufacture (Indian only), and in "distribution, hotels and catering, repairs." All of those of New Commonwealth (and Pakistan) origin and their descendants were underrepresented in the growing sector of banking, finance, and other services.

The first half of the 1980s brought some significant changes in these employment patterns, as the amalgamated rounds of the government's regular Labor Force Survey for 1985–7 show. First, ethnic minority employment has shifted out of metal manufacture into other forms of manufacturing while simultaneously moving into services. For white men services now account for 27 percent of the total, while for ethnic minorities it has risen to 21 percent (UK Department of Employment, 1988b). Among women the concentrations are equally clear. There is a dramatic overrepresentation of Afro-Caribbean women in service jobs. There is also a slight overrepresentation of Asian (Indian) and Afro-

Caribbean women in the transport sector. By 1985–7, there was a growing concentration in the service sector. For example, 52 percent of white women workers are in the service sector, compared with 47 percent of minority women.

Unfortunately it is not possible to measure with the precision available in New York the degree to which the flight or retirement of native whites has opened up job possibilities for relative newcomers in London. But longitudinal data for 1971–81 show that by the latter date only Asians were still overrepresented in manufacturing, as can be seen from table 6.4. For Afro-Caribbeans of either gender the secondary services sector provides the emerging employment concentration.

These data show that overall the major change in the employment of the 1971 sample over the following decade was the growth in business services, particularly for men (up 57 percent), and in the public sector, particularly for women (up 115 percent). Professional services also showed a modest gain for both genders but otherwise the picture was one of job loss. Manufacturing led this decline (by 42 percent overall) but the retail and personal services sectors also showed major falls. In terms of socio-economic category, the unskilled categories of operatives and laborers showed the greatest declines for men and women. They constituted 21 percent and 9.8 percent respectively in 1971 but fell to 11.3 percent and 2.5 percent a decade later.

As in New York, comparison among the groups reveals substantially different job trajectories. First, the total size of the white UK group fell by proportionately more than other groups but did not substantially alter its distribution across jobs or sectors. Second, the Afro-Caribbean population, when considered as a whole, moved out of declining manufacturing and into white-collar jobs in the public sector. Even by the end of the decade, however, it had achieved only three-quarters of the representation in higher white-collar jobs compared to the population as a whole. Finally, the Asian population, although clearly divided into a more "middle-class" Indian population and a more "working-class" Pakistani/Bangladeshi group, had shown very different forms of adaption. Rather than exposure to manufacturing declining, the Asian population had sustained or even extended its overrepresentation in this sector, although from a very low level, but there were no signs of greater engagement with advanced services. These findings are consistent with a population of more recent migrant origin, sometimes lacking fluency in the dominant language.

Table 6.4 Changes in job configuration, London 1971–1981 (thousands)[a]

	Employment		Index of representation[b]	
	1971	1981	1971	1981
All groups				
High white collar	931	891		
Low white collar	1,249	968		
Manufacturing	1,157	669		
Advanced services	935	943		
Public sector	322	694		
White UK				
(non-NCWP)[c]				
High white collar	890	844	1.01	1.01
Low white collar	1,206	918	1.02	1.01
Manufacturing	1,055	607	0.97	0.97
Advanced services	885	836	1.00	1.01
Public sector	311	654	1.02	1.01
Afro-Caribbean				
High white collar	19	23	0.63	0.75
Low white collar	24	28	0.58	0.84
Manufacturing	51	28	1.34	1.08
Advanced services	33	41	1.09	1.13
Public sector	8	26	0.71	0.96
Indian				
High white collar	19	21	0.96	1.07
Low white collar	17	19	0.72	0.92
Manufacturing	39	26	1.75	1.72
Advanced services	14	14	0.80	0.66
Public sector	32	12	0.52	0.74
Pakistani				
High white collar	4	4	0.82	0.83
Low white collar	3	3	0.43	0.58
Manufacturing	13	9	2.07	2.21
Advanced services	2	2	0.37	0.36
Public sector	1	3	0.45	0.67

[a]Employment figures given are estimated from a 1 percent longitudinal sample. Although they correctly portray trends, they do not give accurate numbers for 1981 since they do not include individuals lost from the sample.
[b]The index of representation, which measures the extent to which the distribution of a subgroup mirrors the overall distribution (1.00 reflects identical representation in one category), will inevitably tend towards parity when one group predominates. Thus, the "white UK" category shows little difference from the population overall since it comprises more than 90 percent of this total.
  Ethnic origin as given in 1971.
[c]New Commonwealth with Pakistan.
Source: Census: Longitudinal Sample, 1971–81

MINORITIES IN THE POSTINDUSTRIAL CITY

New York

In both the housing and the labor markets various native minority and new immigrant groups occupy distinctive niches. In the educational system, in contrast, they share a common institutional system. Close to half New York's dwindling proportion of white youth is enrolled in private schools, with the great majority of this group in parochial schools. The public schools are the domain of minority and immigrant youth: no more than one-sixth of any major group is enrolled in the private/parochial sector (Berne and Tobier, 1987).

Unfortunately it is difficult to determine how this common experience affects group-specific outcomes. Performance measures for schools are notoriously unreliable and inconsistent, making comparisons over time difficult and often misleading. Moreover, the data produced by the schools disaggregate by broad ethnic categories (black, white, Hispanic) and do not provide the detail on nativity with which we are interested. Nonetheless, several generalizations can be made. First, the performance of the public school system as a whole is inadequate, though the current state of affairs is not new, but rather a problem that has persisted for two decades. Second, within this environment there are some significant differences among ethno-national groups. At the minimal level, that of maintenance of enrollment, immigrants appear to do better than their native-born counterparts. Indeed, from age 16 on, both black and Asian immigrants maintain higher enrollment levels than whites and substantially exceed the enrollment levels of native blacks and particularly of native Hispanics. Third, the educational attainment of all non-white groups, with the exception of Asians, lags far behind that of native whites. To be sure, there has been a substantial improvement in the school performance of blacks: between 1970 and 1980 the percentage of native blacks aged 25–30 with at least some college education more than doubled, while the proportion of similarly aged native Hispanics almost tripled. But schooling levels among comparably aged whites increased as well, with the result that, relative to whites, the black and Hispanic schooling lag barely declined, despite the sizable increases in black and Hispanic education attainment.

The differing economic and social fates of New York's diverse minority groups have their political ramifications as well. Though blacks and Hispanics have long made up a coalition in local politics, that coalition is uneasy at best, characterized by constant competition, and always subject to break-up and internal conflict. For most of the 1980s, fractiousness, not coalescence, appeared to characterize black–Hispanic internal political relations. New York's dominant political figure of the period, Mayor Edward I. Koch, played successfully on these fissures, showing considerable skill in fomenting internal competition. Koch also benefited from genuine substantive differences: the issues of particular importance to Hispanics, for example immigration and bilingualism, rank considerably lower on the black political agenda. Since Hispanics are more conservatively inclined than blacks, they were also more likely to be in ideological convergence with Koch as well (Falcon, 1988). Thus, in the 1985 mayoralty election, 70 percent of the Hispanic vote, but only 37 percent of the black vote, appears to have gone to Koch. Part of this split reflects immigrant/native differences: immigrants were more positively inclined towards Koch, who in turn invested substantial campaign funds to mobilize immigrant voters (Mollenkopf, 1988a, 1988b).

Immigration also diminished the political impact of the city's demographic transition. Only citizens can vote in local elections, and since legal permanent residents must wait at least 5 years to apply for naturalization, entry into the political arena is automatically delayed. This assumes that immigrants naturalize as soon as they can, which is most certainly not the case. In fact black and Hispanic immigrants have naturalization rates that are a good deal below the national average. And the population of illegal immigrants further increases the numbers of new New Yorkers who are barred from electoral participation (Waldinger, 1989).

Nonetheless, in fall 1989 New Yorkers elected the city's first African-American mayor, David Dinkins. To some extent Dinkins's victory drew on factors external to the issues at hand, in particular the fallout from an unending series of scandals that weakened Mayor Koch from the early days of his third and final term. Dinkins also proved successful in building ties with Hispanic leaders, thus averting the in-fighting that doomed an earlier attempt at unseating Koch. And Dinkins could further appeal to a sizable population of white, mainly Jewish voters, although the great bulk of white votes were cast for Koch (see chapter 8).

Ultimately Dinkins built on a coalition that drew mainly from black and Hispanic voters. That base suggests that the city's minority population may indeed be more than a mere collection of demographic aggregates. Clearly a major factor transcending the cleavages we have emphasized is the influence of class. Blacks and Hispanics, whether immigrant or native, whether employed or not, have on average lower incomes than whites. That common economic condition produces sufficient policy alignment to make these groups viable political partners (Waldinger, 1989).

Nonetheless, differences among the new New Yorkers remain the source of continuing conflict. Ever since his electoral victory, Dinkins received criticism for paying too little attention to Hispanic concerns and for providing too many of the spoils of office to blacks. Long-simmering frictions between Korean small storeowners located in black communities and neighborhood activists and shoppers erupted during 1990 in long-term boycotts of two Korean stores in Brooklyn, effectively denying them any patronage. While the Korean retail owners' association sustained the stores during the boycott, ultimately one closed and the other changed ownership. In the summer of 1991 decades-long conflict between African-American and Hasidic residents reached an incendiary level as riots broke out after a Hasidic driver accidentally ran over and killed a black child. Apparently in retaliation a Hasidic rabbinical student, visiting from Australia and unconnected with the earlier incident, was stabbed to death. Although Mayor Dinkins did little to settle the Korean grocery dispute, he exerted a significant influence in calming the Crown Heights situation. The volatile nature of relationships among low-income ethnic groups suggests how fragile is the coalition under-pinning the electoral coalition of any minority mayor.

London

Beyond the labor market, the 1980s saw several changes of decisive importance for ethnic minorities in London. First of all the city continued to push relentlessly towards a postindustrial future (see chapter 8). Central government undertook a major effort to reassert the dynamics of the market over the evolution of planning and administration, leading to the abolition of the Greater London Council and the Inner London Education Authority and the dramatic curtailment of local authority budgets which now compete with private-sector resources in providing urban services. Before looking at the implications of these changes, however, another dynamic element must be assessed.

Ethnic minority populations are constantly in change, even if they are not replenished by new inflows from abroad. Like any other group, minorities respond to opportunities in the economic climate as a whole, and to local circumstances. Of the many adaptive responses possible, the most important is the degree to which visible minorities are able to utilize the educational and training system in order to get the skills required by a rapidly changing labor market.

Numerous studies of pupil performance in London schools, most of them conducted by the Inner London Education Authority, abolished n March 1990, provide data needed to assess this question. Although these studies vary enormously in the size of the samples, in design and method of analysis, they yield strikingly similar results concerning the performance levels of various ethnic groups. For example, when we compare the proportions of each group in Inner London passing five or more "O" levels or their equivalents (the exam taken at the age of 16 which triggers entry to higher-level schooling and hence to postschool education), we find that Afro-Caribbeans lie in the range of 0–5 percent, whereas South Asians are in the very highest range of 17–18 percent. The total population (which is, of course, mainly white) falls well below this, in the range 3–10 percent.[8]

These results, which show that South Asian pupils are out on their own in performance terms in Inner London, have been confirmed by a 1990 Inner London Education Authority report which showed that only the poor Bangladeshi communities of East London were an exception to this pattern (Inner London Education Authority, 1990). If data existed for Outer London, it would probably reveal a closing of the gap between South Asians and whites since national data suggest that these two categories score about the same at this level of the educational process (Drew and Gray, 1991). These performance levels imply that South Asians are at least as well equipped as whites to respond to the growth of lower level white-collar work. In all likelihood this relative advantage will extend to managerial and professional positions.

These educational disparities add further weight to the evidence of ethnic economic differentiation that we have already uncovered. Consequently the policy agenda, and therefore the pattern of political preferences, is likely to reflect the heterogeneity of minority interest. In Greater London, for example, the results of capital-wide elections for local councillors in May 1990 tended to show a consolidation for the ruling Labour Parties in Inner London (for example, in Haringey, Lambeth, Lewisham, and Southwark) and a more complex pattern entailing pronounced shifts to the right in the outer boroughs (for example, in Ealing and Brent).[9] We do not know yet whether this reflects a growing disenchantment by South Asian voters with the welfare orientation of traditional Labour policy, but it is not improbable that this is so. Certainly there is evidence that in the gradual emergence of ethnic politics the two main groups are stepping down divergent paths (Fitzgerald, 1988). For Afro-Caribbeans, whose inner urban political agenda focuses on public services, unemployment, and the police, the struggle is for recognition within the Labour Party. Asians, in contrast, are split more by social class and in other ways, too, have a spread of political concerns more characteristic of the majority. Inevitably, therefore, there is a greater tendency toward mirroring the spread of political support found nationally. This process is constrained, however, by the particularistic loyalties of ethnic politics which, in the case of Britons of Asian descent, would certainly include intervention to combat racial harassment and a concern about whether or not national political parties support policies to sustain cultural traditions. In the wake of the so-called "Rushdie Affair," it is precisely the lack of such support that has prompted the faltering beginnings of ethnic minority-based political movements.

CONCLUSION

Ethnic differentiation is the theme of this chapter; this process, we argue, is bound up with the transformation of the New York and London economies. Research on this issue generally falls into one of two camps. One argument offers a "tale of two cities," according to which the city's advanced services have rendered useless those minority residents with low skills who earlier had been recruited for manufacturing jobs, now irrevocably gone. The second argument contends that the middle of the labor market is disappearing; what remains is a polarized arrangement in which growth is concentrated in either high-level jobs requiring higher education or in low-level positions in services, retailing, and the remnants of a depressed manufacturing sector. It is in the latter group that minorities are largely confined.

This chapter suggests another answer. Neither the metaphor of dislocation (or "mismatch") nor that of polarization captures the impact of the postindustrial urban transformation on ethnic minorities. Both these approaches concentrate on demand-side issues to the exclusion of a supply-side approach. They assume that the loss of white city residents is the source of urban disaster, when in fact the outflow of white people in the two global cities considered here is what gives some newcomers their chance. During economic downturns whites have left the city at rates that outpace the rate of decline. And when the economy has reheated, the outward flow of whites has slowed, without ever truly stopping. Proportionately whites have thus been in constant decline. This shift in ethnic proportions creates a "replacement demand" for other groups up and down the hierarchy of jobs, especially in those segments of the labor market where employer requirements are not too high.

But who benefits from replacement demand, and under what conditions, are not straightforward matters. Thus, our treatments of New York and London emphasize the emergence of distinctive ethnic niches. In general a complex of factors – skills, predispositions, informal networks, and group resources – interacts with the demand for replacement labor to disperse ethnic minorities into distinct concentrations. In New York, for example, the public sector has become a stronghold for native blacks, but an area of little immigrant employment, in part because discrimination is less pervasive than in the private sector, but also because black political mobilization has gained institutional access to public-sector jobs. In contrast immigrants have moved heavily into manufacturing, a sector in which black representation, never high, has further declined. In this instance the circumstances of migration circumscribe newcomers' search for better opportunities, while the networks between settlers and new arrivals provide for rapid integration into the factory workplace.

Similar patterns appear to characterize London. As manufacturing decline hit the city, unemployment rates among ethnic minorities rose dramatically. As restructuring took over, Afro-Caribbean minorities relocated to the public sector, although at lower levels than remaining whites. South Asians, in contrast, have tended to remain in the private sector, both as employees and, increasingly, as self-employed. They have increased their concentration in manufacturing and also advanced in private-sector services. These differences are becoming increasingly reflected in spatial and social class terms. South Asians are moving into private properties left by the departing white middle class in areas of the city that have retained a manufacturing capability and where private-sector services provided by petty entrepreneurs have formed a newly available niche. The South Asian population of London reveals a social class pattern which is bimodal, even when compared with that of native whites. They are overrepresented in the professional and managerial sectors of the middle class *and* in the lower echelons of manual labor.

Despite these similarities, there are also important differences between London and New York. Most striking is the disparity in the flows of immigrants to the two cities. In New York, as we have noted, the trend has been continuously upward for a 25-year period. Immigration on this scale has linked New York-based ethnic communities, with their established niches in the housing and labor markets, to sending areas around the world. With such networks in place, immigration becomes a self-feeding and self-sustaining process. In the absence of new and unexpected legal barriers to immigration it is difficult to imagine the circumstances that would diminish the immigrant stream. London is also a magnet for immigrants, notwithstanding many attempts to restrict entrance, especially to newcomers from the Third World. Indeed, Great Britain, like most other European countries, has seen an increase in foreign immigration over the past few years. But the scale of immigration to London will remain much smaller than in New York. Consequently the ethnic issue agenda is shifting from matters associated with the arrival and settlement of foreign populations to those related to the concerns of a second generation of settlers.

Other demographic changes also distinguish the two cities. Most notable is the extent of net white out-migration in New York and the occupational repositioning of those whites who remain. These patterns reflect the extraordinary improvement in the standards experienced by the white population in the United States over the past 40 years – not fully paralleled in the United KIngdom. In the labor market the consequences are that the impact of local economic decline is largely offset by the still greater decline in the size of the white population and a sustained demand for nonwhite replacement labour. The implications of greater white population loss emerge again in the discussions of housing and politics.

In the end, however, despite these differences, it is the commonalities in the experience of ethnic minorities in these two cities that most impress us, especially the emerging ethnic differentiation between groups. Though analysts often assume that "minorities" are influenced in uniform ways by processes of economic and social change, that presumption is clearly misplaced. Theories of urban change which deny the reality of ethnic differentiation fail to grasp a key component of the postindustrial urban form. Race and ethnic groupings are clearly becoming a more salient feature of the new urban landscape, but the resulting shapes and structures create a complex mosaic, the results of new demands and old ways being served in specialized ways. The ethnic division of labor is, in this sense, the central division of labor in the postindustrial city.

NOTES

1 Calculated from US Department of Commerce, 1988, table 1.
2 These population figures, for the Chicago, Los Angeles, Miami, New York, and San Francisco metropolitan areas, are based on calculations from the 1980 Census of Population, Public Use Microdata Sample.
3 Data for New York City calculated from US Bureau of the Census, 1985b, table 116.
4 Data calculated from Immigration and Naturalization Service, Public Use Tapes.
5 Data calculated from the 1987 Housing and Vacancy Survey, Public Use Sample.
6 1980 data calculated from 1980 Census of Population, Public Use Microdata Sample; 1987 data from the 1987 Housing and Vacancy Survey of New York City, conducted by the US Bureau of the Census, Public Use Tapes.
7 Calculated from the Census: Longitudinal Sample, 1971–81.

8 The studies from which these data are drawn are Maughan and Rutter, 1986, Mabey, 1986, and Kysel, 1988. They are all based on surveys conducted in Inner London boroughs. For an overview of these and other studies see Drew and Gray, 1991.

9 Voting in the major local election was also strongly affected by the community charge (or "poll tax" – the replacement for local property taxation introduced in 1990); variations in the level of this tax levied locally led to pronounced distortions to this pattern.

7

Housing for people, housing for profits

Michael Harloe, Peter Marcuse, and Neil Smith

THE GLOBAL ECONOMY AND HOUSING

In 1987 land for luxury housing in Central London was being sold for up to £30 million per acre and the apartments built on it for £1.5 million (Brownhill et al., 1989, p. 21). At the same time around 30,000 households were *officially* accepted as homeless (many more were actually homeless) and an estimated 12,500 people were squatting. House prices soared by 170 percent between 1983 and 1988. Meanwhile, the stock of subsidized, council-owned housing – the main source of lower-income accommodation – shrank because of privatization and the virtual prohibition on new building.

The housing predicament in New York City was even more extreme. Even conservative critics bemoan the "third-world city living uneasily with the city of the twenty-first century" (Sternlieb, 1986, p. 83). While Fifth Avenue apartments in Trump Tower sell for over $10 million, an estimated 60,000 to 70,000 live on the streets (Marcuse, 1989c). In public housing more than 35,000 households are illegally doubled and tripled up. Although it collects the statistics, the New York City Housing Authority refuses to evict the doubled-up households, knowing that most evictees would end up homeless.

Economic restructuring has not benefited most housing consumers in either city. The boom in residential property vastly enhanced the profits of landlords, developers, and housing financiers. It did not expand the supply of affordable housing. Instead, the middle and working classes find it an ever greater struggle to meet monthly housing payments. New entrants to the housing market are hard pressed to find any affordable housing. For the poor the housing crisis is even worse and deepens daily. Whether in the desolate South Bronx or in the misery of Inner London's euphemistically labeled "hard to let" public housing estates, whatever the market around them does, tenants' experience is the same: rising costs, deteriorating conditions, insecure neighborhoods.

Changes in the global economy have affected the two cities' housing markets in at least three ways. First, the concentration of multinational financial and other corporations leads directly to an increase in the small but significant demand for luxury housing in both city centers. The inflated prices paid for land and housing at the top of the market act as a price leader throughout, rippling out geographically from Central London and New York and filtering down, resulting in inflated price levels in other parts of the market. A second, and related, consequence of globalization is that investment in the built environment, including housing, has become an increasingly attractive option for large-scale financial and other capital, building almost exclusively for the higher-income groups working in the financial and producer serpices sector. New building and structure conversion have been moving "up market," and those who cannot afford its products – the majority of households – are increasingly forced out of the city or down market to buy or rent. The third consequence of globalization, not specific to London or New York, is the deregulation of home mortgage finance and its integration with the globally organized money and capital markets (Florida and Feldman, 1988; Ball, 1990). In both Britain and the US home mortgage interest rates were far higher in real terms in the 1980s than in previous decades (D. Smith, 1989). Home lending is big business and the opportunities for profit have encouraged many new types of lenders to emerge. In London a substantial amount of mortgage money now comes not from the traditional lenders but from major national and foreign banks (London Research Centre, 1989c). Competition for mortgage business has become so intense that lenders have been willing to take on even riskier loans. This has helped to fuel the house price boom, raised housing costs/income ratios, and led to an increasing level of mortgage defaults and arrears – especially when interest rates rose sharply in 1988. Likewise, in New York, especially in the suburban counties, such nontraditional sources as General Motors and the Sears Corporation account for an increasing proportion of mortgages.

In both cities housing policy traditionally combined strong support for private housing suppliers and for better-off households with some measure of provision for lower-income working-class households. In New York, federal tax laws strongly subsidize private homeownership, while the whole apparatus of zoning and other controls has generally favored homeowners along with middle-class and better-off working-class renters. The latter have also been assisted by such initiatives as the long-running and extensive Mitchell–Lama program, which provides state subsidies for units for moderate- and middle-income households. Lower-income working-class households have benefited from the rent control and public housing programs, but their coverage has been limited and selective. Public programs as a whole do not target the poor and working class. In London planning policy and controls have also aided suburban homeownership while public housing and, less importantly, rent controls have aided broader sections of the population than in New York.

In the rest of this chapter we shall examine some aspects of the London and New York housing markets which are linked directly or indirectly to their role as global cities. There are significant similarities as well as differences in how these markets are constituted; we proceed first to outline these.

THE TWO HOUSING MARKETS

With 2.70 million and 2.68 million households respectively, New York City and London have similarly sized housing markets (Stegman, 1988; London Research Centre, 1989c). After significant population declines, both cities experienced population growth in the 1980s, although this may have ended in London as the escalation of house prices has forced many to move out in search of affordable homes (*Guardian*, 1989). There are similarities as well in household type and structure; for example, the low proportions of families with children, the large numbers of elderly and adult households without children. New York, however, houses a higher proportion of single-adult households and single-parent families than does London (table 7.1(a)). The two populations also differ in their racial and ethnic composition (table 7.1(b)). While in both cities racial discrimination is as evident in housing as in employment and education, the scale and sharpness of racial division is far greater in New York (S. Smith, 1989).

The data on tenure show that New York is mainly a city of tenants while in London most households now own (or are buying) their homes (table 7.1(c)). Within the rental sector, public housing predominates in London, the private landlord in New York. In London private rental housing is now a minority tenure, important for many young households and a declining number of the elderly, but for few other groups. In New York public housing is the minority rental tenure, housing less than 10

Table 7.1   Comparison of housing markets (%)

(a) Houshold type	New York City (1987)	London (1986–7)
Elderly (over 65)	21.3	23
Single adult (excluding elderly)	22.5	13
Single parent	7.2	4
Two or more adults	27.3	34
Families	21.6	27

(b) Race and ethnicity	New York City	London	
White	46.1	White	83
Black	24.0	African	2
Puerto Rican	11.6	Afro-Caribbean/ Black British	5
Asian	4.4	Asian	5
Hispanic (non-Puerto Rican)	11.7	Other	5
Other	2.2		

(c) Tenure	New York City	London
Owner-occupier	30.2	54.1
Public	5.9	30.8
Publicly assisted/ housing association	12.6	5.0
Private rental	47.1	10.0

Sources: Stegman, 1988; London Research Centre, 1989c

percent of the city's tenants. These differences obviously affect the politics of housing in the two cities.

The state plays a far larger role in the housing market in London than in New York, although the difference is eroding. In 1987 8 percent of New York households in private housing received some help with housing costs through the shelter allowance element in welfare payments, although in 63 percent of these cases the allowance was insufficient to cover their full rent. In addition a further 10 percent of households received assistance through the public housing, *in rem*, and Section 8 programs (some in public housing also received welfare payments toward housing).[1] Overall 18 percent received housing and/or welfare payments. In contrast at least 17.9 percent of London households received housing benefits while 26.2 percent received housing and/or welfare benefits (Stegman, 1988; London Research Centre, 1989c).

As this suggests, the sectoral division of housing by income is complex and a source of significant differences between the two cities. These include the following:

1 The majority (private) rented sector houses a wider range of incomes and household types in New York than does the (majority) public housing sector in London. At the bottom of the spectrum, in New York about 26 percent of all renter households had incomes of 50 percent of the renter median or less; in London 20 percent of tenants in the majority rental sector, public housing, had such low incomes. At the other end of the spectrum, in London under 8 percent of renters had incomes of three times the median or more, while the New York figure was almost 17 percent (Stegman, 1988; London Research Centre, 1989c), indicating a larger affluent private rental market in New York than in London.

2 Publicly owned housing is by far the most important source of accommodation for lower-income working-class and poor households in London. Especially after 1945, this tenure replaced the private land-lord as the main working-class tenure (Barlow, 1989; Hamnett and Randolph, 1986; Hamnett, 1990). In postwar New York private housing remained the primary tenure for most poor people.

3 State policies have been largely responsible for the high concentration of low-income public housing tenants, notably in high-rise, high-density estates in Inner London. In New York similar concentrations occur in the private rented as well as the public sectors; both market processes and the concentration of public "projects" result in segregation along racial as well as class lines. Segregation *within* the private rental sector has far more importance in New York than in London.

In both cities issues of security of tenure and rent levels are of central relevance to housing politics and economics. In New York most private rental housing is subject to some rent and security regulation (rent stabilization or rent control). In London, even before recent legislation virtually abolished controls, most new private tenancies were unprotected (Greater London Council, 1986); controls in public housing, however, are significant. Between 40 percent and 45 percent of the total population in each city thus have some degree of rent/security protection. However, in both cities these controls have been eroded in recent years.

One important cause of this erosion is tenure conversion (also discussed later in this chapter). In London and New York this involves the conversion of private rented housing to forms of homeownership (freehold or leasehold tenures in London, co-ops or condominiums in

New York). In London it also involves the sale of public housing for owner occupation; although pressure for public housing sales has existed in New York, it has so far been resisted. Between 1981 and 1986 almost 205,000 units of private rented housing were converted in New York; in London 104,000 council houses were sold between 1980 and 1986 (Stegman, 1988; London Research Centre, 1989c). In New York about two-thirds of the units sold were bought by nonoccupants. In London most sales were to sitting tenants, but many were then resold. In both cities the sales involved a loss of rental accommodation and substantial increase in the costs of housing for lower-income households. In New York conversion has involved the displacement of many lower-income by middle- and upper-income occupants. In London, among sitting tenants, the better-off bought initially. For vacant council housing sold on the open market, the profile of purchasers is much like that of co-op/condo purchasers in New York (i.e. disproportionately higher-income and professionals). This tendency has been accentuated by the *resale* of council houses (Murie, 1990); by 1986 about 40 percent were owned by outsiders.

The burden of escalating housing costs is high in both cities, but much more severe in New York than in London. Whereas Londoners pay approximately 14.4 percent of their income in public housing, the average New York renter, public and private, devotes 29 percent of income to rent (far more than the London figure, even allowing for the fact that the latter figure includes utilities costs). Americans have traditionally spent higher amounts on rent (Board of Trade, 1911; Harloe, 1985), and the gap shows no signs of lessening. In 1987 47.5 percent of all renter households in New York paid 30 percent or more of their gross household incomes in rent. In London at least 38 percent of public housing tenants and a similar proportion of private tenants pay 20 percent or more. The most serious difficulties are more prevalent among those in low-paid jobs or outside the labor market, and among those who do not qualify for welfare or other state benefits, although this is no longer a problem confined to the poor (table 7.2). The housing crisis is migrating up the economic ladder: in New York by 1987 even those in the fifth decile of household income distribution had gross rent/income ratios of 33 percent, and only those in the top three deciles paid under 20 percent. In London a recent survey found that 20 percent of those in the highest paying occupations and 29.6 percent of owners with a mortgage found it "very" or "fairly" difficult to make housing payments.[2]

In both cities, then, issues of *access* and *affordability* are of central importance. Questions of *quality* also remain important, especially overcrowding and lack of basic amenities, and these severely affect poorer

Table 7.2 Rent/income ratios in New York City and London (%)

London (1986–7)

% of income paid as rent	Local Authority (raw)	Local authority (boosted)	Private rental (raw)	Private rental (boosted)	Housing association (raw)	Housing association (boosted)
< 10%	18	30	18	24	30	48
10–< 20%	25	32	29	29	28	26
20%–< 30%	19	22	17	14	16	12
30% or more	38	16	36	22	26	14

New York (1987)

Income decile	Renter households with gross rent/income ratio over 40%	Median gross rent/income ratio
1 low	85.4	85
2	67.9	58
3	69.3	51
4	50.4	40
5	27.9	33
6	8.9	27
7	7.4	24
8	1.9	19
9	0.8	16
10 high	–	13

London income figures boosted by 50 percent to allow for under-reporting.
Sources: Stegman, 1988; London Research Centre, 1989c

households. Theoretically quality in the private market is inversely related to access and affordability: as price rises, quality is also expected to rise. But as the housing crisis becomes more severe, prices rise with little increase in quality, and for poorer residents quality declines absolutely. In both cities elderly and female-headed households, single-parent families, and minority households, as well as the poor working class and those outside the formal labor market, suffer the most from poor housing quality (Stegman, 1988).[3]

The following sections attempt to make historical and geographical sense of this initial comparative portrait in the New York and London housing markets. We begin with an examination of contradictory political and economic trends on the production side, namely the destruction and reconstruction of residential built environments, then consider the social and economic stratification of the housing market. Following a discussion of the simultaneous trends towards globalization and localization, we conclude with an assessment of the political fabric of the housing system.

DESTRUCTION AND RECONSTRUCTION

In both New York and London there has been simultaneous disinvestment, reinvestment, and new investment in residential property and neighborhoods. There are, however, significant differences between the New York and London experiences, especially as regards disinvestment. In New York disinvestment has been led by the private market. In areas such as Harlem disinvestment already took place in the early years of this century, whereas in the South Bronx it began in earnest only in the late 1950s. The peak period of disinvestment, however, came between 1968 and 1976 in reaction to several simultaneous events: a sequence of national and local recessions, the uprisings of the late 1960s, and the New York City fiscal crisis of the mid-1970s. Disinvestment is notoriously difficult to measure, but as indicated by tax delinquency levels, it peaked in 1976 when over 7 percent of the city's residential buildings were in tax arrears (W. Williams, 1987). Abandonment, the most extreme form of disinvestment, also peaked in the mid-1970s. Geographically, disinvestment has been highly concentrated in inner city neighborhoods such as the Lower East Side, South Bronx, Bedford Stuyvesant, Harlem, and East New York. In Harlem, by the early 1980s, fully a quarter of residential properties were abandoned (Schaffer and Smith, 1986). City-wide, 14.4 percent of rental units had three or more serious maintenance and/or equipment deficiencies in 1987.

Disinvestment in public housing has involved a significant reduction of funds for badly needed modernization and even repairs and new construction has come to a standstill. The reductions began after the 1971 Nixon moratorium on selected housing subsidies, but was dramatically accelerated by the Reagan administration, which reduced the housing budget for the Department of Housing and Urban Development (HUD) from $32 billion in 1979 to under $8 billion in 1988. Nor has the nonprofit sector – much vaunted by Republican administrations – been able to pick up the slack; fewer nonprofit starts were accomplished throughout the 1980s than were built by the federal government in any single year of the 1970s (Zipser, 1989).

In London massive disinvestment has also occurred in private rental housing. However, the timing and nature of this disinvestment has been different, and it has involved minimal abandonment (Allen and McDowell, 1989). Well before the 1980s, there had been a major shrinkage in London's private rental housing (down from 42 percent in 1961 to 22.6 percent in 1976). The private rental sector did not receive the government subsidies that flowed to council tenants and homeowners, yet it was constrained by rent control. Landlords sold properties either to sitting tenants or to local authorities, but with the virtual cessation of public house-building in the last decade local authority purchases no longer occur. Landlords' most profitable recourse now is to sell (with "vacant possession") or to "convert" and modernize the property for upper-/middle-income occupancy (Hamnett and Randolph, 1986).

Private-sector disinvestment is now overshadowed by public-sector disinvestment, a deliberate policy of the Thatcher government, continued under John Major, but begun in the mid-1980s under the preceding Labour government. In the 1970s and even into the 1980s, the sharp reductions in public expenditure on housing were driven more by budget crises amidst a failing British economy than by political dogma. By the mid-1980s, with a massive public-sector budgetary surplus, policy was more purely driven by ideology – the attack on collectivism and state provision (Harloe, 1990).

There have been two elements to public-sector disinvestment. First, the sharp reduction in new building: starts in London fell from almost 20,000 in 1977 to just over 2,000 by 1988, and even more sharply in the Outer Metropolitan Area and the Outer South East (UK Department of the Environment, various dates). Public housing starts amounted to 35 percent of all starts in London and the South-East in 1980, but only 10.8 percent by 1988 (see table 7.3(b)). As in the US, central government has claimed that the private sector could replace much of the public-sector building, but attempts to provide lower cost, state-assisted private housing have achieved virtually nothing (Malpass and Murie, 1987).

Table 7.3   Housing production in the 1980s, London and New York

(a) Housing units authorized, 1980–1987, New York metropolitan region

	Total permits		Percentages	
	New York	*Suburban ring*	*New York*	*Suburban ring*
1980	6,001	26,700	16.9	75.0
1981	8,436	25,912	23.1	71.1
1982	7,485	27,270	20.0	73.0
1983	11,795	43,543	20.7	76.5
1984	11,566	53,655	17.1	79.5
1985	20,332	68,497	21.8	73.3
1986	9,782	72,520	11.5	85.4
1987	13,764	61,332	17.5	78.1
Total	89,161	379,429	18.2	77.3

(b) Housing starts, 1980–1989, Greater London and the rest of the South East (Outer Metropolitan Area and Outer South East)

	Total starts		Percentage share	
	GLC	*OMA/OSE*	*(all starts) GLC*	*(Public housing starts) GLC/ OMA/OSE*
1980	8,216	35,396	18.8	35.0
1981	9,131	37,514	19.5	23.4
1982	13,521	47,477	22.2	25.6
1983	14,050	60,261	18.9	22.0
1984	12,849	53,283	19.4	20.0
1985	11,062	55,718	16.6	16.6
1986	13,895	56,287	19.8	15.1
1987	14,843	59,061	20.1	13.7
1988	15,291	63,086	19.5	10.8

Sources: Stegman, 1988; UK Department of the Environment, various dates

Private-sector output has not numerically compensated the loss of public units. Further, new private housing is increasingly built for the luxury market, not those on council waiting lists. Indeed, it took the massive house price inflation of the mid-1980s to bring about even these levels of private output, and as the boom burst in 1989, in the face of soaring homeowner costs, output dwindled.

Disinvestment also affects the remaining council stock. The sharp reductions in subsidies and the more general fiscal crisis of many local authorities mean that the long-term pattern of underinvestment in repair, maintenance, and modernization has been intensified (Malpass and Murie, 1987; Malpass, 1986).

New investment in housing has taken several forms in both metropolitan areas. Quantitatively the most significant component is the rapid suburban expansion that accompanied postwar development and continued, if unevenly, through the 1970s and 1980s. In 1980, amidst the 1979–82 recession, only 6,001 housing units were authorized in New York City but 26,700 were authorized in the suburban ring, representing 75 percent of new building permits in the region (table 7.3(a)). By 1987 the suburban ring accounted for 78 percent of authorizations, or 61, 332 units (Hughes and Sternlieb, 1989, p. 66). In South East England London's share of private starts was around 20 percent in the 1980s (table 7.3(b)). In both cities metropolitan growth has pushed dramatically out from the center city. In London restrictive planning policies such as the Green Belt have provoked leapfrog development. In both cities a massive growth of long-distance commuting (50 to 100 miles is no longer uncommon) permitted the integration of distant housing markets into the metropolitan space economy (Cervero, 1986; Fishman, 1987; Hall et al., 1973; Herington, 1984; Lake, 1981; Muller, 1981; D. Smith, 1989). But it is only a partial integration. First, in both metropolitan regions, but most sharply in New York, the exclusionary politics and economics of suburban expansion severely restrict minority and poor people to only a few suburbs. Second, with dramatic suburban decentralization of jobs, an increasing proportion of suburban residents work as well as live outside the urban core.

The other focus for investment remains the central urban cores. Classical gentrification was first identified in London three decades ago with the rehabilitation of working-class housing and neighborhoods and the displacement of their residents by middle-class homeowners (Glass, 1964). In the intervening quarter century the gentrification process has expanded beyond classical rehabilitation and is no longer restricted to the most elite segment of the market. A number of other processes are involved: tenure conversion (rental to owner occupancy or cooperative status), functional conversions (from nonresidential uses), and new construction, often on former nonhousing sites, usually at the luxury end of the market. Whatever form it takes, gentrification involves a systematic displacement that is integral to the restructuring of urban space, not simply an unfortunate side-effect.

In London tenure conversion was virtually unknown up to the early 1970s, but by 1981 there were at least 58,000 converted units (almost half the national total). In Inner London, in particular, conversions are now the single largest source of "new" housing output, with at least 60 percent of *gross* "additions" to Inner London stock between 1987 and 1991 expected to come from this source (Hamnett, 1990). These properties are concentrated in the arc of boroughs (Camden, Westminster, and Kensington) which lie west and northwest of the City of London and include the central retailing and commercial district of the West End. And as conversions, of course, they usually involve a *net* reduction of total housing units.

Conversions are much less common in Outer London and even rarer beyond. The impetus for conversion, and gentrification more generally, comes from (and adds to) escalating property prices, the concentration of professional employment, and a suitable stock of devalorized land and housing (N. Smith, 1987; Marcuse, 1986, 1989a). As the stock of centrally located housing and available land is consumed, gentrification spreads outward. In London, as a result, even converted flats, the cheapest form of homeownership in the capital apart from council housing purchased by its tenants, are becoming ever less affordable by moderate-income households even as their quality declines. Thus, between 1978 and 1985 building society data suggest that the average incomes of those who bought converted flats shifted from 6 percent below average London household income to 12 percent above (Barlow, 1989). This growing exclusion of lower-middle-income households from access to even minimal levels of homeownership is one clear indicator of the more general polarization in London housing.

In New York City classical gentrification persists on a large scale in inner city neighborhoods such as the Upper West Side, Clinton, East Harlem, the Lower East Side, Brooklyn Heights, Park Slope. As in London, the process is diffusing outward geographically, and now affects Hoboken, across the Hudson River, as well as lesser-known neighborhoods in Brooklyn (Barry and Derelvany, 1987). Tenure conversion also occurs in New York City; between 1981 and 1986, 205,000 housing units were converted to either co-op or condominium status in the city (almost 8 percent of the city's housing stock), generally leading to increased costs and often to displacement (Stegman, 1988, p. 173). In addition, functional conversions occur in previously industrial and warehousing areas like SoHo, Long Island City, and elsewhere. An array of city, state, and federal programs lubricates these various forms of gentrification. Most notorious is the J-51 tax abatement program, under which almost 380,000 private rental units were rehabilitated in the 1970s (New York City Department of City Planning, 1983, p. 25). Under pressure from grassroots housing movements, which objected to government subsidy of gentification, the J-51 program was rendered inapplicable to Manhattan below 96th Street, the main presumed location for gentrification, in 1983. Today the program still fuels gentrification outside this area.

New investment in housing also takes the form of demolition of existing uses and construction of housing targeted at the new upper-income demand created by the expansion of global city functions. In London the prime site for such housing lies in an area of industrial disinvestment, to the immediate east of the financial center in the vast area of abandoned docklands, now being redeveloped for residential and business uses with the aid of substantial state investment (Brindley et al., 1989; A. Smith, 1989). By 1988 new housing output in this area accounted for over a quarter of all new private-sector housing in Greater London (and a far higher percentage in Inner London) (Department of the Environment, various dates; KFR Research, 1988). Within an area of traditional working-class employment and residence, both the new housing and the new jobs have little or nothing to offer the local docklands population. Despite the (now diminishing) allocation of a very limited number of houses for moderate-income local residents, most housing is for the upper-income market. By 1988 one-bedroom apartments with a riverside view ranged in price from £100,000 to £275,000, depending on location; even less favored inland properties started at around £65,000 (KFR Research, 1988).

Morover, this housing is "not ideal to raise a family." It is, however, ideal as a five-day "pied-à-terre, for single people, young professional couples, and those past the child rearing age." An important element in successfully marketing this housing to such populations has been the provision of facilities which are by design or in practice for the exclusive use of the new residents. As the consultants further remark: "the additives can consist of unique design; sporting, leisure or shopping facilities or catering for the trend to do home-based office work. The buyer does not just buy a house or a flat, but a life-style" (KFR Research, 1987).

New upmarket housing development is closely connected to the financial restructuring of the City of London, which has increased the number of well-paid jobs but has also lengthened the working day as the City embraced "competition in international financial markets." Consequently the demand for luxury residences within short commuting distance has grown as the strong competitive demand from overseas buyers and from investors converting houses into "high rent company flats" has temporarily reduced the supply of good quality residential accommodation in Central London (KFR Research, 1987).

A growing polarization is evident, with the new clusters of offices and upper-income housing uneasily coexisting with the legacy of the docklands' earlier economic and political history – concentrations of working-class households, many now unemployed, living in deteriorating high-rise, high-density public housing. Even the real estate consultants acknowledge the "increasing disparity between high quality housing developments and local authority housing estates in need of refurbishment" (KFR Research, 1987). As a recent study concludes: "the private sector regeneration of Docklands is producing a collage of private realms, each barricaded behind its own security system. The social exclusiveness of the new houses and offices is mirrored by the physical exclusion imposed by the buildings themselves" (Brindley et al., 1989, p. 120).

New York presents a similar picture. Between 1980 and 1987 35,718 new housing units were authorized in Manhattan alone, virtually all of them high-rise luxury homes (Hughes and Sternlieb, 1989, p. 314). Dominant here was Battery Park City, which added nearly 6,000 residents in 19 new residential buildings between 1982 and 1989. Mean household income exceeds $100,000. Battery Park is exclusionary as much as it is exclusive, enhancing the socio-geographical polarization of the city (see chapter 8 for further discussion on the Docklands development and Battery Park City). Metrotech in Brooklyn and other city-subsidized projects intended to produce jobs and housing for middle- and higher-income people will have similar effects.

SOCIAL AND ECONOMIC STRATIFICATION

In social terms the restructuring of housing provision and consumption now occurring in the two cities is resulting in two interconnected trends. There is, first, a concentration of the housing crisis among the poor and a growing segment of the working class, with repercussions among the middle class. Second, there is a polarization and restratification of the urban population in terms of access to housing, both financially and in terms of its location. As one of us has suggested, "quartering" may be a better word for the process, for it has different effects on the very rich, the new professionals (the "gentrifiers") the middle and working class, and the very poor (Marcuse, 1989b). These trends are really parts of a single process of spatial and social restructuring in which housing provision is becoming increasingly oriented towards the needs of an upper middle class of professional and managerial elites. Lower-middle-income groups and manual workers find increasing difficulty in gaining access to affordable housing, while the unemployed and more marginal sectors of the labor force are left trapped in poor housing and deteriorated neighborhoods with little or no prospect of a better housing future. In the frank, if self-interested, formulations of *Business Week* (1984): "No relief seems in sight for spiralling housing costs, which are out of reach in Manhattan for all but the very wealthiest newcomers, pushing the middle class into the suburbs, and locking the poor in the ghettos."

We have already referred to several aspects of the changes which have occurred. The upward spread of the housing crisis concerns first of all the rapid increase in housing costs in relation to income. An increasing number of people are paying a greater percentage of their income for less and less housing. A second manifestation is public and private disinvestment from housing and the concentration of new investment in key executive and managerial markets connected to the expanding nexus of financial and other services. At the other end of the spectrum homelessness, and housing poverty in general, is growing more intense.

Only the intensity of the housing crisis is different between the two cities. London – with a larger, albeit shrinking and deteriorating, public housing sector, a national housing allowance scheme, and a national welfare system not yet as gutted as that in New York, and a legal system that obliges local authorities to house some categories of the homeless – does not as yet display the same degree of deprivation as New York. Although the courts have interpreted New York State's constitution to impose a similar rehousing obligation on the city, the ruling has produced almost as much litigation as housing for the homeless. With an estimated homeless population of between 60,000 and 70,000 (Marcuse, 1989c), New York City has shelter space for less than 20,000 individuals. The destruction of marginal housing, its conversion through gentrification, and evictions have increased the homeless. Between 1970 and 1983 the number of single-room occupancy units fell by a staggering 89 percent from an estimated 127,000 to only 14,000. During the mid-1980s gentrification alone displaced between 25,000 and 100,000 each year (Marcuse, 1986). In 1988 alone 21,000 households (an estimated 70,000 people) were evicted from New York City housing, and, according to the city's Human Resources Administration, at least 26 percent of the homeless have become so immediately through eviction (Swanstrom, 1989). But the differences are of degree only. In both cities similar processes are at work.

The geography of this stratification and quartering is evident in the landscape. There are two spatial dimensions to the phenomenon. One is the long-established division between the core city and the expanding outer areas. The second is the increasingly visible and spreading division between the affluent and the poor within the inner city. In London privatized public housing is concentrated on the lower-density single-family estates in and beyond the outer boroughs. By contrast high-density public housing blocks in the inner boroughs experience accelerating disrepair allied with high levels of poverty and insecurity. However, in the inner areas the second sort of polarization also exists. The paradigmatic case is that of Docklands, where, as we have already noted, there is an uneasy juxtaposition of new private housing and run-down, high-rise public housing projects. But such a division exists more widely: for example, a recent research study found that 25 local authority areas in Great Britain combined above average levels of unemployment *and* of house prices (CES Ltd., n.d.), indicating clear polarization. Thirteen of these were London boroughs, covering almost all the inner city. A similar polarization characterizes New York, where, according to the 1980 Census, the wealthiest tract, with an annual household income of over $121,000, lies in the Upper East Side, less than four miles from the poorest tract (in the Bronx), with a per capita income below $4,000.

The future evolution of this latter polarization is unclear. The current divisions may be no more than a transitional stage in a new "colonization" of the central city by sections of the professional and managerial classes, and the exclusion of the poor, or at least their confinement to an ever more tightly circumscribed, deprived, and neglected rump of "welfare" public housing, at a safe distance from the new middle-class enclaves. Some have argued that the heightened geographical polarization represents a secular "third worlding" of the central global city (Franco, 1985; Koptiuch, 1989). At present, however, the empirical evidence clearly supports the notion that a limited convergence in urban structure is occurring vis-à-vis London and New York, at least as regards class locations (N. I. Fainstein and S. S. Fainstein, 1982).

In terms of race, however, there are important differences in the stratification of housing provision between the two cities (see also chapter 6). Segregation by race is far greater in New York than in London. While high segregation indices are to be found in a few areas of London at the block or street level, at more aggregated levels nothing in London compares with, for example, Central Harlem, which had a 1980 population of over 105,000, 97.3 percent of whom were black. New York contains a mosaic of highly segmented local housing markets. African-Americans and Latinos are especially segregated, ghettoized in the larger inner urban concentrations of the Lower East Side, Harlem, South Bronx, Brownsville, Bedford Stuyvesant, and East New York. Recent Third World migrants also cluster there, as well as in Chinatown and in newer neighborhoods further out in Queens and Brooklyn, where disinvestment has made housing of declining quality available to poorer renters.

Geographic and economic ghettoization of housing and job opportunities are among a complex of factors persuading some researchers of the existence of an American "underclass," demonstrated by its physical isolation from the rest of society (Wilson, 1987). Whatever its validity in the US (Holcomb, 1989–90), the underclass argument is hardly applicable in London. There minority groups face widespread racially based discrimination and disadvantage in the housing market, as in the labor market and education (C. Brown, 1984; S. Smith, 1989), but geographic separation is far less. Two patterns predominate in London, corresponding to the two main nonwhite minority groups. Households of Asian origin are highly concentrated in mainly poorer quality, owner-occupied housing. With most such housing located in the middle suburbs, the Asian population is more dispersed than the other main minority, Afro-Caribbeans. The latter are highly concentrated in public housing, especially in the high-density estates in Inner London. In general, however, both Asians and Afro-Caribbeans normally live in close proximity to similar lower-income white households. This is not to say that there is not a racial dimension to housing deprivation; whites clearly tend to occupy better public housing stock than do black tenants. Rather, with only 5 percent of the population Asian, and 7 percent African, Afro-Caribbean, or Black British, geographical interspersion is less limited in London than in New York, as is everyday social interaction across racial boundaries. The varied patterns of geographical segregation are implicated in the rise of racism in both cities in the 1980s. From London's East End to Howard Beach and in tens of other neighborhoods, attacks on minorities and political responses to racism are closely identified with specific residential enclaves. While New York experiences nothing as organized as British Movement racism, as noted in chapter 5, white hostility and fears are much more extensive than in London.

The housing crisis also clearly affects people asymmetrically according to gender. Among the housed, an increasing proportion of those ghettoized in minority and/or working-class neighborhoods in New York are single women, often with children. Among the homeless, by recent estimates, 34 percent, an all-time high, are women. In London the feminization of housing poverty is equally real. For example, a study of homelessness in London found six times more female-headed than male-headed homeless households living as "concealed" households with others (Austerberry et al., 1984).

GLOBAL CITY/FRAGMENTED CITY

The housing markets in both New York and London are being restructured in ways which reflect the new fault lines in the urban economy, created by the growth of global city functions in both places, which have been described in earlier chapters. The global economy has directly affected the demand for housing, through changes in both the labor market and the production and financing of housing. At the upper end of the market luxury townhouses, condominiums, and rental properties are increasingly advertised internationally, and significant foreign capital has flowed into the land and property markets of both cities. In addition, a good deal of development capital has been raised on international markets. By 1987 Japanese investment alone in New York City real estate exceeded $7 billion, with an estimated $1.5 billion of new investment in the first eight months of 1988. British, Canadian and Dutch capital owns a further $6.2 billion (Burstein, 1989, p. 30). Given the complexity of investment patterns and the difficulty in assigning definitive national origins to capital, estimating precise levels of foreign financing in residential real estate is difficult.

Luxury housing accounts for only a small proportion of the total housing stock in both cities, albeit a critical part of new construction. Yet its growth has provoked escalating land and property prices throughout the metropolitan housing markets. In the Isle of Dogs area of Docklands, for example, residential land values rose from about £80,000 per acre in 1981 to around £3 million by 1986 (KFR Research, 1987). Luxury housing in London's West End or in the Trump Tower on New York's prestigious Fifth Avenue now forms part of an international rather than a city-wide housing market. Yet the escalation of prices at the top both inflates the market lower down and diffuses outward geographically from the centre.[4] In this sense, globalization ripples down and out through the market.

Globalization, ironically, also leads to a sharpening fragmentation and localization of housing production and consumption. New residential enclaves are defensively cordoned off from the environments into which they are inserted. Sometimes the barrier are physical, as with the wall "protecting" St Katharine's Dock from London's East End; sometimes it is a political barrier, such as the stringent security force removing "unwanted" people from Battery Park City, which ensures a privatization of public space. Further, the penetration of global capital down the market leads to an ongoing redifferentiation of the residential geography. Capital seizes on some neighborhoods, converting them into new "frontiers of profitability" (N. Smith, 1986, 1990). Thus, real estate capitals, in drawing frontiers round their new investments, using the full medley of cultural, social, and political infrastructure to hype "new" neighborhoods, also concentrate disinvestment and devaluation in discrete geographical pockets where deterioration intensifies. This sharpening of geopolitical boundaries in the real estate market also enhances the fragmentation of urban space. Finally, existing neighborhoods defend themselves against conversion by global or at least supra-local capital. The cultural, social, and political defense of communities also enhances spatial fragmentation insofar as struggles remain local and are not effectively linked (see chapter 8 for further discussion of these issues).

These, then, are some of the principal ways in which the housing markets in the two cities are increasingly enmeshed in the global economy and thereby also further fragmented. Dramatic rises in land and property prices have severely circumscribed the available residential locations for the vast mass of people working in the central cities, forcing longer and longer commutes without appreciable improvement in the transportation system. For lesser-paid workers the financial burdens of this commuting are severe, with substantial price increases in public transportation (and, in New York, increases in bridge tolls) now routine in both cities. Even for better-paid workers who can afford such costs, the social as well as work-related opportunity costs of such commuting are high and rising (Lyons, 1987). In the words of London real estate consultants, long-distance commuting is "an increasingly archaic arrangement," especially given longer work hours in the City with its increasingly global role (KFR Research, 1987). In New York the transportation system makes the commute even more archaic. The use of chartered point-to-point private Express buses for upper-income commuters and an antiquated public mass transit system for poor people mirrors residential segregation in a segregated (stratified) transportation system. In London the image of the new enclaves of luxury housing in Docklands adjacent to – but a world apart from – the deteriorating high-density public housing estates encapsulates this development. In New York a similar contrast is to be found, for example, on the Lower East Side, where an international art scene, stretch limos, and chronic homelessness emerged together in the pores of a hot real estate market in the 1980s.

DIVIDE, SEDUCE, AND SIPHON: THE POLITICS OF HOUSING

Political processes modify and stimulate housing market processes, sometimes blunting their unequal distributive effects, sometimes reinforcing them. In both cities during the 1980s the main trajectory of housing policy was to reinforce rather than blunt inequality. While in New York housing policies have traditionally been aimed at subsidizing the working- and middle-class households rather than the lowest income population (Marcuse, 1988), in London a more complex and fluctuating history has accompanied the greater role of the Labour Party and a nominally socialist politics.

"Divide and seduce" is the traditional policy of conservative governments toward working-class demands for housing.[5] Its essence is to divide the working class into subcategories and deal with each differently. Those who are necessary to the continuing functioning of the economy and/or who have some actual or potential political voice need to be provided for, but are divided from those seen as superfluous, marginal, or redundant, who can be residualized or excluded without basic damage to the prevailing economic and political order. Government housing programs focus on the key groups with the aim of seducing them to identify with the social situation and housing needs of those immediately above them in the economic hierarchy. With federal and local programs in New York especially, this attempted seduction has long been accompanied by the siphoning upward of housing funds, purportedly targeted at low-income households but in practice benefiting an officially designated middle-income population. Some recent policy trends in London also fit this description. Far from integrating them into the system of housing provision, housing policy effectively neutralizes an already marginal population, reinforcing patterns of discrimination and racism. We look at the politics of housing first in New York, then in London.

Within the United States as a whole only when grassroots political movements have threatened established power has the federal government provided housing for the poor. Thus, economic and social control questions have guided the formulation of public housing policy. For the better-off working and middle class, postwar federal policy heavily encouraged homeownership, promoting suburban expansion around central cities. Federal subsidies also established slum clearance: while much cleared land was used for commercial and upper-income residential developments, urban redevelopment had to provide some public housing for those displaced. The Reagan administration's dismantling of housing policy in the 1980s left the suburban subsidies intact but effectively dissolved federal subsidies for public housing or inner city rehabilitation. Existing housing subsidies, most prominently the large Section 8 programs, were gutted; efforts to instigate a voucher system were cynical in inspiration and ineffective in practice, with most of the small proportion of eligible New Yorkers who received vouchers returning them as insufficient to enable them to afford housing on the private market. Reagan's HUD was revealed by the end of the decade to have been mired in corruption, funneling tens of millions of dollars to benefit Republican officials and their cronies rather than the poor. Geographical segregation of existing public housing was accentuated, and isolation from employment opportunities increased.

With the new federalism, New York City government depended increasingly on private developers and public/private partnerships for the provision of new and rehabilitated housing. Unveiling its neighborhood redevelopment strategy in 1982, the Harlem Task Force verbalized a city-wide policy: "With drastic reductions in federal housing and economic aid . . . the private sector . . . would have to play a pivotal role" (New York, City Harlem Task Force, 1982, pp. i–ii). The partnership between developers and the city was explicit. As the *New York Times* observed: "developers have been scrambling for position in the newest real estate game in town. Mayor Koch is playing quarterback" (Scardino, 1986, p. 35). The city housing policy responded to market conditions rather than need: gentrification, increasingly, *was* the housing policy of the 1980s.

"Linkage" was part of the new policy. In return for subsidized or free land, tax abatements, or assorted zoning variances in the construction of market rate and luxury buildings, developers would agree to provide some linked developments for the public good. Developers have refurbished parks, streets, and subway stations and also produced some housing rented at or below cost. Often referred to as 80/20 schemes, these developments involve units, 80 percent of which are rented at market rates, the remaining 20 percent of which are subsidized or "affordable" housing. Significantly the 20 percent subsidized housing need not be situated at the same site, nor indeed in the same borough. Further, there is often no specification that the subsidized units be made affordable to lowest income people. Thus, in New York in 1988, according to federal guidelines, "middle income" refers to households earning between $35,000 and $53,000, and middle-income households are eligible for public subsidies in the 80/20 schemes. They are clearly the developers' favored tenants.

Mayor Koch's 1986–95 $5.1 billion housing plan reflected these priorities (table 7.4). Of a total of 83,870 new units (new construction and gut rehabilitation) scheduled for completion, almost 40 percent were planned for middle-income tenants while less than 19 percent (15,600) were to be set aside for the homeless. The plan also envisaged a moderate rehabilitation program with almost 70 percent of the affected units under low-income occupancy. A mere 160 of 168,900 such units were designated for the single homeless. The city's plan, which actually incorporated a variety of ongoing programs in addition to new initiatives, continued the tradition of divide and siphon; there was insufficient effort to deal seriously with the most dire effect of housing crisis – homelessness – while the most concentrated expenditure in new construction would have benefited households with annual incomes up to $53,000. New York's new black mayor, David Dinkins, began on entering office to develop significant modifications to the Koch plan, an attack on which had been part of the campaign with which he defeated Koch in the Democratic Party mayoral primary.

The crisis of affordability has led to other struggles over housing. New York's rent control and stabilization laws, which regulate tenancy

Table 7.4   New York City housing plan 1986–1995

	Income category				
	Homeless	*Low*	*Moderate*	*Middle*	*Total*
Production programs					
Gut rehabiliation	15,600	17,430	12,990	1,170	47,190
New construction	0	460	5,070	31,150	36,680
Subtotal	*15,600*	*17,890*	*18,060*	*32,320*	*83,870*
Reservation programs					
Moderate rehabilitation	160	117,420	51,320	0	168,900
Total	15,760	135,310	69,380	32,320	252,770

Source: City Limits, 1989

and allowable rent increases in 58 percent of the city's rental stock, are under continued assault by real estate owners, who have argued aggressively that, rather than keeping rents down, rent regulation causes homelessness by holding units off the market. Elsewhere the Real Estate Board has taken out large newspaper advertisements asking: "Is gentrification a dirty word?," hoping to equate gentrification with "giving homes to working people."

New York's housing struggle is rough. In 1984 a 22-person gang was indicted and jailed for having organized a "routine of terror" (as the Manhattan District Attorney called it) aimed at emptying 21 apartment buildings. Hired by a group of landlords for $100,000, the gang "installed drug addicts, prostitutes, thieves ... to commit burglaries and assaults against tenants" up to and including death threats (Shenon, 1984). In another case an ex-judge was found guilty of racketeering and tenant harassment (Buder, 1987). In a more gruesome case Bruce Bailey, an aggressive tenant activist in Upper Manhattan's Columbia Tenants' Union, went missing on June 14, 1989. The next day his dismembered body was discovered in trash bags in the Bronx; his head was never found. Although no one has been charged with the murder, the police, newspapers, and tenant activists openly speculated that landlord opponents were responsible (Burr, 1989). While no evidence confirms this suspicion, the breadth of speculation bespeaks the seriousness of New York's housing struggles.

Political struggles around housing are characterized not only by the aggressiveness of landlord and developer groups but also by the very localized nature of many tenant and neighborhood groups and demands, with little overall city-wide cohesion. However, in 1988 the city government sought to impose a curfew on Tomkins Square Park (traditionally used by homeless people as a place to sleep and live) as a means to remove the homeless and encourage gentrification. In the wake of a police riot there on August 6, 1988, political opposition was galvanized, with increased links between homeless, squatter, and other tenant organizations. Following the riot, a substantial homeless settlement was built in the park, dominated by shanties and tents. However, on December 14, 1989, after several unsuccessful attempts and with the blessing of incoming Mayor Dinkins (New York's first African-American mayor and a democratic socialist), police in riot gear moved into the park, destroying all existing structures and displacing between 150 to 300 people.

If the problems and causes are broadly similar, the politics of London's housing are different. In Inner London, under the leadership of first the London County Council and later the Greater London Council and the mainly Labour-controlled boroughs, there was a strong commitment to public housing. In sharp contrast, the suburban Conservative-controlled jurisdictions restricted public housing to a minimum and encouraged private homeownership (Young and Kramer, 1978). Successive national governments, whether Labour or Conservative, essentially sustained this division, although from the 1960s onward Labour increasingly shared the homeownership goals of the Conservatives, in part as a response to the shift in its core electorate – the organized, more skilled and unionized working class – into homeownership.

Labour's fading attachment to social housing was accelerated between 1974 and 1979 by economic crisis and the recourse to monetarism and deflationary public finances. But many inner city Labour authorities remained strongly committed to public-sector construction and the principle of low-rent housing. The qualitative shift in policy came with the Thatcher government in the 1980s. As in New York, the clearly stated objective, under Thatcher and then Major, has been to reduce and then break up public housing, to extend homeownership down the income distribution, and to minimize help for the poor ("targeting help on those who most need it"). Apart from any economic consideration (the sale to tenants of public housing has been the largest privatization program in terms of the revenue collected), public housing is widely seen as one of the refuges of that collectivism and local socialism which the government aims to eradicate (see, for example, Henney, 1985; M. Brown et al., 1985). There are many other aspects of this strategy: the forced privatization of other local authority services, the imposition of a poll tax, the removal of local authority financial autonomy, the abolition of the GLC, and so on (Pickvance, 1990). Today London (and other) local authorities, which remain committed in principle to social housing, have been reduced to virtual impotence, unable to build or even maintain their existing housing stock properly, desperately trying, and mostly failing, to act as houser of last resort for the homeless poor (Dibblin, 1989).

Sales of public housing to individual tenants, a primarily political effort to cement individual loyalties to a "nation of property owners" and to the Conservative Party, have been followed by legislation aiming at wholesale transfer of the remaining stock to private for-profit or nonprofit landlords. Both sorts of transfer involve the siphoning off, and up, of housing benefits. Thus, as individual tenant purchasers sell off their properties, bought with the aid of massive discounts, they are lost forever by the groups for which they were originally intended. A similar "upgrading" is likely to occur in much of the stock slated for wholesale transfer. Insofar as reduced subsidies are available for new building and rehabilitation, these are now targeted not at the marginal poor but increasingly on the production of "affordable" housing for moderate-income households (combining, for example, shallow public subsidies with private-sector money) (Page, 1987). The removal of any semblance of effective private rent control is aimed at stimulating the production of new rental housing for the professional and managerial employees of the growing financial and related sectors who were increasingly unable to locate in the city due to escalating house prices. In Docklands, housing schemes reserved for "local residents" and sold at below market prices have often favored this same group, as proof of local residence, the basis of eligibility for these units, has been obtained by the purchase of "accommodation addresses" (Gosling, 1987; Brindley et al., 1989).

All this contrasts with the treatment of the marginal poor. Many of the homeless can expect at best a long period of residence in privately owned "bed and breakfast accommodation" followed by eventual relocation in deteriorating public housing. Here they may enter limited self-help programs aimed at resolving "problem estates," but, as with parallel self-help initiatives in New York, the result is double-edged. They can genuinely tap residents' powers of collective organization and action, but may also be seen as an invitation for the marginal poor to manage their own confinement to a sort of inner city reservation.

Such minimal housing provision characterizes other aspects of housing policy. Rules of eligibility and benefit levels in the housing allowance and related welfare systems have been increasingly restricted. Rent levels in public housing have been increased sharply, especially in the early 1980s, both to encourage tenant purchase and to shift the burden of costs to tenants. In some places, indeed, council housing accounts began to make "profits," used to subsidize general local expenditure (Malpass and Murie, 1987). New arrangements for local housing finance now ensure that a proportion of the rent allowances paid to the poorest tenants will be drawn directly from the rents of other public tenants (Grant, 1988).

Outside the central city the contradictions and inadequacies of contemporary housing policy are also manifest. In addition to the familiar erosion of the public sector, the outer areas are especially affected by market-borne problems. Escalating house prices restrict accessibility and are reinforced by financial deregulation. Since 1988, however, the collapse of the housing market has exacerbated the problems. Following the government's adoption of a high interest rate policy, in response to inflation led by house price rises and changes in tax laws, increasing numbers of homeowners who had stretched their finances to the limit found they could not afford the massive increases in mortgage payments. Nor could they sell without incurring capital losses. Mortgage default and repossession rose sharply in the late 1980s.

Such policies have been divisive politically. The loss of many better-off tenants to owner-occupation, the changing role of public housing from accommodating the mainstream working class to housing the marginalized poor, and the increasing concentration of minorities in public tenure have all contributed to a distinct ghettoization, politically and geographically. More generally the growth of what Forrest and Murie (1986) have aptly called "subsidized individualism" limits the possibilities for a collective response to commonly experienced housing problems. The reduction of much housing-related policy to welfare policy, treating social problems as the individual pathologies of deprived "clients" or "cases," has the same consequence. Nor is there much sign as yet of a collective response by homeowners struggling to avoid foreclosure on their suburban housing. Ironically, perhaps the most evident collective response and resistance to policy has come from a conservative middle rather than radical working class; in the Outer Metropolitan Area and the Outer South East government encouragement for large-scale private-sector residential development and a commensurate loosening of planning regulation have met with stiff resistance from its own heartland electorate, existing resident homeowners. Although often fought under the environmental banner, the real basis of this reaction against developers is the preservation of the local environment and property values. Such suburban resistance may be seen more appropriately as a symptom of intra-class division; not only do the suburban middle class exclude the poor, they also fight to exclude newcomers of their own class.

Despite the distinctively different history of housing policies in the two cities, there has been a striking degree of convergence between them in recent years – the decay of even the previously inadequate commitment to the housing of lower income households, the accentuated skewing of such subsidies as are available to the better-off (and to the benefit of the housing industry), and the clear concentration of the remaining housing assistance (often combined with private capital) on small-scale schemes for middle-income groups. In London, with the demise of the "new urban left" and the lack of new thinking by the Labour Party nationally, the prospects for any major change in this situation seem dim. In New York too, despite the expanded public involvement occasioned by the Koch housing plan, a significant reorientation toward the neediest sectors seems unlikely, despite the reevaluation of this plan by Mayor Dinkins, noted above.

CONCLUSION

The overriding conclusion that emerges from this study is that as the housing systems of both cities devolve into greater crisis, marked by their inability to provide affordable, quality housing to larger and larger segments of the population, they are converging toward a broadly similar model of housing supply and demand. New construction services the upper middle class while the public sector withdraws from housing provision for the poor and many of the working class. Throughout the 1980s a segmentation in the housing market according to class, race, and (in a more restricted sense) gender was the clear result. For many people in both cities the housing system has broken down. The failure of the housing system can be traced both to the intensity of economic pressures that have accompanied the emergence of London and New York as world cities, but also to specific policies since the 1970s which are only in part a response to this globalization.

The convergence of the two housing systems will never be complete, of course. Without extraordinary shifts in federal, state, and city policy, it is difficult to conceive of a New York with 35 percent public tenancy, and without an equally unlikely expansion of the British property market it is also unlikely that London's private rental sector will have six-fold growth. The possibility of such dramatic upheavals – the cessation of business as usual – ought not to be dismissed too lightly however. In both cities there is the growing recognition that the housing system is failing the majority of residents, that economic recession is a growing threat, and that community protest over housing may well increase. In precisely such circumstances as might emerge in the 1990s, the housing system can be radically transformed. Increasingly bound together in their role as world cities, New York and London can be expected to continue their pattern of housing convergence, yet the conditions under which a dramatic restructuring of their housing provision might occur are also so intensely local that it would be foolish to dismiss other possible outcomes.

NOTES

1   The *in rem* program is specific to New York City. It involves some of the many blocks of deteriorated low-income private rental property which have come into the ownership of the city council as a result of legal proceedings to collect unpaid property taxes from defaulting landlords (hence the legal terminology). Minimal city resources are provided to enable the tenants of such properties to form cooperatives and carry out basic repairs and improvements.

   Section 8 (of the US Housing Act 1974) was the main program of federal assistance to low- and moderate-income housing in the 1970s and 1980s. It involved payments to meet the gap between the assessed rent-paying capacity of tenants and the officially estimated "fair market rents" in local private rental markets. In the 1970s a considerable number of new units were built with the aid of these subsidies, although they were originally intended mainly for use in connection with existing housing units. Section 8 subsidies were sharply cut back under the Reagan administration, which tried, with some eventual success, to convert them into a program of "housing vouchers." Widespread racial discrimination in letting, and the general shortage of lower rented units which are eligible for inclusion in the program, have prevented many potential recipients of Section 8/housing voucher assistance from taking up this benefit.

2   Unpublished data taken from the Greater London Council's 1986 survey of Londoner's Living Standards. Overall almost 20 percent of households surveyed found it "fairly difficult" and a further 7.5 percent "very difficult" to meet their housing costs. Unlike New York, the figures for those on low incomes are very much less than they might be, due to the impact of welfare benefits.

3   For example, the GLC survey (see n. 2 above) found that 25 percent of all public housing in London had four major defects (damp, vermin, internal and external building defects). All the groups mentioned in the text are overrepresented in this tenure.

4   Recent UK research shows this clearly. An analysis of over a million mortgage transactions enabled house price changes between 1983 and 1987 to be mapped onto 280 local labor markets. London had the highest annual average house price inflation at 17.62 percent. In general, house price variance reflected local labor market conditions, being highest in "areas with many jobs in the financial services and banking sectors . . . [a]nd in areas with large proportions of professional people at the upper end of the socio-economic spectrum." However, house prices were not just influenced by conditions in each local labor market, "[t]he team also identified the independent influence of London: proximity to the capital has an additional effect on local rates of house price inflation with a strong trend for prices and price inflation to fall as the distance from London increases." The "ripple out" effect from Central London was evident from computer mapping (Hurst, 1989).

5   For an historical account of such policies in Europe and the USA, see Harloe, 1991, and also Topalov, 1985, and Magri and Topalov, 1988. For New York, see Marcuse, 1988.

8

Politics and state policy in economic restructuring

Susan S. Fainstein and Ken Young

In the period since 1978 the governing regimes of both London and New York have actively sought to promote growth in output and employment. Their dedication to social amelioration over the same time-span has been less certain. During the 1980s New York's mayoral administration and the British central government that bore ultimate responsibility for governing London displayed strikingly similar social philosophies (S. S. Fainstein, 1990; Barnekov et al., 1989). As well as defining governmental planning and regulation as inimical to economic vitality, they regarded real estate development (in contrast to job training or infrastructure investment) as their primary strategy for stimulating expansion. They identified global city status as the hallmark of their economic advantage and fostered those forms of development – especially first-class office space and luxury housing – which responded to the needs of the upper echelons of the financial and advanced service industries participating in world economic coordination. The two regimes also resembled each other in confronting conflicting political agendas at subordinate levels of government as well as among outside groups. At the same time the two metropolises continued to have quite different governmental structures, resulting in important dissimilarities in local autonomy, political expression, and planning.

This chapter examines the system of political institutions since 1978, the relationship between politics, state policy, and economic and spatial development within the two metropolises, and the kinds of political conflicts that have occurred. The chapter concludes by analyzing the extent of convergence between development politics in the two metropolises and the factors causing existing biases in public policy.

INSTITUTIONAL STRUCTURES

Differences in the governance of the London and New York regions stem fundamentally from national differences between the United States and the United Kingdom. A federalist, presidential system, checks and balances, and home rule have traditionally strengthened local representation in the US and made it more possible for urban regimes to adopt policies opposed by the national party in power.[1] The nonprogrammatic nature of political parties and extreme jurisdictional fragmentation, however, militate against the adoption of broadly redistributive strategies at the local level.

Centralized parliamentary government under party control has consistently limited the autonomy of local government within the UK (Loughlin et al., 1985; Hambleton, 1989). The principle of party control and executives drawn directly from legislative bodies makes national party programs determinative both through the mechanism of parliamentary supremacy and, for the national oppostion parties, through the party machinery. Responsibility for local planning rests ultimately with the cabinet minister who heads the Department of the Environment (DoE), and the power of central government to set the general level of local expenditures further constrains local authorities. In both London and New York traditions of limited government reinforced by recent conservative tides restrict the public role in economic planning, meaning that for both regions private investment decisions determine their economic fortunes.

New York's political institutions

Within the New York region municipalities compete to capture the generators of growth and to exclude those populations and facilities that impose financial, social, or environmental costs without commensurate benefits (Danielson and Doig, 1982). It is not possible to discuss both suburban and New York City politics simultaneously, and this chapter will focus on the political history of the city. Nevertheless, it is important to remember that the character of political activity in each is strongly influenced by the existence of the other. Suburbia appeals to residents and industry through offering lower densities and more amenities than the city; its political leaders seek to maintain this competitive advantage. New York City's leaders justify the large subsidies they offer to private business locating within the city by the need to remain cost competitive with surrounding areas.

The continued heavy dependence of localities on tax revenues based on the assessed value of property within their boundaries exacerbates the competition.[2] The tri-state division of the New York region, moreover, allows the creation of tax differentials much greater than those that typify other US metropolitan areas.[3] Suburban residents constantly rationalize their exclusivity by evoking the specter of the dirty, crowded, crime-ridden, high-tax city that they have fled. The city, which cannot share in the tax base of its suburban ring, must forever strive to keep revenue-generating people and industries within its borders so as to stay fiscally solvent. Even if, from a regional viewpoint, it were economically most rational to move manufacturing, back office, and warehouse facilities outside the city limits, the city's structural position forces its government to oppose such moves.

Planning in the New York region

Outside the city itself few institutional mechanisms exist to provide a framework for regional planning or the resolution of territorial inequities. The Port Authority of New York and New Jersey has responsibilities on both sides of the Hudson, but its mandate is limited to transportation and some development activities. It operates autonomously and gives first priority to maintaining the fiscal soundness of its investments. The only democratic check on its operations is the requirement that the minutes of its board meetings (and therefore any decisions it might take) be approved by the governors of New York and New Jersey. The Metropolitan Transportation Authority plans and operates public transit in the New York State suburbs as well as the city. Its purview, however, does not extend to either Connecticut or New Jersey. New Jersey's Meadowlands Authority wields planning powers over a number of communities in northern New Jersey and has succeeded in promoting large-scale commercial and residential development as well as a major sports complex despite friction with subordinate municipalities. Governmental units within its boundaries share the tax revenues from new development. New Jersey, as well, is developing a state land-use plan that seeks to channel growth within certain municipalities while restricting development elsewhere.

Overall, however, peripheral expansion continues unplanned. The most egregious example is the growth along the Jersey side of the Hudson River. This area was the principal recipient of overspill development from the Manhattan business district during the boom period of the eighties. Each of the numerous municipalities that line the waterfront has virtually total responsibility for construction within its borders. Millions of square feet of office and residential space have sprung up in the narrow band between the river and the palisade behind it. There is no north–south transit along this strip; road connections are limited; east–west road access is made difficult by topographical barriers; and east–west transit provision touches only a few points. The main roads coming into the area must also serve the three trans-Hudson crossings to Manhattan. While the New Jersey state government makes occasional statements of intention concerning improving the traffic situation, it finds itself unable to mobilize the financial resources to do so. In the meanwhile each locality continues to accept further development, in part to increase tax revenues, but also because of the pervasive influence of real estate interests within municipal governing bodies.

The city: shifting alliances

New York City resembles other large American metropolises in having a mayor–council form of government. Until 1990, however, it also possessed a unique body called the Board of Estimate that wielded extraordinary power in the city's affairs.[4] Consisting of the mayor, with three votes, the city council president and controller, with two each, and the borough presidents, with one vote a piece, it had final authority over all land-use and contract matters. The city council, which is elected by district, therefore had relatively weak powers. The borough presidents, who exercised legislative power when sitting on the Board of Estimate, also held some executive power within their own boroughs. There was not, however, a corresponding borough legislative body. The establishment in 1977 of 59 community boards, with advisory power over land-use and capital budget matters within their districts but no executive authority, allowed for some decentralization within the city government, but far less than was the case for the London boroughs (Marcuse, 1987).

During the 1980s the public–private partnership became the chief vehicle of urban redevelopment (S. S. Fainstein, 1991). The Public Development Corporation (PDC) acted as the lead agency in development planning, while the Department of City Planning was relegated to a limited research and regulatory function (N. I. Fainstein and S. S. Fainstein, 1987). Established as a quasi-independent local development corporation with a board of prominent business people, the PDC played an entrepreneurial role in spurring construction. With a staff of 200 and a $95 million annual budget obtained through a contract with the city, the PDC acted primarily as a financial intermediary, putting together packages of land improvements, tax abatements, and funding for specific development sites (New York City Public Development Corporation n.d., p. i). In its larger projects the PDC worked together with New York State's Urban Development Corporation (UDC). This entity, originally established to develop housing for low- and moderate-income groups, had been reconstituted as an economic development agency. Within New York City it retained its original power to override local zoning and citizen participation requirements; its i volvement in projects, therefore, permitted a steamlined process of regulatory approvals.

As a general rule, district-based representatives, including state legislators as well as city councillors, frequently played ombudsman roles in city affairs and lobbied for neighborhood concerns. Since none of them had formal responsibility for land-use decisions, however, the most they could do in this crucial arena was put pressure on the city-wide elected officials and borough presidents. These policy-makers usually responded to more highly organized and wealthier constituencies and almost uniformly supported large development projects. The dominant role played by the Board of Estimate in the governance of a city of over 7 million people made it extremely difficult for community-based representatives to make names for themselves and attain sufficient financing to seek higher office.

The Democratic Party has dominated postwar electoral politics within the city.[5] It is, however, divided into reform and regular wings, with the regulars devoting themselves almost entirely to allocation of nominations and patronage. Whereas in the 1960s the Reform Democrats had strong, liberal policy positions, their influence and ideology have both waned during the ensuing decades. In general, in both city and suburb the party system exists primarily for the purpose of contesting elections rather than of programmatic control and has largely failed as a vehicle for representing neighborhood or minority interests (Mollenkopf, 1988b). Many of the suburbs are Republican strongholds, reflecting their upper-class social composition. In suburb as well as city, however, incumbency rather than ideology defines electoral success. We cannot describe a party program, whether in the city or the rest of the region, because there is none. Hence, when we contrast New York and London, we cannot compare Democrats with Labour or Republicans with Conservatives on this dimension or on the evolution of ideologically based internal party divisions.

New York, compared to other US cities, had an unusually active governmental sector, rooted in a strong labor movement and a long tradition of paternalism and civic endeavor by New York's upper classes (see chapter 2). Mobilization by low-income minority groups in the late sixties, however, strained the alliance between low-income groups, labor, and progressive civic associations; the fiscal crisis of 1975 marked its demise.

Fiscal crisis and its aftermath

The immediate cause of the 1975 fiscal crisis was the refusal of banks to refinance New York's short-term debt once the city lost its approval by the principal investment bond-rating firms. Unlike the nation, New York had not recovered from the recession at the beginning of the decade; as a consequence, it revenues were falling, but there had been no correlative decrease in financial commitments. It increasingly borrowed for current expenditures, backing its bonds with mythical or otherwise committed anticipated revenues. Once the banks refused to continue lending, New York had no alternative source of funds by which to meet its obligations. Essentially the fiscal crisis resulted inevitably from the effort to sustain a strongly interventionist public sector within a situation of economic contraction without increased support from the national government. Interventionism comprised both large subsidies to capital and major commitments to social welfare; its costs were further expanded by relatively high total compensation for municipal employees.[6]

Radical critics blamed the city's plight on overspending for capital accumulation and the rapacity of banks and political insiders (Tabb, 1982; Newfield, 1976); they argued that the crisis was deliberately created in order to force discipline on the city's government (Marcuse, 1981). Liberal defenders pointed to obligations like public hospitals and welfare borne by the city government for which higher levels of government took responsibility elsewhere (Morris, 1980). They argued that the crisis would not have happened if New York State had shouldered its appropriate burden. Popular interpretations, however, reinforced by conservatives within the national government and aspirants for local office in the 1977 campaign, attributed fiscal demise to the squandering of resources on the undeserving (and predominantly black and Hispanic) poor.[7] Thus, the racial divisions that increasingly demarcated political and policy conflicts became incorporated in the discourse surrounding the very survival of New York – if the city were not totally to founder under its fiscal burden, its government had simultaneously to spur economic growth and eliminate the wasteful expenditures which were forcing it into bankruptcy. The fiscal crisis thus had an important ideological effect. It delegitimized the role that the city government had long played in assuaging the frictions between classes and ethnic groups through patronage and welfare provision. Simultaneously it made achievement of economic growth and fiscal solvency rather than of service provision the test of governmental legitimacy (see Pickvance, 1990).

The period between 1975 and 1977 marked an interregnum in New York's political life as control of public policy shifted from the caretaker regime of Mayor Abraham Beame to the agencies that had been established to restore fiscal integrity (Shefter, 1985; Morris, 1980). The loss of its acceptable bond rating had completely cut New York off from capital markets. Negotiations to provide new capital and keep the city from formally declaring bankruptcy resulted in the creation of a number of business-dominated bodies to oversee future spending. These included the Municipal Assistance Corporation (MAC), the Financial Control Board (FCB), and the Office of the Special State Deputy Controller for New York City. The MAC had been guaranteed a revenue stream against which to borrow and was entrusted with the job of restoring the city's credit. The FCB, which was an agency of New York State, oversaw and had veto power over the city's financial plan, while the Deputy Controller acted as its staff and auditor. Businessmen chaired the MAC and the FCB, which consisted of public officials and business and civic leaders; the MAC board had one black member, whereas the FCB included no members of minority groups. The criterion these boards used for evaluating city policies was their effect on the balance sheet. They determined the city's budgetary priorities for a number of years, tilting them toward economic development at the expense of social welfare objectives.

The new regime cut thousands of municipal jobs, drastically curtailed services, halted all major capital programs, ranging from school to subway building, froze civil service salaries and public assistance levels, introduced tuition in the City University while shifting responsibility for its financing to the state, and deferred routine infrastructure maintenance. The municipal unions, whose strikes and strike threats had enabled them to wring billions of dollars of concessions from the Wagner and Lindsay administrations, grudgingly agreed to purchase the MAC bonds that no one else showed much interest in buying. Their leadership began to meet regularly with bank executives in order to work out mutually acceptable strategies for city expenditures.

The resolution of the fiscal crisis through the creation of new institutions to insure solvency on terms set by business provided the context for the development politics of the next decade. Thus, even before the conservative tide swept over the US national government after the Reagan election of 1980, New York had installed a regime determined to control governmental extravagance, which was interpreted as spending for consumption rather than accumulation. While the path of institutional change in London during the same period was quite different, the set of constraints on local initiatives that emerged was remarkably similar.

London: politics and institutional change

London's population primacy, in addition to its status as national political as well as economic capital, makes its affairs much more prominent within the country than New York's, and therefore much more the subject of national political attention. Nevertheless, despite the domination of London policy-making by the national government, there are recurring and, as it were, "local" themes which are distinctive to London. Foremost among them are the east–west inequalities, inner–outer tensions, and metropolitan–local confrontations. Each of these draws its fuel from the underlying opposition of expansion and containment. The manner in which they are handled and resolved owes much to the patterns of political representation and leadership throughout the region, the values and interests that local regimes express, and the styles and strategies they adopt. These are the basic patterns, upon which institutional factors – the formation of collaborative arrangements for the region, the working of a metropolitan authority, the promulgation of a regional strategy, the aspirations of problem-solving Secretaries of State for the Environment – are more or less significant overlays.

Geography and politics

Each of the three major territorial divisions of London has its particular politics. Differences in social composition, party dominance, and institutional traditions produce different issues and responses in the three territories: Inner London, Outer London, and the Outer Metropolitan Area (OMA).

Within Inner London the historic West End–East End tension has defined party positions. Because their support was concentrated within the city's core, Labour leaders have typically eschewed a more inclusive metropolitan vision and have sought to solve their problems at the local level (Young and Garside, 1982).

Although the differences between the parties have remained stable, the character of Labour leadership has undergone profound changes. In the mid-sixties, based on tiny ward organizations, self-selection for office, patronage and spoils, and the rigorous exclusion of middle-class outsiders, the closed regimes of the Inner London boroughs were accurately characterized as "sclerotic" (Butterworth, 1966). The Conservatives in the anti-Labour swing of 1968 displaced the representatives of older working-class communities and trade union organizations who had formerly controlled most of these solid Labour areas. After these defeats intense political struggles occurred within the Labour Party between the liberal-left, largely homeowning, university graduate activists and the residue of the right-wing manual workers, with the former generally triumphing (Glassberg, 1981; Chamberlayne, 1978). In some parts of Inner London – notably in south-Thameside Southwark – the old Labour regimes proved remarkably resilient, only to give way suddenly when the new activists gained power in the ward parties and challenged sitting councillors (Goss, 1988). The regimes which these newcomers instituted, however, being more politically open and discursive, proved vulnerable to more overtly socialist successors who displaced them in turn; and the intra-party conflicts which ensued were alleviated in some cases only by the founding of the Social Democratic Party and the defection of the old right and disgruntled intelligentsia alike.

Elsewhere in Inner London the sizable local black populations also found a medium of political expression through the Labour Party, and a modest-sized cadre of black local politicians gained rapid prominence, attaining thereby their springboard to national politics. From the impact of these black politicians, from the parallel emergence in Inner London of socialist women leaders and a well-organized gay and lesbian movement, from a confrontational style and from occasional financial ineptitude there arose a concern about Labour's electability and the perception of a "London problem" for Labour which had taken root in the capital's local government.

The contrast between the Inner and Outer London boroughs is subtle and deep-seated and goes beyond simple differences in party dominance. Unlike the historically weak, Labour-led inner boroughs, most of those in overwhelmingly Conservative Outer London inherited a tradition of considerable municipal autonomy and substantial experience in running a broad range of services on behalf of their counties. The politics of territorial defense quickly emerged to top the local political agenda in such boroughs.

For the most part these outer suburbs began life with leaderships that paralleled those of the inner boroughs: a well-entrenched and slow-moving aldermanic group of strong local connection and long municipal service. Yet, from 1970, a number of the outer suburbs saw the rise to prominence of new, younger, and politically ambitious Conservatives with more professional skill and a sharper and more partisan cutting edge. The Conservative solidity of the wealthier of these boroughs concealed regime contests every bit as intense as those which occurred within the urban core. The territorial threat posed by the Labour- (and indeed at times the Conservative-) controlled GLC aided their rise, for they generally nailed their colors to a more vigorous defense of local characteristics than had been offered by their predecessors.

A more continuing threat, however, was posed by a renascent suburban Liberalism growing out of grassroots ratepayer discontent and
which had successfully challenged the Conservatives in some parliamentary elections. Accordingly, Conservative Central Office was careful to
nurture the new breed of suburban leaders, whose sharp political
antennae were respected there. For their own part the new Conservative
politicians quickly gained influence within the London-wide political
and governmental networks and it was from them – and from their
allies among Inner London's Conservative ultras – that the pressure to
abolish the Greater London Council (GLC) and to accord complete
autonomy to the London boroughs was to come.

The OMA was largely insulated from the intense pressures detailed
above. The Green Belt acted as a political cordon sanitaire, while
local politics in the tidy, well-regulated commuter towns of the region
contained its own subtle checks and balances. The OMA has, however,
long been caught in the grip of development pressures that arise from
the strategic significance of the region in the national economy, pressures
which are accommodated, amplified, and channeled by the development
of the motorway network, and most profoundly by the prospect of the
channel tunnel and its projected London rail link.

House prices and labor shortages are among the preoccupations of
the OMA's county leaders. The prices, congestion, and environmental
conditions that drove both households and businesses out of London in
the 1960s and 1970s threaten now to engulf them in the OMA itself.
The struggle to restructure public provision that has been a source of
political agony in London now preoccupies OMA leaders, who fear that
they can no longer reconcile their traditional commitment to low tax
rates with inherited commitments. Arguably, the politics of ad hoc
resistance to occasional development proposals is giving way to a more
generalized political movement as the residents of the OMA discover
the virtues of the planning process as a constraint on unwelcome development. The development backlash is, however, acquiring political force
at the very moment when the development pressures seem most inexor-
able.

As the politics of development intensify, pressures similar to those
which occurred in London suburban politics threaten the counties of
the OMA also. Nevertheless, the region still contains three distinct
political entities. They are forced into coexistence by the interdependenc-
ies of the region, by the strategic policies and institutional forms that
give it expression, and increasingly by the promotion of development
proposals whose scale is such as to affect the region as a whole, and to
underline its national importance.

Metropolitan structures

The London region increasingly resembles the New York area in comprising an uncoordinated mass of governing bodies ranging from elected borough councils to appointed authorities and public benefit corporations. The London metropolitan area, however, lacks a dominant local entity in no longer having a single municipal administration comparable to that in the city of New York. First the London County Council (LCC), which had responsibility for Inner London, then the GLC, which included the outer boroughs in its remit, acted as the metropolitan governing body. So far as central government was concerned, the creation of the GLC in 1965 was expected to overcome the gap caused by the limited geographic scope of the LCC in managing metropolitan strategic development. In setting up this body, the permanent officials of the then Ministry of Housing and Local Government chose metropolitan government as the alternative to governing London directly themselves. Their advocacy of reform coincided with the political imperatives then facing the Macmillan government, not least of which was to overthrow the apparently permanent Labour regime based in the LCC. In such a fashion, and subject to such high expectations, was the new metropolitan structure born (Young and Garside, 1982).

The GLC never possessed the authority of New York City's government since ultimate decision-making power rested with the central government, while primary responsibility for publicly provided housing and most land-use planning remained with the boroughs (Self, 1971). Most important, the GLC produced the opposite political effect from that intended by its Conservative progenitors. Party control of its council passed initially to Labour, and thereafter switched back and forth, mainly in tandem with changes in national control. In 1981 Labour returned to power and, under the leadership of Ken Livingstone, used the GLC as a base for opposing Thatcherite policy in planning, transport, social welfare, and revenue raising (O'Leary, 1987a). This conflict proved intolerable to the Thatcher government, which, under the guise of administrative efficiency, but actually in response to long-standing and intense internal party pressures, abolished the GLC along with the other metropolitan authorities in England (O'Leary, 1987b). In many ways the ideological and practical impact of the successful Conservative attack on a local governmental body that was viewed as profligate and too radical resembled the outcome of the New York City fiscal crisis – it subdued opposition to business-oriented growth strategies and made proposals for redistributional measures seem far-fetched.

From a planning perspective the shortcomings of the GLC structure were several, but two proved fatal. The first was that the GLC's limited geographic scope left unresolved the relationship between the new authority and the rest of the metropolitan region. This might have been overcome, had not the GLC initially maintained the outdated planning stance of the 1944 Abercrombie plan, which established the Green Belt with the aim of containing urban London. Even by 1960 many saw the Abercrombie plan as irrelevant to the postwar dynamics of growth in a booming region. Thus, by the time the GLC was established, the Home Counties – the circle of counties around Greater London – were calling for "a new Abercrombie" and had taken steps to recreate the wider regional planning framework of the prewar Standing Conference on London Regional Planning (Buck et al., 1986). At the same time the central government had established the South-East Regional Planning Council, an appointed body charged with the responsibility of producing the regional component of the national plan. From its inception, then, the GLC struggled to find a role in a region which, while it clearly required a single overview, was handicapped by two bodies claiming to provide it: the appointed Planning Council seeking to restructure the region for growth, and the (indirectly) elected Standing Conference seeking to contain and channel the growth process within the existing infrastructure.

The second unexpected shortcoming was the failure of the GLC to implement the roads plan that lay at the heart of its strategic posture and for which, in the eyes of central government officials, it had been established. It began life with bipartisan consensus on the need to create the urban motorway system proposed in the Abercrombie plan, which was intended to provide rapid movement around the region and link it effectively to the national motorway network. But once internal political changes within the Labour opposition had forced Labour to disown the motorways, the Conservatives could promote them only at their electoral peril. By 1973 the Conservatives were distancing themselves from the roads plan, which had been subjected to a humiliating and unfavorable public inquiry; by the 1977 GLC election it was clearly on the back burner. The episode seemed to prove that a locally accountable body could not implement restructuring on this scale.

Central government's role

After the Conservative victory of 1979 authority over planning for the London region shifted decisively to the central government. The Secretary of State for the Environment had previously held veto power over London planning.[8] Now, however, he virtually usurped the function of plan-making itself rather than simply acting as a final arbiter. Previously preparation of the overall Greater London Development Plan was made at the metropolitan level; now the Secretary of State would provide it. The boroughs would prepare their Unitary Development Plans (UDPs) in the context of his guidance and submit them for his approval. The Secretary of State could call in any of the UDPs, modify or reject them. He could intervene where a borough was preparing an "inappropriate" plan, commission his own plan in its place, and charge the expenses of this exercise to the borough concerned. At the same time central government could claim that – unlike under the GLC – strategic guidance was now framed at a level where the interrelatedness of Greater London and the wider metropolitan area, indeed of the region itself, could be taken into account (Hebbert and Travers, 1988).

The planning philosophy of the Thatcher government was expressed as follows:

> London's future depends on the initiative and energy of the private sector and individual citizens and effective co-operation between the public and private sectors, not on the imposition of a master plan. The role of the land-use planning process is to facilitate development while protecting the local environment. (UK Department of the Environment, 1989 p. 5).

It implemented this stance through the system of appeals against the refusal of planning consent. If local authorities refused planning applications on grounds not shared by the ministers at the DoE, they could then be overruled on appeal. The operation of the appeals procedure has been a powerful influence shaping implicit planning policies in London, as local authorities, when making development decisions, tend to anticipate the minister's response to an appeal. But the process has other constraining aspects as well. The minister has the power to "call in" an application which seems to him to raise issues of larger policy, a device which can be used to preempt a local authority's refusal. In practice, large development applications are bargained with the local authorities, who commonly seek to secure local gains as a price of acceptance. The developer has a fall-back in this process, as he can terminate the negotiations and place a formal application, thus triggering ministerial intervention, if the concessions which the local authority seeks to exact are too onerous.

The key role in speaking for London on strategic planning issues now rests with the London Planning Advisory Committee (LPAC), which was established as a 33-member joint committee of the boroughs, with one nomination from each. The government was concerned to ensure that no locally based planning body emerged in a form that could claim to fill the gap left by the GLC, and most commentators were confident that LPAC would fall far short of this. Its most important decisions, those which deal with budgeting (and thus with building the professional base from which LPAC might play a long-term role), require a two-thirds majority. This, in London's narrowly balanced politics, is hard to come by. During the period between 1986–1990, the Committee – reflecting as it must the political control of the London boroughs – lacked even an overall majority of any party. Indeed, many have viewed the location of the LPAC office, with its small team of 25 staff at the easternmost fringe of London, as symbolizing the extent to which London-wide planning has been marginalized since 1986. (New York, of course, has no office of metropolitan planning at all.)

The contribution of locally elected bodies to the planning process was, then, intentionally limited and, in the absence of a single area-wide local authority, was indirect as well as advisory. The Department of the Environment did not, however, take on the planning role for the metropolitan region in the sense of establishing a powerful professional team or of acting as an overall coordinating agency, bringing the many metropolitan actors together. Rather, in line with the Thatcher program of permitting the market to do its work without interference, both bottom-up and top-down planning were minimized.

POLICY AND POLITICS IN NEW YORK

Development politics under the Koch regime

In 1977 Edward Koch, promising an activist administration that would foster growth, manage the bureaucracy, and care for the middle class, won the Democratic mayoral primary and met no serious opposition in the regular election. Koch's political strength was based singularly on his personality. His virulent attacks on political opponents, unceasing commentary on events within the city, and self-promotion brought him continuous media coverage. He achieved broad support from business and the white electorate, especially from the Jewish community. His strong stance against crime and "poverty pimps" was interpreted as antagonistic to minorities; nevertheless, he was not wholly without minority support, especially among Hispanics (Shefter, 1985). Originally a reform Democrat (i.e. opposed to the regular Democratic organization), he forged ties not only with the Democratic clubs and county organizations but with the Republicans as well, receiving Republican endorsements in later elections. His campaigns received large financial contributions from real estate developers (Sleeper, 1987).

The London region offers no comparable position to the mayor of

New York that would allow this kind of development of personal political power. When Ken Livingstone headed the GLC, his personal style did to some extent mobilize his following and galvanize his opposition (Mackintosh and Wainwright, 1987). But he never possessed the executive authority that would have allowed the translation of style into program. The apposite comparison to Koch would have to be the national cabinet ministers concerned with London (usually the Environment Secretary but sometimes even the Prime Minister); the power of the cabinet, however, so greatly exceeds that of the mayor as to make this correspondence faulty.

At the onset of the Koch regime the mayor arguably had little room for maneuver, and his active personal style may well have been a necessary element in the compromises necessary to attain solvency. Once city government no longer had resources for public programs, the common interests shared by bureaucrats and their clients, working-class homeowners and renters, Jews and blacks, dissolved. By defining himself as the leader of the middle class, Koch (1984, p. 221) created a supportive constituency for his cutbacks; at the same time, however, he reinforced the division of the city along racial and class lines.

During the initial years of his administration almost the only development activity within the city involved the renovation and conversion of existing residential and factory buildings into middle- and upper-income domiciles. These took advantage of already existing tax subsidy programs which substantially reduced costs to new occupants and stimulated the gentrification of parts of Manhattan and Brooklyn (Sternlieb et al., 1976; Zukin, 1982; Tobier, 1979). Housing and neighborhood revitalization programs, except for the *in rem* program, which operated buildings taken for tax delinquency, were terminated as the federal dollars on which they depended were withdrawn.

To Mayor Koch's great good fortune the New York economy began to revive just after he took office. By 1980 New York was speeding toward recovery. It easily weathered the sharp national recession of 1981–2 and began a dramatic economic expansion brought on by the stock market boom of the middle eighties, the sharp growth in mergers and acquisitions on Wall Street, and the influx of foreign investment (see chapter 3). The response of city government to economic growth was a revival of investment in infrastructure, enlargement of the municipal workforce, and further encouragement to real estate developers. As growth accelerated, Koch was able to take credit for balancing the city's budget while rescinding most of the service and capital expenditure cuts caused by the fiscal crisis. He thus could claim to have restored New York to financial health without demanding significant additional sacrifices from the populace.

Major projects

While retention of manufacturing jobs and improvement of neighborhood retail strips received some rhetorical and financial support, the
main thrust of the mayor's economic development program was the
stimulation of office construction, principally in Manhattan. The largest
of the various publicly sponsored projects was Battery Park City. A
counterpart to the Canary Wharf development in London's Docklands,
Battery Park City exemplifies the accomplishments of the Koch years
while raising questions about the potential of even the best top-down
development and about the designation of the financial sector as the
engine of economic improvement.[9]

Initially conceived as a new town to be constructed on a 92-acre
landfill in the Hudson River, the original 1969 plan for the project
provided that two-thirds of the housing units built would be subsidized
for low- and middle-income occupancy. During the 1970s, however, the
Battery Park City Authority (BPCA), an agency of the State's UDC with
the power to issue bonds, could not attract a developer. It therefore
redesigned the project, eliminating the provision for on-site subsidized
housing but pledging some of the proceeds from the development to
low-income housing in other parts of the city. The giant Canadian
developer Olympia & York, also the sponsor of London's Canary
Wharf, committed itself to the entire commercial portion of the venture,
and a number of other major developers agreed to construct luxury
apartments expected to add 14,000 units to Lower Manhattan. The
BPCA, which retained ownership of the project and paid no taxes,
participated in profits from the enterprise; in 1987 it promised $1 billion
for low-income housing throughout the city as well as $50 million for
general revenues (Schmalz, 1987).

Battery Park City succeeded in attracting such prestigious tenants as
Merrill Lynch, Dow Jones, and American Express; it provided the
congested Wall Street area with a widely praised waterfront park and
indoor botanical garden open to the general public. Its construction
caused no displacement, and the conditions of its ownership and financing resulted in much greater returns to the public till than the usual
development project. Nevertheless, except for transient visitors, it
remained the fiefdom of big business and wealthy, mainly childless
households. The firms that moved into the new buildings left vacancies
behind, adding to the surplus of office space that currently afflicts
downtown Manhattan.

Battery Park City is forthrightly a trickle-down project, although it
differs from many other similar endeavors in New York and other cities

in that there are benefits specifically earmarked for low-income recipients rather than simply assumed to disperse to them. To that extent it contributes to the welfare of lower-income New Yorkers. Nonetheless, it operates in a context where the most desirable urban locations are reserved for those best-off, and large amounts of public subsidy are used directly to stimulate private investment in order for some of the cash-flow produced by that investment to be reinvested in other uses. The upper-income families that have moved into its residential buildings presumably could have found housing elsewhere; the development does not directly add to the supply of low-cost housing within the city. The jobs it has generated present the familiar dichotomy of upper-income professional and managerial and low-income clerical and janitorial positions. The future of all of them is dependent on the health of the financial industry.

Many of the city's efforts were directed at retaining already existing businesses such as NBC and the Chase Manhattan Bank. These particular cases involved the granting of enormous tax abatements and other subsidies to avert threatened moves to New Jersey, within the region but outside the city's taxing authority. In return for a $100 million abatement, NBC agreed to remain in and renovate its present headquarters in midtown Manhattan (Finder, 1987). For almost twice as much in various inducements, the city enticed the Chase Manhattan Bank to move its back offices to downtown Brooklyn. The rationalization for the deal was that in addition to fending off the threatened move, it would anchor a major development node outside Manhattan.

Only at the end of 1987, a decade after his initial election to office, did Mayor Koch announce a low-income housing program (see chapter 7). To be financed from Battery Park City revenues and city borrowing, the plan represented a substantial increase in the commitment of the city government to redistributive programs. It resulted from a combination of intense lobbying by housing groups, pressure from community boards, widespread disgust over the evident nature of homelessness, fears that lack of housing would create labor market problems for New York industry, and the ultimate realization that the federal government was unlikely to resume funding for subsidized housing in the foreseeable future. The first years of the program demonstrated a major acceleration in city-sponsored housing activity. Nevertheless, the revival of fiscal problems at both state and city level in 1989 and their ensuing escalation, neighborhood resistance to the increased densities that some projects would create, and the difficulty of finding competent sponsors to implement development made attainment of the program's targets uncertain.

The housing initiative, however, did represent an extremely unusual commitment for a US municipality. Few US cities directly subsidize low-income housing, relying for this purpose entirely on grants-in-aid from federal and state levels of government. Some have used linkage programs, requiring contributions from developers of commercial and market-rate residential construction, to create funds for affordable housing. These efforts, however, are wholly dwarfed by the scale of the New York program. The New York endeavor also contrasts with London. There governmental support of housing never ebbed to the extent it did in New York between the mid-seventies and mid-eighties, but neither did it show any increase despite soaring housing prices and the growth of homelessness.

The Dinkins administration

In 1989 David Dinkins, an African-American, defeated Edward Koch in the Democratic primary election and then went on to a narrow victory over his Republican opponent. His regime encompasses a different governing coalition in terms of class and ethnic characteristics and thus might augur a shift in development policy. His appointments of deputy mayors and department commissioners were far more heterogeneous in terms of race and gender than Koch's, and some members of his administration were drawn from community groups that had opposed the economic growth juggernaut. In addition, the new Manhattan borough president, who took over the position Dinkins formerly occupied, had a history of skepticism toward the claims of developers. The revised city charter vests more planning power in the community boards and the city council than formerly had been the case. So far, however, Dinkins has continued to promote large-scale, Manhattan-based development as avidly as his predecessor and has shown no reluctance to use major subsidies for this purpose. It remains to be seen what will be the impact of institutional changes in the planning process. As of this writing, a calamitous decline in New York's economic situation, of which a major real estate slump forms a part, will limit the mayor's options when confronted with the demands of developers.

Political divisions within other policy arenas

Housing is one area where the administration is under widespread pressure to act in ways that would benefit lower-income people. Similarly the low quality and physical disrepair of the eductional system cause considerable discontent among corporate employers as well as the system's clients. The politics of race and trade unionism, however, cross-cuts the pressure for educational efficiency. As in other urban educational systems with large numbers of low-income, minority students, the solution to the educational deficiencies of New York's schools, even with the investment of considerably more resources, is elusive.

The long history of conflict over who should control New York's school system and who should have jobs within it limits the possibilities of reform. The battle over decentralization was settled through the creation of community school districts but with continued staffing of the central board of education; tensions between the central and local boards continue, exacerbated by recent discoveries of corruption within the community school boards. The prerogatives of the various unions, including supervisors and school custodians, as well as teachers, are well protected within the New York State Legislature, which has ultimate legal authority over the schools; concessions on work rules, use of national rather than special exams to determine qualifications for positions, and flexibility in the appointment of school principals are strongly resisted both in the legislature and through the courts.

The new school chancellor, of Puerto Rican extraction, has succeeded in overcoming some of these barriers to change (Traub, 1990). He has achieved some limitations on the autonomy of building custodians, obtained the right to transfer incompetent principals out of schools (although not to fire them), eliminated the board of examiners, whose special licencing exams limited recruitment of personnel, and removed authority over school construction from the Board of Education to an independent authority. Whether these institutional changes will improve educational quality, as hoped, is unknown. At best, they make the operations of the New York City school system more closely resemble those in other US cities.

Drugs and crime, in addition to housing and schools, constitute the policy areas of greatest concern to New York residents. Because they are such salient issues to the voting public, electoral candidates outdo each other in their promises of toughness. (Liberal candidates usually pledge to temper toughness with enlargement of treatment and rehabilitation programs but also emphasize the importance of expanding police, prisons, and courts.) The intractability of the problems, however, means that although anger by the general public at the quality of life in New York makes up the context of electoral competititon and of popular evaluations of the governing regime, nobody receives credit for effectively dealing with these issues. Instead public frustration mounts, and the general feeling that the city is ungovernable persists. The defeat of Edward Koch, who dropped from a favorable rating among 67 percent of all registered voters in 1985 to 31 percent in 1989, reflected that disenchantment (Levin, 1989).[10]

Community politics

Issue-oriented politics in New York has typically been mediated through community movements rather than the party system. In the past citizens have mobilized around bases of race and ethnicity, client status, and neighborhood; when, as in the movement for community control of schools, these bases combined, social movements took on a significant force (N. I. Fainstein and S. S. Fainstein, 1974). More recently gay and feminist organizations have also mounted protest activities. On the whole, however, movement politics has been replaced by routinized community politics (S. S. Fainstein and N. I. Fainstein, 1991). Even race, the most divisive question in contemporary New York, has, except within the City University, not produced an identifiable social movement or a specific set of objectives. Racial discontent has, however, spawned a number of demonstrations connected with widely publicized incidents of violence against blacks and ensuing trials. Within the City University, with its predominantly nonwhite student body,[11] students and faculty demanding increased minority hiring, improved retention of nonwhite students, cultural diversity in the curriculum, and no tuition increases have succeeded in forcing some personnel and curricular changes; and in 1989 student unrest blocked a proposal to raise tuition.

The most prominent, client-based group is the Coalition for the Homeless. It focuses primarily on bringing law suits to protect the rights of the homeless rather than on building a mass following. While its constituency consists of New York's most indigent population, its composition is mainly professional advocates. Thus, while it can point to important achievements in forcing the city to offer shelter to those without it, it remains an advocacy and service organization, not a mass movement.

Neighborhood groups are the most visible representatives of New Yorkers seeking to divert city resources from large-scale redevelopment to community improvement. These include block associations, merchants' groups, housing and economic development corporations, and police precinct councils. Their aims center on affordable housing, physical facilities, service provision, community economic development, and protection from crime and drugs. They pursue their agendas through the community boards, by lobbying legislative and administrative offices, and by raising funds from public and private sources. Neighborhood politics has a disjointed, issue-specific character and varies considerably from one part of the city to another. Its effectiveness depends on the entrepreneurial abilities and political connections of community leaders. Despite the commonality of issues affecting neighborhoods and the

existence of various coalitions of neighborhood groups, no widely visible, city-wide organization to press neighborhood interests exists.

Within both electoral and community politics the perception of social
disorder permeates the discourse of New York, whether the topic be
homelessness, schools, housing, or crime. Whereas the political right
blames the situation on a lax criminal justice system and the cultural
characteristics of the poor, the left attributes it to worsening inequality.
The left, however, lacks a vehicle for pressing its viewpoint other than
the variety of groups mentioned above. Moreover, it has no political
strategy to remedy the situation, although liberal candidates offer a
variety of specific programs aimed at social melioration. The absence
of a national Democratic Party agenda for addressing the issues of
economic growth and equity means that local leaders are on their own.
Within the context of New York City alone, given its fiscal limitations,
racial divisions, and ideological backlash against the poor, liberals cannot offer very much beyond less abrasive personalities and a more
humane version of the Koch program.

New York contrasts with London in that conflict centers on the
actions of particular individuals and is highly issue-specific rather than
party-oriented and programmatic. Nevertheless, the cleavages that divide
the cities and the influence of economic restructuring on them are
similar. In London as well as New York government has placed high
priority on global city functions, and the politics of planning has been
generated by the tensions among development, equity, and environmental preservation.

POLITICS AND PLANNING IN LONDON

London's status as a global city has long been recognized and celebrated.
Since 1974, in particular, the need to maintain its world city status has
provided much of the impetus for modernization; this effort, however,
has produced major development conflicts. The first of these conflicts,
running through the 1970s and revived only recently, was the attempt
to improve movement through and around the capital by constructing
an urban motorway network. The second was the great eastward expansion of the City, maintaining London's financial and commercial centrality through the redevelopment of the derelict docklands area. The
third has been the pressure to achieve greater economic integration with
Europe by building a direct physical link through the construction of
the channel tunnel and its rail connection to London.

Development policy under Thatcher

Mrs Thatcher's first administration was skeptical as to the abilities of local authorities to facilitate the development process and strongly in favor of shifting the emphasis from social to economic considerations. Consequently it introduced a series of changes aimed at opening up the process to market forces. Much of the existing Urban Programme[12] was recast, and ministers withdrew from detailed involvement in the process of grant aid for development projects. A US-style urban development grant was introduced to lever private investment for major developments through local authority negotiations, only to be effectively displaced by the city grant scheme, which brought private investors into a more direct relationship with central government funding, bypassing the local authorities. More significant perhaps were the creation of Urban Development Corporations (UDCs) modeled on the appointed corporations which had built the New Towns since 1946. The UDC model, like its New York counterparts, was intended to speed up land assembly and development and, more subtly, cut it free of the constraints of local interests. By 1990 the Thatcher administration had largely succeeded in enforcing its priorities upon local authorities through financial and legal controls.

Large projects: The docklands and King's Cross

The London Docklands Development Corporation (LDDC), a UDC similar in powers to New York's Battery Park City Authority, was established in 1981. Fiercely resisted by the affected boroughs, the LDDC inherited a huge territory of derelict dockland, together with the planning powers of the local authorities. The preexisting Docklands Joint Committee, consisting of representatives from the affected boroughs and the GLC, had moved laboriously through its own planning and consultative processes, the effect of local political preferences being clearly apparent in the priority given to social housing and local employment opportunities. Relations with the LDDC, which immediately scrapped the existing plan, varied from outright noncooperation on the part of some boroughs, to covert gratitude on the part of others. But the LDDC made few concessions to local feeling in the first years of its life, achieving instead an astonishingly rapid transformation of the western portion of its territory, and the Isle of Dogs isthmus, site of Olympia & York's Canary Wharf, in particular.[13]

The docklands thus became the showpiece of the Conservatives' inner city regeneration policies, aided by a substantial preexisting land bank, a simplified planning system, tax breaks for business location, burgeoning demand for eastward expansion from the City of London, unrivaled opportunities for high-income housing via conversion of redundant warehouses, and substantial injections of public funding for infrastructure development. Initial lines of polarization between the LDDC and the local authorities, caused by LDDC's exclusive focus on physical development, became more blurred. For a time the Corporation shifted its emphases, as it began formulating a compensatory social program, endeavored to work more closely with community groups, and pursued equality of opportunity issues within the limits of its developmental rationale. Moreover, it soon became clear that the high-profile market-led development of the Isle of Dogs was unlikely to be replicated further east, causing a search for an approach less dependent on private initiatives.

By late 1989, however, Britain's faltering economic growth and high interest rates brought the housing market in the docklands close to collapse. The shift from infrastructure development to social purposes was read as a dilution of the government's intention to transform the docklands. The autumn 1989 economic statement revealed a reinjection of development funding for the LDDC; the Minister for Local Government sent a reassuring letter to developers reaffirming the government's commitment to docklands regeneration; and early in 1990 the Corporation reportedly came under central government pressure to swing funding away from its social schemes towards further infrastructure improvement.

Outside the docklands, local authorities retained the primary responsibility for decision-making regarding development. The major development projected for King's Cross, at the time of writing in abeyance due to the financial difficulties of the development consortium, involved lengthy negotiations between the borough authority and the development group. Here, however, as elsewhere, the borough's negotiating stance was constrained by the central government's directives concerning encouragement of private initiatives. Moreover, local planning intersected with the largest restructuring decision concerning London to be taken by the central government in the 1990s – the channel tunnel rail link. The crucial policy choice here was whether that link would be to King's Cross, and thus into the hub of the national rail network, or to Stratford in the East London borough of Newham. The progress of the King's Cross development scheme rested crucially upon that decision, while the docklands' development would have benefited from the Stratford location.

British Rail sought to preempt the consultations by announcing that it had chosen King's Cross, a congested site requiring extensive demolition of homes and businesses. Ultimately the government overruled its selection, but the time-consuming altercation over this key decision also illuminates the third and largest question: that of strategic planning for the metropolitan region and the current struggle to control that process.

Strategic guidance: the struggle for influence

At first sight, the central government role in preparing strategic guidance (i.e. a planning framework) for London constitutes the long-predicted final usurpation by central government of the role which the GLC was established to play. The DoE, however, cannot exercise this role without a substantial analytical and informational input from London itself. And this dependence of central upon local government makes the issue one not of absolute but of relative power.

The LPAC's principal role, for which it was established under the 1985 Act, was to advise on the content of the strategic guidance which the Secretary of State for the Environment must provide as a framework for the locally prepared unitary development plans (UDPs). In July 1986 Environment Secretary Nicholas Ridley invited the LPAC to offer advice on the distribution of housing, commercial and industrial development, transport and land-use, Green Belt and open land, minerals and urban design. The LPAC contested this list and early in 1987 further topics were added. To some commentators this promised a fragmented, issue-based approach rather than one which took a comprehensive view of strategic problems (Hebbert and Travers, 1988); others believed that the DoE had a clear interest in disaggregating the issues to prevent the emergence of a coherent overall view of London's future. Meanwhile, the Labour-controlled boroughs looked to the LPAC to renew the fight for the policies which the Livingstone GLC had written into the revisions of the Greater London Development Plan, policies which had already been decisively rejected by the government.

In the event, the LPAC presented advice that was more than the aggregate of 33 local views. Agreed on by the boroughs with surprising unanimity, the LPAC document (LPAC, 1988) was far more than the "lowest common denominator of planning platitudes" expected by some commentators. In particular, it set out the case for remedying developmental imbalance in the metropolitan region and overheating in the western Thames Valley by means of major planned development east of the docklands in the East Thames corridor. It identified the principal opportunities for the development of further strategic centers, several of them within east London, and for the rejuvenation of run-down town centers; it identified the need for infrastructure improvement, for further investment in public transport, and for the coordination of business development throughout the capital.

The government, however, showed itself unresponsive to this advice. First, the Department of Transport published the four consultants' studies of road options for London which had been commissioned at the time of GLC abolition; the proposals not only appeared to resurrect aspects of the old roads plan, but they also conflicted directly with the LPAC advice to the DoE. Next, months later, the Department of Transport published its central London Rail Study, the rationale of which was again at odds with LPAC. Finally, the draft guidance which emanated from the DoE in 1989 as a response to the LPAC submission largely ignored the LPAC's recommendations. The key theme was that the London boroughs should "adopt a positive, flexible and realistic approach to business development throughout London" (UK Department of the Environment, 1989a, p. 4). Of the LPAC's "visions," only the concept of London the world city was grasped, and that as a text for the legitimation of major commercial development. The identification of East Thames growth points was discarded, as was the inclusion of a social policy framework for London local government.

Despite widespread criticism of the draft, the revised guidance document (UK Department of the Environment, 1989b) made few concessions to the critics. Still, the content of London policy can no more be regarded as settled than can the institutional framework for its expression. The LPAC's achievement was to produce a plan that not only united the disparate parts of London but also received general acclaim as an appropriate strategy for the capital. The great irony is that its rejection by the government was followed by the award of the Royal Town Planning Institute's Silver Jubilee Cup for "an exceptional level of planning achievement." The endorsement of the planning profession ensured that the LPAC plan will continue to wait in the wings until, in a more favorable policy environment, it is taken forward as the basis for Greater London planning in a revised strategic guidance.

Political divisions with other policy arenas

The restructuring of planning and local government has constituted only one of several recent major transformations in London's institutional framework. In particular, Conservative changes in modes of local taxation and finance, as well as the abolition of the Inner London Education Authority, the last of the institutions of metropolitan government, have provoked considerable political controversy. Indeed the reaction to the imposition of the poll tax was a major component of Margaret Thatcher's downfall.

The politics of central–local government relations during the Thatcher years was dominated by attempts to constrain local expenditure. Initially no more than a concern (inherited from the Callaghan administration) to restrict aggregate public expenditure and borrowing through imposing cuts and cash limits on local councils, the pursuit of financial constraint turned into a trail of strength between government ministers and the renascent socialist strand in the Labour Party, entrenched as it was in the town halls. The partisan and ideological divisions colored the subsequent attempts to make a succession of financial regimes work. First came a complex mechanism of expenditure targets and penalties; later, selective direct control over local rate (property tax) levels, the so-called rate-capping which led to the most bitter confrontations and accelerated the process of judicializing central–local government disputes.

Rate-capping fell most heavily upon Labour's Inner London boroughs, but was for some time adroitly evaded by the disposal or mortgaging of assets to raise additional local revenue. Fervent opposition to "cuts" provided local Labour groups with effective propaganda material, increasing the Conservatives' electoral nervousness, radicalizing Labour, and raising the political stakes. Moreover, the continuous introduction of new controls to close loopholes unwittingly created in the previous set threatened to ensnare ministers in a guerrilla war over the determination of local expenditure in which anything less than a show of full attention to local facts and circumstances in making an order could be challengeable at law.

By 1986 Prime Minister Thatcher had decided it was necessary to change the dynamics of the decision process and expose "spendthrift" councils to local, rather than central, pressure. Hence the radical departure of the abolition of local rates and the introduction of a local flat rate per capita "community charge," which, despite the government's most strenuous efforts at euphemism, remains immortalized as the "poll tax." The original notion was based on a massive simplification of the grant-aid structure aimed at achieving a standard level of service in each area through comparable levels of community charge; beyond this, further expenditure would be constrained by the newly sharpened pressures of local electoral accountability. Yet the scheme, despite the increased equity provided by the removal of local business rates and their translation into a national uniform rate to be centrally distributed, produced very large variations in projected local charge levels, with extreme gainers and losers, requiring a panoply of safety-nets and transitional arrangements.[14]

The conflict continued, with the inescapable inequities of a flat-rate charge proving highly unpopular, while the administrative difficulties of collection threatened substantial revenue shortfalls and thus still higher rates of taxation. Anti-poll tax campaigns revitalized the left at street level, to the considerable discomfiture of the Labour leadership. The factors which had led to the dreaded "London effect" of left extremism alienating working-class voters now reemerged not just in London (where anti-poll tax riots were of a ferocity unprecedented in this century) but across the country. Finally, and perhaps fatally for the Conservative aim, the government's determination to let the fiscally conservative dynamic of the poll tax work to its long-term benefit faltered. If the government had simply allowed local authorities to set the community charge at whatever level they deemed appropriate, high-charge councils would have had to face voter backlash. Instead, however, the government attempted to "cap" poll tax levels, thereby sliding into a new round of confrontation and intervention evocative of the rate-capping episode and marked by humiliation in the courts. Ultimately the conflict over local taxation forced Margaret Thatcher's resignation, and the Major government planned to rescind the tax.

Popular dissatisfaction with investment in London's public services had helped consolidate Labour's constituency there. But in one respect at least – the changes in the structure of education in Inner London – the Thatcher government's changes appeared to move with the tide of discontent. Inner London education has long been an administrative anomaly. Although the Macmillan government eliminated the LCC in favor of the GLC in 1963, the civil servants in the Ministry of Education, with the support of their minister, resisted the abolition of the LCC's education service. As a result of the ensuing compromise, the LCC education structures were continued unaltered under the control of an ad hoc Inner London Education Authority (ILEA) with a secure Labour majority. The arrangement was intended to be temporary, pending the devolution of education powers to the London boroughs. But a Labour government struck out the crucial "review" clause in 1967 to remove any uncertainty about ILEA's future.

Throughout the 1970s pressure from the Conservative grassroots for ILEA abolition continued. As Education Secretary in the Heath administration, Margaret Thatcher had the task of deflecting these pressures. But by the time she reached Downing Street, Conservative distaste for Labour education policies had grown, while the accumulation of evidence about underperformance in ILEA schools made abolition of this hybrid body politically advantageous. Even so, the issue was forced by backbench pressure, not by government initiative, ministers apparently realizing only late in the day that there was popular mileage in dissolving ILEA and constituting the inner boroughs as education authorities. In many respects the contemporary politics of education in London resembles New York's in the late 1960s, when proponents of educational reorganization contended that administrative decentralization of the school system would force schools to respond to the particular educational problems of the inner city. In New York compromise resulted in decentralization of some powers to community school districts roughly comparable to the boroughs but a failure to dismantle the central authority, with predictable central–local tensions.

At the time of writing, the tenor of London press comment is beginning to emphasize the downside of abolition of ILEA, spotlighting the inadequacy of the arrangements made by some of the boroughs, the lack of experience of some of their officials, and the newly recognized high cost of duplication of local services. Meanwhile, the balance between education authorities, on the one hand, and schools and parents, on the other, is itself being transformed by the Education Reform Act, the effects of these two forms of decentralization being to pose a major political and intellectual challenge to Labour's local policy-makers. But although their ability to shape education outcomes is now severely constrained, the politics of education may well continue to exert a more powerful impact upon elections in London than any of those potent, yet less visible, issues which arise from the processes of economic restructuring.

STRUCTURE, POWER, AND PLURALISM

Governmental commitment to attracting private investment in the built environment was the context for development politics in both New York and London during the eighties. In both places forces attempting to constrain growth in the name of either equity or the environment have primarily been voiced at lower levels of government: community boards in New York and local authorities in London. The capacity of these levels to regulate development has been limited by the creation of development corporations that have powers to override local decisions, are largely insulated from public oversight, and measure their accomplishments by the amount of money invested. These corporations are structured similarly to private concerns, with boards that represent business interests. They are exempt from partisan conflict and democratic participation; within them the ideology of growth is unquestioned.

Commonalities and differences

Until the end of the decade development politics in both metropolises operated within a situation of economic restructuring and rapid growth in financial and advanced services industries. Real estate development itself was one of the engines driving the boom. By 1990 both metropolises found that the financial industry was cutting back; the real estate market was extremely weak; and there were high vacancy rates in both luxury residential and commercial space. During most of the eighties there were enormous private-sector pressures on government to accommodate expansion; in the present period of doubt government feels compelled to stimulate the economy. In London, central government has provided large infusions of funds to the financially troubled consortium that is constructing the channel tunnel and has agreed to enormous investments in transportation infrastructure to service the docklands. In New York the city government continues to press for a massive, controversial, tax-subsidized project to redevelop Times Square, and a consortium of city and state development corporations has proposed an equally large scheme for development of Hunters Point, part of the borough of Queens just across the East River from Manhattan.

The two metropolises are similar, then, in having had, for more than a decade, governments supportive of unimpeded development and willing to use taxpayers' money to foster it. Nevertheless, their differing institutional and party structures, as well as variant planning traditions, mean that politics, policies, and outcomes are not identical. Despite Margaret Thatcher's emphasis on the enterprise economy, Britain retains a commitment to urban containment that never prevailed in the New York region (Savitch, 1988). And the very existence of strategic planning guidance, advisory planning bodies for the region, and borough plans reveals a level of governmental coordination virtually absent in New York.

New York City's government is embedded in a number of structures that restrain its capacity to produce either an efficient or an equitable city. Caught in the web of federal policy, buffeted by regional competition, faced with the consequences of social inequality generated by the world and national economic system, the governing regime can at best hope for improvement rather than transformation. Its objectives for the last ten years, however, have been shaped not just by outside forces compelling certain actions, but also by the internal politics of the city. These especially have privileged property developers, whose exceptional access to the regime has profoundly affected the city's recent trajectory. The most prominent dynamic element in city policy has been the drive to construct ever larger buildings. Pluralism is evidenced in the city's politics by the occasional capability of community groups to block or modify development projects, usually through the courts.[15] The veto power of these groups, however, does not imply that they participate in policy-making. Until the announcement of the housing program, the city government of the eighties largely avoided the program initiatives called for by neighborhood advocates.

Within the New York suburban ring, as in the outer portions of London, proponents of growth confronted defenders of the environment. Almost every suburb contained forces strongly opposed to increased densities and the building over of open space. Except in areas of special state and national concern like the coastal zone, however, conflicts over preservation occurred within individual municipalities and did not form the basis for unity as occurred within the London OMA. Moreover, New York's suburban municipalities had far fewer legal tools with which to overrule development proposals than their London counterparts. As long as their plans fit within the municipal zoning ordinance, which must permit some form of remunerative development on all privately owned land, developers may proceed "as of right"; in London local authorities may yield to pressure from central government to make concessions but there is no assumed right to develop.

Within London conflict over the character and content of development is much more likely to be played out through the party system than in New York. Divisions within the Labour Party as well as among the parties have reflected different views on the extent to which development should be promoted, the type of development, especially as between housing and industrial/commercial construction, and the appropriateness of particular sites. The Labour Party remains the force calling for investment in manufacturing, employment schemes, and affordable housing. Labour, however, has not presented a coherent program for sustained economic development. Its record rests primarily on oppositionism rather than a program that promises enlarged prosperity to the employed working and lower middle classes, dependent as they must be on an infusion of investment capital. Consequently, while many voters may not like the social and environmental impacts of state-sanctioned, developer-driven growth, they do not see an alternative to which they can readily profess allegiance. The absence of such a formulation, rather than simply the organizational and financial power of the right, constitutes a formidable barrier to the electoral success of groups opposed to the present regime.

As in New York, within Inner London elements opposing development have largely conceded their original position and instead opted for concessions from developers as the price for support. In the outer boroughs and the OMA, however, environmental preservationists exceed their New York area counterparts in influence. Despite deteriorating infrastructure and obvious homelessness, London remains a more civilized and governable city than New York.

Economic restructuring, social forces, and policy

In both New York and London economic restructuring and global city status shape politics and policy. Although the mode of interest representation differs between the two places, changes in political allegiances in both can be traced to the fragmentation of the old working class. In New York the working class never was organized through a single powerful institution like the Labour Party. Nevertheless, unions were significant promoters of distributive programs and provided the foundation for Democratic Party power. The weakening of union power attributable to the decline in manufacturing employment resulting from economic transformation and the failure of unions to organize the white-collar proletariat is an important factor in the close relationship between city government and business interests. Moreover, while the left-liberal coalition still exists and presses for increased social welfare spending, its elements have become more disparate, and priorities based on gender, ethnicity, territory, and race have increasingly become more prominent than class as the underpinning for action.

In London, likewise, a relatively unified business-oriented grouping confronts a disorganized opposition. The break-up of the old Labour machine in Inner London reflects the demise of a solidaristic, white male-dominated, unified working class (Gordon and Harloe, 1991). In its place has arisen a similar constellation of interests as in New York. While those displaced from their economic niches or their housing comprise disadvantaged groups, they do not share an identity and consequently do not agree on a common program. Thus, in London as in New York the success of conservative forces arises less from consensus on their aims than from the inability of those in opposition to constitute a widely acceptable alternative.

The economic growth of the eighties seemed to validate governmental policies based on little planning, incentives to private investors, and encouragement of restructuring. The end of the speculative boom in real estate and the general economic downturn, especially in New York, may subject these policies to far closer public scrutiny than had previously been the case. At that point disaffection among elite groups may produce yet a new political realignment and a less market-oriented strategy. It is, however, still too soon to tell.

NOTES

1 A prime example of this capacity is New York City's system of rent regulation. Anathema to the national Republican administration, it nevertheless endures despite, under the Reagan presidency, efforts to cut off federal aid to cities that controlled private-sector rents. These efforts never got very far, primarily because they would have constituted federal intervention in a local matter and thus strongly contravened federalist principles whereby cities are creatures of state rather than of national government.

   While federalism has enhanced the capacity of local regimes to enact policies different from those of the national government, it has typically protected private enclaves of power from national regulation and limited the development of the national welfare state (Robertson and Judd, 1989).

2 In 1985 47 percent of general revenue for New Jersey and 28 percent for New York state municipalities derived from local property taxes. Only about 5 percent came from the federal government, while about a third derived from state aid (Advisory Commission on Intergovernmental Relations, 1987).

3 Until 1990 New Jersey's income tax was considerably lower than New York State's. Connecticut had no income tax at all. New York City has its own income tax on top of the state's; residents of suburban municipalities typically pay no local income tax although they must pay state income taxes as well as an earnings tax if they work in New York City. There is wide variation in property tax rates, licenses and users' fees, and nuisance and sales taxes among municipalities and between the states.

4 This body was declared an unconstitutional violation of the principle of one person-one vote by the US Supreme Court in 1989. The equal voting power possessed by the borough presidents gave the same representation to Brooklyn with its 770,000 registered voters as to Staten Island with 170,000.

5 John Lindsay's victory as a liberal Republican in 1969 marked the last time a Republican won the mayoralty; although Rudolph Giuliani, the Republican nominee in 1989, lost the election by a close margin. The city council is overwhelmingly Democratic.

6 McCormick et al. (1980), after comparing 12 large cities, conclude that New York City pays neither the highest nor the lowest, although in examining seven job categories they find New York's employees predominantly within the upper half.

7 A number of commentators attributed Gerald Ford's loss of New York in the 1976 presidential election to the famous *Daily News* headline that declared. "Ford to City: Drop Dead." While Ford had, in fact, not used these words, he had initially refused to endorse a federal loan to assist the city in meeting its short-term debts.

8 The GLC's Greater London Development Plan was subject to the ultimate approval of the minister, an approval which had been withheld in the case

of the Livingstone Council's attempt to rewrite the strategy; and the power to "call in" a local plan had been used against the borough of Southwark in order to thwart proposals which countered central government's preferred vision for the docklands.

9 Sharon Zukin (1992) comments: "Despite great differences between the political systems of New York and London, and different relations between their financial communities and the national economy, both major projects of contemporary new construction – Battery Park City and Docklands – show the same trajectory of a landscape of power (p. 218).

10 Ratings of the mayor fell among all population groups, and most among whites and Hispanics. In 1985 he received a favorable rating of 78 percent among white registered voters and 66 percent among Hispanics; the figures dropped to 33 and 32 percent respectively in 1989.

11 The total enrollment of the City University exceeds 200,000, of which over 60 percent are minority.

12 The Urban Programme was originally created in 1968 and funded a number of social and community projects in local authorities with a 75 percent matching grant from central government. After 1977 its brief was extended to include industrial, environmental, and recreational as well as social projects (Lawless, 1989, pp. 40–1).

13 A considerable literature exists concerning docklands redevelopment, including, inter alia, Marris, 1987, ch. 3; Brindley et al., 1989, ch. 6; Church, 1988; S. Smith, 1989; S. S. Fainstein, 1991.

14 In the United States no one any longer expected the national government to make up New York City's revenue shortfall, despite the necessity by 1991 for drastic service cuts if the city was to live within its revenues. By contrast, assumptions of continued maintenance of services in the UK forced a central government response.

15 Savitch (1988) characterizes the New York political system as corporatist-pluralist, referring on the one hand to the influence of the growth machine and on the other to the veto power of non-elite groups. Corporatist, however, is not an accurate term to describe the pro-growth coalition, since it consists only of two parties, government and development interests, and does not involve compromises with representatives of the mass of the population.

9

Conclusion: The divided cities

Michael Harloe and Susan S. Fainstein

In the first chapter of this book we outlined the process of restructuring which has occurred in the global economy and referred to its differential impact on cities. Our concern has been with the consequences of restructuring in two of the three world cities – London and New York – which, both in their respective nations and internationally, stand at the apex of the urban hierarchy. We noted that there are apparent similarities in the socio-political outcomes of the parallel economic changes which have occurred in both places, despite their differing political and institutional traditions. At the same time we rejected any simple, deterministic link between economic change and its consequences for the populations of these cities, arguing that opportunities existed for policies which would modify the negative social and economic consequences accompanying the supposed "renaissance" of London and New York.

We also questioned the way in which recent commentators have tried to encapsulate the outcome of economic restructuring in terms of "duality," "polarization," or "marginality." Such formulations skate over the surface of complex processes of social and economic change. Moreover, as the controversy over the concept of the "underclass" or the more distant example of "marginality" and "modernization" in cities of the Third World illustrate, such approaches can be used to stigmatize those worst off, thereby legitimizing policies which do little to alleviate the problems caused by restructuring and may even intensify them. Still, the contention that both cities have experienced a sharpening of social inequality in the past two decades and that this is a direct consequence of the type of economic change which they have been experiencing can hardly be denied.

In this book we have described and analyzed some of these processes.

Our aim has been to provide answers to five key questions concerning the economic restructuring and urban revival evident in both "global cities" in the 1980s, namely:

1 In what sense, if any, was there an urban revival?
2 For whom was there an urban revival?
3 To what extent was the revival of the eighties a consequence of the fact that London and New York are global cities?
4 What role have public policies played in urban revival?
5 Is the revival of the two cities sustainable and can its distributional outcomes be modified, by state or other action?

In trying to answer these questions we have, of course, been constrained by various problems which were outlined in chapter 1. Our conclusions are tentative and limited. Key evidence is frequently lacking, especially on an easily comparable basis, and we need to know much more about the linkages between the economy and urban social and political structures. In this chapter we shall summarize our findings and discuss their implications. First, we return to the five questions outlined above; then we consider other recent analyses of urban change in the light of our findings; finally we discuss some salient policy issues and options.

To a considerable extent we shall concentrate on the similarities between the two cities and on their development over the past 20 or so years. Nevertheless, distinctive local circumstances, many of which derive from previous periods in their histories, shaped the present situations of London and New York. These include the following:

– The primacy of London in the UK economic and urban system. In contrast, New York has always been in competition with other major centers in relation to the domestic and, to some extent, international markets, while London and now its wider region dominates the British economy and its urban hierarchy. There are no UK equivalents to cities such as Chicago, Los Angeles, or Houston as locations for some of the advanced industries and as centers for the control and organization of global capital.
– The role that London plays as the center of national government. Like London, New York is the cultural capital of its nation, but the focus of the federal and state government lies elsewhere. Consequently New York lacks not only the direct, economically stabilizing effect of the presence of national governmental institutions, but also that of the related public and private organizations and the employment that they generate.

- The status of New York as the nation's premier destination for long-distance migration. The impact of late nineteenth-century and early twentieth-century migrations from Europe, together with that of blacks from the South, did much to shape the social and political structures of the city as they still exist today. As every chapter of this book shows, the renewed post-1965 migration, from the Caribbean, Asia, and elsewhere, has also had a profound effect. In contrast, although London too is the premier location for long-distance migrants to the UK, this has always been on a far smaller scale and has had less significance for the development of the city (although, as we also show, the impact has not been negligible).
- The considerable differences between the two cities in relation to political institutions and organization. Both New York and London lack regional government and planning. However, local government has both more autonomy and more authority in the US than in the UK. London has a long history of particularly weak urban government; as the capital city it has always been under the watchful eye of national government. Nevertheless, too much should not be read into these contrasts when considering the scope for urban policies, given the far greater history of intervention by both central and local government in housing, transport, urban planning, and social welfare within the UK. In other words, despite weaker local government, London has had a history of stronger state intervention.
- The recent histories of their respective national economies. Although the challenge from countries such as Japan and Germany is now severe, the US economy is still the largest and one of the most prosperous in the world. In contrast, Britain's economic position continues to decline – a long-term process which has, if anything, been accelerated by the events of the past 10 to 15 years. Even the London region, the nation's most prosperous area, has, as we have shown, been severely affected by this decline.

THE FIVE KEY QUESTIONS REVISITED

In what sense, if any, was there an urban revival? As chapter 2 described, by the 1970s both cities were widely regarded as being in decline. The simplest indicator of this was the loss of population due to selective out-migration, although this was a long-established trend in London. More significant were the collapse of large sections of manufacturing industry, disinvestment in the built environment, the growth of the multi-faceted "inner city problem," and the failure of urban policies which attempted to reverse such trends or alleviate their consequences. The timing and detailed nature of the changes differed between the two cities, largely due to the differences which were highlighted above. Unlike New York, London had no fiscal crisis, although the subsequent cuts in the public services by the Thatcher government, together with its abolition of the Greater London Council, provided a functional equivalent. Likewise, the social and ethnic composition of those most severely affected by decline varied, as did the nature of their political representation. But although such differences affected the intensity and timing of decline, a recognizably similar process was underway.

The indicators of revival in the 1980s in the two cities also had a good deal in common. First, there was the reversal of previously accelerating population loss, although this may have been no more than a temporary upturn in London's long history of decline (given the tight restrictions which still inhibit the entry of migrant workers to the UK). Likewise, New York's gains may well have been temporary, at best indicating stabilization of the core and some growth in the outlying areas. A more significant change is the shift from employment loss to gain, in New York from 1977 and in London from 1983. Chapter 3 described these changes, noting that job growth has been limited and has not fully compensated for previous losses, that growth in the rest of the two regions has surpassed that in the core, and that the new jobs, in services rather than manufacturing and associated activities, are very different from those which they have partially replaced. Also in the early 1990s this growth was checked; in the 18-month period up to June 1991, New York City lost 100,000 jobs (Malanga, 1991). There were signs, however, of stabilization and predictions of an increase. In the UK the severe recession of the early 1990s began in London and the South East, only later spreading to other areas. In 1991 output fell by 5 percent in Greater London, over double the UK average, and in the 18-month period to the end of this year employment fell by 250,000. Further job reductions were forecast for 1992–4. By early 1992 it was predicted that weak and slow growth might commence at the end of this year but it would be far less vigorous than in the late 1980s. A key element in the severity of the London recession was the collapse of the commercial property market in 1991, after the speculative overproduction of the 1980s. The huge surplus of office space in the capital was likely to persist for several years (Cambridge Econometrics, 1992, pp. 1–2). Such changes in the nature, level, and location of economic activity and jobs suggest that there has been no simple revival of the previous urban space economy, as occurs after a downturn in the business cycle for example, but rather a more radical restructuring and reordering of this economy (together, of course, with some cyclical changes).

Chapter 4 spelt out some of the consequences of these changes for the two labor markets. It showed that, again, there has been a break from the past with the transition from a period of relative labor market stability, which some analysts associate with the "fordist" regime of accumulation, to a much more "flexible" labor market. The new jobs which have been created in the two cities have many common features, for example they tend to be occupied by women rather than men, they provide a significant number of well-paid jobs for the highly qualified and many more low-level jobs (although in many cases more modest levels of qualification are also required for these) but few intermediate-level jobs for skilled manual and supervisory staff. This results in a polarized distribution of earnings. So there has been a change from the more "balanced" distribution of jobs and incomes that existed in the previous period.

There are, however, some important contrasts between the two cities. To a considerable extent these derive from New York's role as a center for migrant workers and the lack of any real parallel to this in London. In New York the "spaces" left in the city's labor markets by the out-migration of white workers have been filled by blacks and the new ethnic minorities. However, there has not been a balance between inmigration and the demand for replacement labor, leading to high levels of unemployment among the latter two groups. In London outmigration has not been accompanied by massive inmigration and the complex pattern of sectoral growth and decline has not led to such extensive and persistent unemployment as has occurred in certain sections of the population and extended geographical areas in New York. Despite this, some groups have suffered from a lack of employment opportunities, notably unqualified school-leavers. Another consequence of the migrant labor phenomenon in New York may have been its declining wage rates in relation to the national average. This has stimulated some growth in lower paid manufacturing and other jobs. London's wages rates have remained high, adding to the cost pressures inducing manufacturing firms to decentralize.

A feature of both labor markets is the growth of much less stable employment conditions. Both cities have historically had quite high levels of labor turnover but the new jobs are often on a short-term or casual basis, employment protection for the worker tends to be far less than in the "fordist" era, and in New York especially there is large-scale informal or unregulated employment. Especially at the bottom of the labor market the balance of advantage has shifted toward the employers, notably in declining sectors of manufacturing and in the only major source of jobs for the unskilled, private consumer services. Job losses in the public sector and the increased resort to "contracting out" the more routine public-service jobs have intensified the situation.

One of the most visible consequences of economic restructuring is the reinvestment which has occurred in the built environment of the two cities. Large-scale projects such as the docklands development in London and Battery Park City in New York and the high volume of investment elsewhere in new offices, retail facilities, entertainment and leisure complexes, and housing, together with the necessary (and largely publicly funded) infrastructure to support them, would have been inconceivable 15 or so years ago. As chapter 7 showed, this reinvestment was tied to the needs of the growth sectors in the two urban economies and the consumption demands generated by those employed in the better-paid jobs which have been created. In contrast there is continuing disinvestment in those parts of the built environment, notably nonluxury housing, which accommodate considerable sections of the rest of the population.

For whom was there an urban revival? The answer to this question has already been touched upon. Above all the changes have benefited the financial and producer services industries, associated higher-level consumer services and the "new service class" which works in these parts of the economy. In addition, throughout the 1980s real estate investors amassed large fortunes; however, the slump in real estate markets that ended the decade in both cities resulted in sudden financial crises and even bankruptcies in this sector. For a far larger section of the population, what Pahl many years ago referred to as the "middle mass" in the context of a study of the London region, the outcome is more ambiguous. A good deal of the prosperity generated by growth has been shared by it. Middle-income households, however, have had difficulty in gaining access to desirable housing; urban public services such as education and transport have deteriorated; and public safety, even in London but especially in New York, has become a critical concern. During the summer of 1990 fear of crime reached a fever pitch in New York, causing 60 percent of respondents to a *Time* magazine poll to indicate that they worried about crime "all the time or often" (Attinger, 1990, p. 57). Moreover, the more volatile and less secure employment conditions which affect those at the bottom of the labor market most severely are also experienced by highly paid workers, although the competition which exists for those with relevant skills for the new industries, which has helped them to gain such large salary rises in the past decade, also ensures that the costs of job loss are likely to be less serious for them (Ehrenreich, 1989).

By far the heaviest consequences of economic change have been experienced by those who are outside, on the margins of or at the bottom of the labor market. Of course growth has resulted in an expansion of low-skilled and low-paid jobs, but in industries with a missing "middle," thus limiting chances for upward occupational mobility. One consequence of low-income employment, evident in both cities, is the rise in the average number of members in working low-income households who are in full- or part-time work.

As chapter 5 showed, there has been a significant rise in the proportion of the population of both cities which is in poverty, around a quarter in each case. The impact of poverty, however, differs within the cities as a consequence of the more extensive availability in London of state-provided services, especially medical care, which is of crucial importance to the working poor. The provision of public housing and rent subsidies on a large scale has been particularly important in this city, and is quite low by comparison in New York. Recently, however, there has been something of a shift, as in the late 1980s New York City embarked on a major program of affordable housing provision. New York's suburban ring, like London's, continues to offer little housing opportunity to low-income people. Moreover, changes in UK policies, discussed below, contributed by the late 1980s to a marked convergence between the two cities, or rather to a rate of growth in income inequality in London which is bringing it nearer to New York's pattern of income distribution. There are other, "softer" indicators of the similar types of deprivation in the two cities, notably large-scale begging and homelessness, formerly confined to people with severe social and personal problems but now experienced by many more, such as the young and unqualified and families with children.

The economies and social structures of both cities are shaped and divided by class, race, and gender. The consequential pattern or system of social stratification is highly complex and this complexity seems to increase as one moves "down" the system. Fairly clearly the "new service class" and the remaining higher status employees in longer established public- and private-sector firms and organizations occupy the "top" end of the system. As is well known, such positions are predominantly filled by white males and, in a wider sense, by their household members. Racial and gender discrimination – though eroding at the edges – still present severe barriers to entry by other sectors of the population, even when they have the necessary skills and training.

At the other end of the system, as several chapters of this book have demonstrated, many positions are now filled by women and by the various ethnic minorities. However, the diversity of situations experienced by these subgroups of the population makes any simple and universally applicable description of their circumstances invalid (Mingione, 1991). This was illustrated by chapter 6, which showed how the out-migration of white workers has opened up a demand for replacement labor at many levels in the occupational and earnings structure. In both cities a combination of skills, predispositions, social networks, and group resources operates to differentially filter distinctive ethnic groups into a variety of employment "niches." Outside the labor market different patterns of advantage and disadvantage also exist. For example, Asian homeowners in London derive some benefit from an appreciating housing asset in comparison with those Afro-Caribbeans concentrated in inner city public housing estates (note though the very different circumstances of Afro-Caribbeans in New York, who have a high propensity to become homeowners in comparison with other ethnic minorities). Public policies also contribute to varying and shifting patterns of disadvantage, for example cuts in welfare benefits in both cities at differing times adversely affected, in New York, poor households with dependent children and, in London, young adults.

As we shall discuss later, these and other factors should make us pause before accepting any simple notion of the "dual" city or any equally simple association of certain broadly defined categories of the population with, in particular, the lower end of the system of social stratification. Despite this qualification, however, we can identify a close link between economic change and intensified poverty and deprivation, alongside considerable prosperity and rising standards of living for relatively limited sections of the population and a more ambiguous combination of costs and benefits for many more.

To what extent was the revival of the eighties a consequence of the fact that New York and London are global cities? To put this question more bluntly, does location at the top of the global hierarchy make a metropolis a winner? This question was addressed in chapter 3 and in several other places in the book such as chapter 7. In chapter 3 six broad changes in the capitalist economic system were noted. These were as follows:

1   the decline in manufacturing and the partial rise of flexible systems of production;
2   the disaggregation of the geography of production which this development, as well as changes in transport and communications, allows;
3   the rise of producer services highly concentrated in large cities such as London and New York;
4   the growth of international financial systems even more highly concentrated in the three "first division" global cities – London, New York, and Tokyo;
5   the growth of public services in such cities to serve the expanding

needs of business and, more problematically, provide services for the low-income population (some proportion of which is attracted to them by the employment opportunities which the growth industries appear to provide);

6 the growth of more specialized consumer services to meet the needs of the high-status, high-income workers in the expanding sectors of the economy, plus the growing demand from international tourism.

Each of these changes has had an impact on New York and London but the extent to which they have *only* or *mainly* had an impact in these places varies considerably. Thus the decline in manufacturing (or, more accurately, the decline in the older manufacturing industries) has been felt across the two national economies and territories, likewise the shift to more "flexible" production systems. It is true that both cities were especially affected by manufacturing decline. However, many other urban areas in both countries were completely devastated by deindustrialization. Again, the effects of the decentralizing geography of production have been especially acute in London and New York but not uncommon elsewhere. To some extent such decentralization can be seen as a consequence of their far from unique status as very large, high-cost urban areas.

The third factor, the high level of producer services associated with the growth in the planning, controlling, and coordinating needs of geographically dispersed production exceeds that of cities further down the urban hierarchy in each country. However, as we have shown, although the absolute levels of such services and their share of the urban economy in the two global cities is higher than elsewhere, their rate of growth (from smaller bases) is greater outside the urban cores and in some parts of other regions altogether. Moreover, there are some important differences between the two cities: London's economic primacy and other factors have resulted in it retaining a far higher proportion of major national (although probably not international) corporate headquarters than New York and, more generally, having a higher proportion of the nation's producer services than that city.

The fourth development, the growth of financial services, is the one which differentiates the two cities most strongly from other locations as the preeminent "global cities" (with Tokyo). Together with the producer services, financial services are characterized by the importance of intensive linkages for the exchange of nonroutine information. Consequently there are great economies of agglomeration in these industries, although the decentralization of routinized "back office" functions, aided by developments in transport, computing, and communications, is evident in both cities.

The fifth factor, the significant expansion of the role of the state in economic management and the provision of social and collective services, is, like some others noted above, not confined to New York and London or even to other very large cities. Nor is the history of especially high levels of public expenditure in these particular cities a purely recent development, as chapter 2 showed. Far more noticeable is the recent switch in the balance of growth-stimulating and welfare-providing state activity away from the latter and toward the former. As other studies have shown (e.g. Squires, 1989; Harloe et al., 1990), this shift is not confined to the two cities but is felt throughout the respective national urban systems. Nevertheless, the scale of the public-sector involvement is greater in the two cities than elsewhere.

The final trend, the expansion of higher-order consumer services, is closely linked to the expansion of producer and financial services. Such services have always been concentrated in the two cities (again London's primacy may have resulted in greater concentration here than in New York) and in recent years they have grown rapidly – stimulated by the high concentration of well-paid employees in the expanding producer and financial services and booming international tourism.

There is, therefore, no simple division between these two global cities and other cities. All of the six aspects of global economic restructuring discussed exist elsewhere, although some, most notably the concentration of financial services, are far less significant in other places. What does, however, make the two cities unique (together perhaps with Tokyo, although see Fujita, 1991, for some important ways in which Tokyo differs from other "world cities") is the scale of the six factors and their combination in a single urban and regional space economy. It is the extent to which both cities have been affected by all six sets of changes – and hence by the interactions between them as well – that really marks them off from other large cities and links their evolving urban and social structures most closely to changes in global economic organization and its consequences.

One of the most important of these interactions flows from the competition for and the high price of urban land. Although such competition has always existed in these large cities, the growth of producer and financial services and of the high-income segments of the population which they employ, together with the more specialized consumer services which they require, has intensified the process. As various chapters have shown, high land prices have forced other economic activities, less able to meet the high costs of urban location, to decentralize to the periphery of the two regions and beyond at a faster rate than from other cities. They have also caused large sections of the population to be priced out of the housing market or to accept higher housing costs, occupy less housing, or endure longer commutes to work than in cities where the transition to the new economic regime has been less rapid and on a smaller scale. The loss of skilled manual and supervisory jobs – evident throughout both national economies – has been amplified by the peculiar conditions which apply in the two cities, leading to the development of the polarized distributions of incomes and life chances to which we have already referred. Evidently, then, placement at the top of the world urban hierarchy does not necessarily result in a generally better quality of life for the populations of these cities.

However, as the second chapter of the book showed, one cannot extract some generally applicable model of the "global city" from the historical context and the social structure and institutions of particular places. London and New York have long histories as "world cities," controlling much economic activity in the rest of their respective nations and internationally. Both have experienced periods of rapid economic change together with their disruptive effects in the past.

If the complexity of the changes in the two cities' space economies cannot be conveyed by simplistic reference to some ideal typical "global city" model, neither can the underlying changes in productive organiz- ation be unequivocally viewed as the consequence of a shift from a "fordist" to a "postfordist" mode of regulation, or of the growth of "flexible specialization." Without making a lengthy diversion into the rapidly accumulating literature on these topics and on their implications for urban and regional space economies (see, for example, the debate between Scott, 1988a, 1991a, 1991, and Lovering, 1990, 1991), we can address some of the difficulties in attempting to typify London and New York as "postfordist" cities.

First, theorists of postfordism and flexible accumulation have focused almost exclusively on changes in the organization of *manufacturing* industry. Yet a great deal of what makes London and New York distinctive is, of course, their *service* industry, and especially that part of it which is directly or indirectly linked to these two locations' global financial role. Even if Scott (1988a, 1988b), for example, is correct in suggesting that "new industrial spaces" are emerging because of the reagglomeration of manufacturing industry due to postfordist organiz- ation of production, the agglomeration of financial and allied services in the two cities is no new pattern and its connection with radical changes in the organization of manufacturing industry is problematic.

Second, whether shifts in the mode of industrial organization caused the decline of the manufacturing sector in London and New York is open to question. Meegan (1988) has, for example, shown that some industries which are organized on classic fordist principles are growing, while others are declining – but less rapidly than some nonfordist sectors. Moreover, "flexible specialization" (which may refer to one or more specific aspects of production and labor market organization) is not, as yet, nearly so widespread a feature of manufacturing industry as is sometimes suggested, nor is the claim that – like fordism before it – it has some sort of hegemonic status entirely convincing. In any event, as Sayer (1989) has recently argued, there seems no necessary connection between the adoption of flexible specialization and economic success in the contemporary world – as the example of Japanese industry's "flexible rigidities" makes clear.

A third point to consider is whether many of the changes which are occurring, for example in labor markets and in the location of industry, may best be seen as the consequences of a shift to a new mode of regulation, or as the adaptations of an old mode of regulation to new circumstances (Meegan, 1988; Allen, 1988; R. Brown, 1990). More generally, Richard Brown and other commentators emphasize the diversity of responses to economic change among firms and sectors, both within and between individual national economies.

Finally, there is the issue of the relationship between the supposed shift to "flexible specialization" and the social outcomes of a more polarized labor force and income distribution that we have observed in the two cities. Much here may depend on what flexibility entails. For example, increased flexibility in workforce size may well result in a more polarized job structure, but this trend could as easily be attributed to a neofordist strategy of adaptation as to a postfordist "system shift." However, the perhaps more distinctively novel adoption of functional flexibility among the workforce does not seem in any very obvious way to require a more polarized workforce. Indeed, Brown (1990, p. 324) has recently argued that deficiencies in British skills training programs will result in the country being "unable to secure the full advantages of functional flexibility and forced to continue to rely on systems of production which perpetuate low skilled and insecure employment for a large proportion of the labour force." He believes that one consequence of this *lack* of flexibility will be increasing labor force polarization.

For these reasons we are not convinced that current theories of postfordism or flexible specialization provide satisfactory explanations of the complex changes which have occurred, and continue, in the space economies of the two cities. Although, with further development, they *may* provide the necessary theoretical tools for such an analysis (as, for example, Scott, 1991a, argues), at present they seem too imprecise and their proponents are frequently inclined to draw general conclusions from a relatively limited number of particular cases of changing industrial organization. As Sayer (1989, p. 666) has rather cuttingly remarked: "[t]he trouble with concepts like fordism, postfordism and flexible specialization is that they are overly flexible and insufficiently specialized."

What role have public policies played in urban revival? In this respect the findings of our research seem clear. In both cities there has been a long history of state involvement – via urban and welfare policies – in the support of economic activity and growth and in the alleviation of some of the negative consequences of this activity and growth for lower-income sections of the population. The scale and balance of these state activities has differed, with far less well-developed state welfare and housing provision in New York than in London. However, following the fiscal crisis in New York and the advent of the Thatcher government in Britain, the use of state support to foster economic growth and the far lower priority given to alleviating its negative consequences has been self-evident. A transparent example of this policy shift concerns the very similar histories of two showpiece projects – Battery Park City in New York and the Docklands development in London. When both were first conceived in the early 1970s, they were seen as offering unique opportunities for the large-scale development of housing (and, in London, employment too) for low- to moderate-income households, those who were suffering most from the decline of manufacturing and associated industries and unable to gain access to affordable housing. The fiscal crisis in New York and the Thatcher government in London caused the abrupt termination of these plans. Instead the sites were to contain offices, retail and leisure facilities, and upper-income housing directly serving the needs of the growing financial and producer services complex and its higher paid employees.

The eighties also saw some significant institutional changes, notably moves to insulate business-oriented state investment from public accountability and democratic influence. The abolition of the Greater London Council and the use of semi-autonomous public development corporations in both cities (participating in private–public development "partnerships") are examples of this trend.

Such developments, lavishly aided by central and local government, contrast sharply with the declining commitment to subsidized housing in London (and, for most of the recent period, in New York too), to planning other than that which serves business expansion, to the maintenance of many public services, and to the support, through welfare systems, of the urban poor. Some have seen these changes as the inevitable consequence of the wider changes in the global economy, together with the pressures which economic recession has placed on public expenditure during much of the last 15 years. In addition in the USA, though less arguably in the UK, the paucity of nationally redistributive policies and the intense competition between localities for

economic development and the revenues which it brings city governments have been used to justify the switch to pro-business urban policies.

Nevertheless, although such factors do constrain all urban governments and policies in the current era, they can hardly account for the
extent of the switch which has occurred. To understand this we must
also examine the impact of economic restructuring on the social basis
of political representation in the two cities. In both cases the (relative)
balance which existed before the current period between policies to
foster growth and those to provide welfare reflected the balance of
political forces. In London, and to a lesser extent in New York, the
social and economic interests of the working class were represented
within the institutionalized structures of urban and national politics.
With some oversimplification, one can characterize this representation
as based on a largely white, manual, male, and unionized working class.
As we have shown in this book, economic changes in the two cities and
processes such as the decentralization of population have largely
removed the previous social basis for working-class organization and
the advancement of working-class interests in policy formation. The
new, much more fragmented working class, divided by ethnicity, gender,
and its location in smaller and/or nonunionized workplaces, has not
been able to replace the organization which previously existed. It has
largely failed to gain entry to the institutionalized political structures,
thus increasing the hegemonic role of business and the better paid
sections of the population in policy-making.

Efforts to counter this influence have occurred principally in individual
neighborhoods or boroughs rather than at the metropolitan or regional
level. Gains have accordingly been slight and often extremely precarious.
Moreover, the disciplines of the market have been reinforced by deliberate actions to disempower and force compliance from groups and political institutions representing the interests of low-income populations.
New York's fiscal crisis, rather than some inevitable consequence of
previous irresponsibility and excessive spending on the urban poor, was
in large part a deliberately engineered event by the city's business and
financial elite to restructure urban policies and expenditures to suit its
needs (Marcuse, 1981). One of the sharpest illustrations of the disciplinary nature of this act was the "forced corporatism" experienced by the
public-sector unions, required to accept sharp job cuts and to invest
their pension funds in city bonds (which the banks would no longer buy)
to preserve those jobs that remained, and to underpin the subsequent era
of pro-business policies.

In London, too, the disciplinary intent behind recent policies has been
evident. In abolishing the GLC, the Thatcher government sought to
eliminate a leading base for political opposition to pro-business local and

national policies. More generally the central government's heightened control over local government and its finances, culminating in the imposition of the poll tax and the capping of "overspending" (almost without exception Labour) councils, was explicitly aimed at the elimination of "socialist" policies in the city.

By the late 1980s – as we noted in chapter 8 – these efforts had mainly succeeded in disorganizing any coherent, large-scale political opposition to the reshaped urban policies. Indeed, even the reemergence in London of an alternative agenda for such policies became unlikely, as Labor local governments had to cut back on their expenditures and come to terms with the era of public–private "partnerships." In New York the situation was somewhat different following the election of Mayor Dinkins, although both the extent of the difference between his program and that of his predecessor and the likelihood that he could implement a more redistributional policy remained in considerable doubt.

Is the revival of the two cities sustainable and can its distributional consequences be modified, by state or other action? This is the most speculative of our five questions. We have already suggested that the economic and social changes which have occurred in the two cities have been influenced by the policy choices made by government. We have also outlined some of the reasons why the policy agenda has been dominated by the objective of fostering economic growth, with a decreasing concern for the distributional consequences of such growth. We return to the question of the potential scope for a different policy agenda in the last section of this chapter.

As noted in chapter 1, by the time of this book's completion there were signs, in both cities, that the rosy optimism of the mid-1980s regarding their revival had faded under the impact of retrenchment in the financial services sector and a recession in the real estate industry. Both industries expanded rapidly in the 1980s, fueled in part by purely speculative activities. In retrospect we can see that such conditions were not likely to persist for any length of time. However, the more fundamental issue concerns the long-term prospects for further growth in the financial and producer services sectors, together with those other parts of the two urban economies which are essentially dependent on such growth. A second issue is whether financial and producer service growth will continue to center in London and New York.

The first point to note is the significance of changes in the regional space economy of which London and New York form a part. As we have seen, much of the remaining manufacturing employment is now located in the outer areas of the two regions, beyond their respective city limits. As was noted in chapter 1, changes in the organization of production and the other factors which have encouraged decentralization have already resulted in a new form of regional structure, with a development of relatively self-contained agglomerations outside the two core cities. Although these core cities retain a unique importance no longer found in many other metropolitan regions, they nevertheless must rely on a narrower economic base than in the past. New York, which lacks London's governmental dominance, particularly suffers from a high level of specialization. Moreover, the expansion of public-sector employment which helped to sustain both economies in the early to mid-1970s has not continued into the 1980s.

By 1991 the British economy was in recession, with no immediate prospects for major recovery. High interest rates were squeezing inflation, at the cost of falling investment and rising unemployment. The property market and the financial services sector continued to be depressed, with, for example, major programs of retrenchment and redundancies being announced by the main banks. The USA had suffered two quarters of economic decline. With this national context New York's position appeared especially shaky as strong negative publicity threatened the previously vibrant tourist industry and placed added pressure on business to move out to more secure locations. In short, the booming economic conditions which underwrote the revival of the two cities in the 1980s were much less in evidence by the end of this decade, nor did their reappearance seem imminent.

In the light of these developments one could argue that the renewed growth of the 1980s was of little longer-term consequence. The relatively stable conditions which both cities experienced in the middle years of this century may now seem, in retrospect, merely an interval separating the period of rapid change up to the First World War and that which began to emerge in the 1960s. The post-Second World War years saw the growth of welfare states, highly regulated patterns of work, and an organized working class – all of which have been seriously eroded since the early 1970s.[1]

We cannot, however, conclude that the last decade was merely an aberration, separating two periods of overall economic decline for the two cities. There are some plausible arguments for suggesting otherwise. Thus, while the real estate market, for example, was by the early 1990s in recession, partly as a result of overspeculation in the 1980s, as a recent survey of New York City shows, in many of its industries there is "little evidence of irreversible decline" (Uchitelle, 1990). There is an evident danger, when commentators respond in an uncritical way to the current crises of the two urban economies, of confusing cyclical and secular changes. Overpessimism in the 1990s may be as misplaced as the overoptimism of the 1980s proved to be. The changes in the economy and labor market that underlay the 1980s revival may have slowed, adversely affecting the institutions and groups that benefited in the 1980s (and further harming those which suffered then), but the general directions taken by economic restructuring seem likely to persist.

Nevertheless, continued economic restructuring may not bring as many benefits to the core areas of the London and New York regions. An important issue here concerns the future location of the existing financial and producer services industries and of possible future growth in them. On the one hand, we have already referred to the reasons why the information-intensive activities have tended to concentrate in Central London and New York City. On the other hand, we noted in chapter 2 that the growth of these industries in the outer parts of the two regions was now far higher than in the cities themselves and that there was a convergence between their proportional share of all economic activity in these two parts of the respective regions. So the new industries which provided the basis for the revival of London and New York in the 1980s are, like earlier established industries, now decentralizing. Developments in transport, communications, and information technology aid this process and the cost pressures in the urban cores are also significant in bringing about decentralization. However, much of this out-migration has involved "back office" functions, leaving behind those activities which still require the advantages of agglomeration in the central business districts. It remains to be seen whether eventually some of the latter will also decentralize.

The increasing direct costs of a central city location are only one set of factors which encourage decentralization. Equally significant is the quality of life which the two cities can offer those who live and work there, especially the more affluent members of the new service class working in financial and producer services. As we indicated in chapter 5, public opinion surveys suggest that residents of both cities regard the quality of life as declining, partly as a result of the cuts in public-service provision over the past 10 to 15 years. In both cities, too, though especially in New York, social tension perceptibly grew in the 1980s and the politics of territorial defense intensified. Developments in the two housing markets have, as chapter 7 showed, resulted in increasing difficulties for many of those who work in these cities, not just the urban poor.

If in the next decade the decentralization of the "new core" industries now located in London and New York does accelerate, both cities may enter another period of relative decline. If residents follow jobs out of the city, the process of contraction may occur without a return to the conditions which marked the inner city crisis of the 1970s. Any out-migration, however, is likely to be selective, given the massive inflation which has occurred in regional house prices, the lack of public or other subsidized accommodation in the metropolitan fringe and beyond, and, especially in New York, the discriminatory barriers which still exist to prevent the out-migration of nonwhite ethnic minorities.

In such circumstances public policies may take an increasingly contradictory form. On the one hand, the state may seek to retain the new industries in the city by offering even greater inducements in the form of infrastructural investments, tax breaks, and so on. On the other hand, these expenditures are likely to be met by further reductions in those public services which are required by the general population, thus adding to the general deterioration of the quality of life and the further out-migration of population. Indeed, this already seems to be happening. As we reported in chapter 8, by late 1989 London's docklands development was in serious difficulties, due to the recession in the real estate market. So, in order to save its showpiece, the central government made a further injection of public investment. But it also required the Docklands Development Corporation to cut back on a social program which it had recently developed, after sustained criticism of its lack of concern for the needs of the lower-income population in this area. In New York, too, the recent history of massive tax abatements and other subsidies in order to retain key industries in the city and encourage new developments seems set to continue under Mayor Dinkins, thus presumably limiting the extent to which he can implement the rest of his political agenda. His efforts to respond to the fiscal crisis through tax increases have met a massive counterattack from business, which threatens to flee the city to lower-tax jurisdictions.

THE NEW SOCIAL DIVISIONS

There is ample evidence, throughout this book, of the ways in which economic restructuring has, directly or indirectly, created new or intensified old social divisions in the two cities. For example, there has been a growth in income inequality and in labor market polarization. Unequal access to housing has been exacerbated by economic restructuring, and new divisions defined, for example, by "race," ethnicity, and gender are emerging. Finally, we have seen how the urban politics and policies of the two cities both reflect and accelerate the development of these and other social and economic divisions.

As we noted in chapter 1, there have been various attempts to encapsulate the totality or some key aspects of these divisions. In particular, the image of the dual (or, perhaps, dualizing) city – highlighted by the supposed division between (what used to be called) yuppies, on the one hand, and an urban underclass, on the other – has been frequently evoked. In chapter 1 we criticized such images. The recent study of New York edited by Mollenkopf and Castells (1991) contains an extended critique of the "dual city" metaphor. Mollenkopf and Castells conclude: "the complexity of New York's social structure cannot be reduced to a dichotomy between the two extremes of the scale of income distribution" (p. 401). We agree with this conclusion, which also applies to London.

An adequate picture of the emergent pattern of social stratification in the two cities is, however, difficult to construct. Mollenkopf and Castells base their account on a six-fold division of the occupational structure in New York City, distinguishing between an upper stratum of executives, managers, and professionals, clerical workers, those employed in miscellaneous services, manufacturing workers, the public sector, and those who are outside the formal labor force. They suggest that, while there are a multiplicity of interactions between these six groups, there is a dominant relationship between, on the one hand, "the upper professionals of the corporate sector [who] form an organizational nucleus for the wider social stratum of managers and professionals" and, on the other hand, "the remaining social strata [which] occupy increasingly diverse positions . . . Neighborhood life thus becomes increasingly diverse and fragmented, hindering alliances among these groups." Thus, "cultural, economic, and political polarization in New York takes the form of a contrast between a comparatively cohesive core of professionals and a disorganized periphery fragmented by race, ethnicity, gender, occupational and industrial location, and the spaces they occupy" (Mollenkopf and Castells, 1991, p. 402).

This contrast, in effect a modified form of the dual city hypothesis, between a core group whose economic, social, and political interests have been served by economic restructuring and a fragmented mass which, to varying degrees, has lost out improves on analyses which merely refer to the "top" and the "bottom" of the system of social stratification. Yet it has serious limitations. For example, the public sector describes neither a coherent occupational category nor a clearly separable social stratum. Those working in the public sector range from high-status, high-income professionals to the poorest paid, unskilled employees. In general, it is unclear where Mollenkopf and Castells locate the vast bulk of the white-collar middle class in their schema, a fact which they perhaps recognize by an admission that the social structure of New York is determined by the interactions between the six segments which they describe "and others not included in this . . . presentation" (Mollenkopf and Castells, 1991, p. 402).

If intended as an account of the pattern of social stratification – not merely a generalized overview of the impact of economic restructuring on the social structure – Mollenkopf and Castells' conclusions are still unduly influenced by the dual city metaphor. Their division between an organized core group and a disorganized, fragmented periphery downplays the extent to which various groups in the latter experience widely varying degrees of disorganization, economic insecurity, powerlessness, and so on. At a later stage in their conclusions, Mollenkopf and Castells modify their argument, characterizing the socio-spatial structure of New York as consisting of "three cities." These are: "metropolitan heaven," the space occupied by the core group described above; "inner city hell," roughly speaking the preserve of low-income workers and those outside the labor market; and "elsewhere," "the stratified differentiation of urban and suburban space" in which the remaining social groups reside (p. 407). They state that the city is structured by two logics, one of segregation, separating the top and the bottom, and one of differentiation, underlying the broad middle of the system of urban social stratification. Mollenkopf and Castells appear to see the division between "inner city hell" and "metropolitan heaven," together with the groups in these locations, as strongly linked to, if not wholly determined by, the new, postindustrial urban economy. "Elsewhere" is the location for groups, of which many members are still involved in declining sectors of the economy.

This new division, however, contains echoes of the earlier, dualistic core–periphery account insofar as it may be read to imply that the "middle" of the social structure (in fact the largest proportion of the city's population) has its location in the urban social and spatial system determined by its involvement in industries which are now of fading significance. The empirical evidence is lacking for such an assertion. As we have shown in this book, economic restructuring has had an impact in both London and New York which is far more complex, socially and spatially, than the dramatic contrast between the new and the old which is at the heart of the three-city model.

To summarize, Mollenkopf and Castells recognize the complex nature of the changes which economic restructuring brought about in the system of social stratification. But their attempts to encapsulate these complexities in a series of striking new images of the city are not entirely convincing. Above all, they provide only a rather limited discussion of "the remaining social strata." In this respect it is surprising that they have, with one or two exceptions, ignored the large body of research and theory concerning the class structures of advanced capitalist societies. After all, New York (and London) are merely specific locations within two such societies, so this literature would seem a useful starting-point. In what follows we provide a tentative attempt to translate what we have learnt about the social divisions in the two cities into a systematic mapping of the class structure. We draw heavily on a recent paper by Runciman (1990) which, synthesizing much recent work on the class structure, performs a similar task for Britain as a whole.

Runciman suggests that "classes are . . . sets of roles whose common location in social space is a function of the nature and degree of economic power (or the lack of it) attaching to them through the institutional processes of production, distribution and exchange" (p. 377). The boundaries between classes are defined by qualitatively significant differences in their economic power. However, this criterion enables one to determine only the structural location of classes. The issue of class consciousness, and hence the potentiality for class-based political or other action, and the extent to which a structurally defined class shares a common level of social prestige are both "logically separate questions to which the answer has to be arrived at empirically case by case" (p. 377).

The research on which this book is based cannot provide adequate answers to these latter issues, although we make some conjectures below. However, Runciman's map of the class structure is based on a series of occupational groupings which is broadly applicable to what we have learnt about the economies and labor markets of London and New York. So it provides a useful starting-point for our attempt to synthesize the findings regarding occupational structures and the other bases for social division in the two cities which we have described in earlier chapters. The relationship between occupationally defined class positions and divisions based, for example, on "race," gender, and household structures are complex and contingent. One cannot "read off" the latter from the former. At this stage we can make only probabilistic statements concerning, for example, the tendency for groups defined by gender or "race" to concentrate in certain structural locations and to hypothesize about effects the resulting configurations of political power might have upon urban outcomes.

Runciman suggests that there are three functionally equivalent criteria of economic power – control, ownership, and the marketability of occupational skills. On this basis he identifies seven classes:

I   An upper class: defined by property ownership, the control exerted by, for example, the chief executive of a major corporation, or marketability as possessed, for instance, by a senior partner in a large law or accountancy firm.

II   Middle classes. Here Runciman proposes a three-fold division.

   II(a)   The new service class; higher grade professionals, administrators and officials in the public and private sectors, the managers of industrial establishments and the proprietors of larger businesses.

II(b) Subaltern or cadet levels of the service class; lower-grade professionals, administrators and officials, managers of smaller businesses and industrial establishments, supervisors of nonmanual employees and higher-grade technicians.

II(c) The more deskilled white-collar employees; clerical, technical, and sales workers who nevertheless have some promotion prospects and who have the "functional 'proximity to authority' which associates them with the direction of the enterprise" (p. 386). If such workers lack either or both of these factors Runciman, like many other sociologists, would assign them to the working class.

III The working classes. Two divisions are suggested, although the difference in economic power between them is much less than between the top and bottom of the middle classes:

III(a) The skilled or, we suggest, the "potentially vulnerable" working class.

III(b) The unskilled and semi-skilled or "actually vulnerable" working class. The reason for preferring the criterion of labor market vulnerability is that the division between these two sections of the working class is no longer, as it was in the past, adequately defined by any objective evaluation of job skills.

IV The underclass; defined as long-term welfare-dependent households, having little or no economic power derived from their occupational position.

Our research suggests that economic change, interacting with other social and demographic characteristics of the two cities, is resulting in the following patterns:

I The upper class has grown significantly, due mainly to the expansion of financial and allied services. While it remains numerically and proportionately very small, it has a major impact on urban processes and patterns. It is a key group politically, and it has seen many of its urban and economic interests increasingly served by urban policies. It is overwhelmingly white and male.

II(a) The new service class has expanded greatly at the top and it has had significant "urban effects." Its political and social interests are closely linked to those of group I. It is frequently tied to international rather than purely local labor markets. Its ability to out-compete other groups in the housing markets of the two cities has had a major impact. Women and ethnic minorities still have only limited representation in this group.

II(b) Middle levels of the service class show a more mixed pattern of growth and decline, depending on the industries concerned. For many in this group and II(c), the more polarized job structure of the growth industries and deindustrialization have posed a threat. Their position is less secure than hitherto. A significant internal divide may be between younger members of this group in the growth sectors, who may reasonably aspire to promotion (the "cadet yuppie class"?) and those who are stuck in "middle management" in the declining sectors, and/or whose skills are being downgraded by new information technologies. Overall, members of this group probably have, or think they have, significant identities of interest with the "higher" groups. Their actions may be guided by the individualist pursuit of interests rather than any workplace-based collectivism, although they do get involved in community-based actions. Minority groups and especially women are significantly represented in this group.

II(c) The lowest service class level presents a rather similar picture of growth and contraction to that of II(b). Some members of this group may fear the possibility of downward mobility to the working class. However, others, such as certain of the ethnic minorities discussed in chapter 6 and some women, may be moving into jobs in the expanding sectors and occupying niches left vacant by others. This group is under much greater pressure than the earlier mentioned groups as a result of the diswelfares of the global city, for example in relation to their housing, the problems of commuting, and personal security. Politically, they may not identify with the interests of the higher echelons of the middle class, but neither do they join with those below them in the class structure, except perhaps if they are in the unionized public sector.

III(a) The skilled working class has contracted, but our evidence suggests that some minorities have moved into the declining but still sizable number of positions here. The group has lost economic and political power, due to the fall in trade union membership and the unions' declining influence. This section of the working class is probably as hard pressed by urban diswelfares as many of those in group II(c).

III(b) New jobs in consumer and producer services created as a result of economic restructuring have enlarged some sectors of the unskilled working class, while many factory- and port-related sectors have declined. Women and minorities constitute a disproportional share of this group. These positions are frequently very insecure and low-wage poverty is widespread. This group has very little economic or political power, but the politically powerful may support their aims, for example for mass transit, if their disadvantage threatens the continued availability of an adequate supply of labor. Some of this group have trade union representation, but their unions are far weaker than they were in New York City before the fiscal crisis of the 1970s and in London before the Thatcher government.

IV Demographic and economic trends, patterns of migration and discrimination have augmented the underclass, which was less prominent in the years of full employment from 1945 to the 1970s. The underclass has little political power or functionality for the two urban labor markets. It contains high concentrations of certain minorities (most notably, of course, in New York), women, working-class elderly, and young unqualified males.

Consideration of this latter group leads us back to the underclass debates outlined in chapter 1. Recently David Smith (1991) has suggested that the structural definition of this group should be separated from its possible social and political characteristics, such as those relating to a presumed culture of dependency. He therefore accepts Runciman's definition of the underclass not as a group which is disadvantaged within the labor market but as "those whose roles place them more or less permanently at the economic level where benefits are paid by the state to those unable to participate in the labour market at all" (Runciman, 1990, p. 388). This definition is, however, influenced by the British situation, with relatively extensive welfare benefits, a limited informal labor market, and a formal labor market which is not as racially divided as that of the USA. It covers a wider section of the population than would, for example, be encompassed by Murray's (1990) definition of the UK (and the US) underclass. At the same time it is narrower than the definition adopted by many others, such as Wilson (1987), who include workers in highly unstable, low-wage employment situations, including those outside the formal labor market. It also excludes the specifically American dimension which involves ecological concentration, as highlighted, for example, by Wilson's recent (1991) suggestion that the term "ghetto poor" might be substituted for "underclass."

In our view the latter, more broadly defined structural definition seems preferable because it more adequately identifies those who are trapped at the bottom of the economic system, who live in the worst areas of the two cities, who suffer most from the costs of urban change. In a recent paper Buck (1991b) uses data from UK Labour Force Surveys to show that between 1979 and 1986 there was a growing proportion of UK households (up from 5 to 10 percent of the working population in this period) who appear not to have had any stable relationship with employment. He also provides a useful discussion of whether groups such as the early retired, long-term sick and disabled, and students ought to be excluded from a structurally defined underclass. He finds that on this definition of underclass membership there are significant correlations with age (young/elderly), educational qualifications, nonwhite ethnic origin, the number of children in the household, and public housing tenure (the latter being particularly marked). Above average levels of such households live in most of the major conurbations and in Wales and Northern Ireland. Interestingly, however, when the high proportion of council housing in Inner London is controlled for, this area had a below average share of underclass households. Buck's further analysis of these data does not support the hypothesis that the concentration of this group in Inner London due to the high level of public housing leads to a process of cumulative causation, an identifiable "inner city effect" which itself increases the level of labor market inactivity.

Claims that the underclass, however defined, shares a distinctive "culture of poverty" cannot be explored on the basis of our research. However, as Wilson and others have persistently noted for the USA, the evidence for these claims is very poor. Moreover, Heath's (1991) analysis of data from the 1987 British Election Study and the 1989 British Social Attitudes survey found no evidence that this group had attitudes which differed from those of the rest of society toward child care or work. There were some more "relaxed" attitudes to marriage and single parenthood. However, in contrast to the assertions made by Murray, for example, there was a greater willingness to take jobs which offered little independence than among the rest of the population sampled. Data on the location of the underclass households showed that, while they clustered in the poorest neighborhoods, the level of concentration never exceeded 25 percent. Thus, in contrast to the USA where this geographic concentration, reinforced by racial divisions in the housing market, is certainly much higher, the UK underclass does not form ecologically defined communities. In addition, having controlled for the level of education, there was no significant difference in the level of participation in politics through voting between the two sections of the population.

To summarize, there is clear evidence in both cities of a growth in a structurally defined underclass. Assertions that this is defined by its adherence to a "culture of poverty" or "socially deviant" attitudes which are in some way self-sustaining are not convincing. However, the racial divide does mean that in New York the underclass forms an ecological community; this seems not to be the case in London. In contrast, as chapter 4 concluded, the "mismatch theory" of underclass formation is not supported by evidence from either London or New York. Beyond this there are some further significant differences in the economic, social, and ecological context to underclass formation in the two cities. The principal differences lie in the greater size of New York's informal economy, New York's much larger minority group component of the population, and London's substantially bigger social housing sector.

If we draw back from this detailed picture, a tripartite rather than a dual division of the social structure seems to emerge. At the "top" there are groups I and II(a) and the potentially upwardly mobile part of II(b); in the "middle" there are the rest of group II(b), together with II(c) and part of III(a); the remaining groups form the "bottom" stratum. Compared to the previous era, power has shifted toward the "top," however this group has expanded. The signficant power resources that the middle group once possessed have eroded. The bottom group, never with much access to economic or other power, has probably expanded in size and has certainly lost out due, for example, to the weakening of trade unions, the decline of redistributive urban policies, and the loss of welfare benefits.

Finally, is it possible to provide a more adequate sketch of the spatial locations of these groups than the tripartite typology suggested by Mollenkopf and Castells? In a paper on New York, which confusingly refers to the "quartered city," Marcuse (1989b) distinguishes between the following:

1 The centrally located luxury city of the wealthy – areas such as the Upper East Side in New York and Belgravia in London which contain high concentrations of group I.
2 Gentrified areas of old inner city housing, the better of which are occupied by group II(a) while the less up-market areas are occupied by younger members of group II(b). It is also important to remember, however, that many in these groups live outside the metropolitan areas altogethr or in areas of new housing such as Docklands and Battery Park City.
3 The suburban city, where much of group II(b) probably live. Note, however, that there are also many less favored suburban areas housing some in groups II(c) and III(a), particularly older households who have been able to save for homeownership and/or who bought at an earlier time when prices were less inflated in relation to their incomes.

4 The inner "tenement city," or more accurately in London the "public housing city," where most of those in II(c) and the two divisions of the working class concentrate.
5 The ghetto. Here, Marcuse suggests, lives the underclass as well as many in group III(c). In the racially divided context of New York City, the distinction between the tenement city and the ghetto seems significant. However, in London the areas of inner city public housing combine the residential functions of New York's tenement and ghetto cities. In New York there still survive areas of lower-income private rental housing distinct from, though in constant danger of becoming like, areas such as the South Bronx.

It seems probable that residents in each of these "quarters" will have distinctive interests, for example with regard to the provision of urban services to their area. But some areas have a very mixed class composition. To judge by past experience purely area-based mobilizations around urban issues will achieve no more than limited, defensive or ameliorative goals unless they connect with significant blocs of mobilized economic power, that is, with class-based groupings. This did occur, for example, in London when the manual male working class was organized industrially through the trade unions and politically through the Labour Party and was concentrated in the "public housing city." Now the economic power base of public housing tenants is weakened and they are more divided, for example by "race" and gender, than in the past. A part of this change has been brought about by ecological succession, with the more secure members of the working class moving out to suburban homeownership. Such changes have also reduced the possibility that class and urban divisions will reinforce each other, leading to successful political mobilizatin. Although the details of these changes are very different in New York City, the resultant decline in the political influence of the working class seems quite similar.

Returning to the tripartite division of the social structure outlined above, in both cities the "top" grouping is least fragmented internally and most powerful in terms of economic power and in the urban system. Global economic change has enhanced its economic position, as well as enlarging the size of the group, and policy changes in the two cities have largely served its interests. When members of this group live outside the two metropolises, their control over local government and urban planning has helped insulate them from the urban costs of economic restructuring.

The "middle" grouping has rather different urban (often suburban) interests. These are likely to be defensive in nature, linked to the pressures created by population growth, out-migration, and the decentralization of economic activity. But the possibilities for cross-suburban mobilization seem limited. Rather, there may be intersuburban rivalry, attempts to deflect the costs of urban change elsewhere but capture the benefits. Fundamentally this broad grouping is split by its differing class as well as its suburban locations. A key issue is whether further economic and urban change might alter this situation and provide a new social base for mobilization. A further concern is whether any successes so achieved would "trickle down" to benefit the bottom grouping, as occurred when both cities had an organized and politically powerful skilled working class. Housing, transport, or environmental issues might provide the basis for such a mobilization, though there is no sign of this at the moment. Moreover, even if the urban basis for a wider mobilization does emerge, it is unlikely to be reinforced by the simultaneous development of a new basis for collective economic action, for example the spread of trade unionism beyond the public sector to the growth sectors of the private economy.

Without the revival of a reformist urban politics among the middle stratum which has some redistributive aspects (or major national policy changes), the prospects for the "bottom" grouping remain grim. Like the middle stratum, this population is very fragmented, both in terms of its class composition and in terms of areas of the city which it inhabits. Those who live in the "tenement city" in New York, for example, are likely to see the ghetto and its inhabitants more as a threat than as potential allies (in London this division exists between and within areas of council housing). In addition gender and, more significantly, "race" are particularly important bases for fragmentation at this end of the urban socio-spatial structure. It may be that individualistic "survival strategies" or ethnically and sometimes gender-based divisions may have more salience as a basis for social action than economic and urban locations.

This relatively brief and sketchy analysis of social divisions in the two cities is necessarily limited in two respects. First, it frequently goes beyond the empirical evidence currently available. In this respect it should be evaluated more as a set of hypotheses which require empirical testing than as an authoritative series of conclusions. Second, it omits some key variables. Principal among these is the level of household resources. As Pahl (1984) and others have argued, a key distinction in relation to changing patterns of social stratification is that between "work rich" and "work poor" households. It is evident, for example, that a move from the "tenement" or "public housing" city to suburban homeownership has become increasingly impossible for most single-earner households in recent years. In general the chances for upward mobility between the broad groupings which we have defined by reference to both urban and class locations are affected by whether a house-hold has several, one, or no members engaged in the labor market. In both cities it is probably now true that only those in the "top" grouping are able to maintain their position with a sole earner. For many in the "middle grouping" rocketing housing and commuting costs mean that maintenance of their position has become increasingly dependent on having a second earner in the household, as has mobility from the "bottom" grouping to this one. Divorce, the death of a partner, and unemployment are all significant causes of downward mobility in the urban system, especially affecting women in the case of the first two of these. Conversely marriage may offer a route to upward movement. Developments such as the growth of unrelated multi-earner households, enabling the sharing of rent or mortgage costs, are an evident response to the enhanced importance of location in work rich rather than work poor households.

POLICY ISSUES

Social fragmentation has constituted the theme of our analysis until now; it also provides the context for policy discussion. To whom are we offering our advice? We have little expectation, in the absence of a strong political constituency demanding public policy less oriented to the accumulation interests of business, that policy-makers will respond to schemes for greater equity. In turn, the weakness of a progressive coalition is less a consequence of a substantial majority of the population doing very well than of the divisions among those who have benefited ambiguously or little if at all from current trends. As we have argued, these social divisions result in part from communal rivalries that mask common economic position; they also, however, are rooted in genuine conflicts of interest as groups differentially are able to compete for opportunity within the restructured urban economy.

We identify growing poverty and associated disadvantages as the principal policy issue created by economic restructuring. The evidence on the consequences of nearly a decade of growth, not just in London and New York but within their respective nations, demonstrates that reliance on market forms of distribution produces increasingly inequitable results.[2] Increases in absolute as well as relative poverty have been a legacy of the eighties.

The negative effects of economic restructuring, however, are not restricted to the poor. The middle strata, while able to qualify for the expanding number of jobs requiring technical and managerial skills, face increasing insecurity, for themselves and especially for their children.

Greater flexibility within job markets causes even very highly paid professional and managerial work increasingly to be dependent on contracting and on speculative activities, reducing the correlation between income and job security. This is especially the case in the highly competitive industries (e.g. investment services, advertising, television, and theatre) that compose the unique core of London and New York. Moreover, even the affluent cannot insure that their progeny will attain either their level of employment or their household comforts (Ehrenreich, 1989). Real estate inflation makes first-time home occupancy increasingly difficult for middle-class offspring. Marital instability combines with the necessity of a two-earner household for the maintenance of middle-class life style to exacerbate middle-class anxiety.

In addition to problems of reproduction for both the lower and middle strata, the restructuring process in London and New York presents obstacles to further accumulation. The hyperdevelopment of centrally located real estate has combined with the withdrawal of government from planning to create acute problems of congestion and pollution. The high price of land, transportation blockages, high levels of taxation, and the further incorporation of these costs into the price of services make London and New York extraordinarily expensive locations in which to do business. In both places, but especially in New York, the social problems resulting from restructuring have become highly visible, acting as a disincentive to further investment. To some extent the glamor of world capitals feeds upon itself, attracting entrepreneurs and wealthy consumers. Yet the presence of the homeless in even the very best neighborhoods of New York reduces the appeal of the penthouses that overlook them, causing executives to contemplate other venues in which to pursue and display success.

Social marginalization is both the foremost policy issue we confront and the reason for the political weakness that makes it so difficult to devise a strategy for overcoming it. Within the terms of the "postwar compromise" that offered welfare state support for the majority of the population in return for labor peace, most people regarded state guarantees of their standard of living as essential to economic security. But increased global economic competition and consequent economic restructuring made problematic the capability of government to maintain its interventionist role. The seeming conflict between welfare provision and economic growth separated the interests of impoverished households from middle groups, to whom continued growth potentially offered a greater return than most state-provided benefits. The incapacity of both Labour and the national Democratic Party to hold onto their middle-class adherents demonstrates the point. And the poor, while all sharing the overriding problem of deficient income, varied according to whether they could take advantage of training programs, required housing assistance, were parts of communal networks, suffered from racial discrimination, had access to low-wage employment, qualified for social service programs, etc. At the same time the split between middle- and lower-income groups became exacerbated by the popularity of ideological interpretations that, in the United States, blamed the poor for their poverty and, in the United Kingdom, identified labor unions as the cause of economic stagnation.

Despite these social divisions there nevertheless are indications that a majority in both London and New York would favor more benign governmental programs than characterized the eighties. In London Labour dominated the GLC until it was abolished, and successive opinion polls showed that a solid majority of the population opposed abolition (Livingstone, 1987, p. 276). The recent victory of David Dinkins, an African-American, reflected not just support for his more liberal policies by an electoral majority in New York but the willingness of racially and ethnically divided groups to compromise their differences. Moreover, although he was a regular Democrat, Dinkins's candidacy represented the aspirations of grassroots groups that had previously largely eschewed partisan activity.

Neither city, then, contains a majority staunchly opposed to a progressive approach to governmental intervention. The two cities, however, resemble each other in lacking, both at the party and at the grassroots level, a force with a strategy for achieving equitable growth. Numerous well-meaning groups press for affordable housing, neighborhood business development, employment training programs, and stabilization of manufacturing employment while opposing large developments that displace low-income residents and small business. Their particular issues, however, do not incorporate a stance toward stimulating investment, except at the micro level.

Two documents sum up the consensual position toward stimulating growth, fostering equity, and improving the environment. While neither are official policy statements, both are the products of nonpartisan groups that received official sanction for their effort. The first, *New York Ascendant*, was the report of Mayor Edward Koch's Commission on the Year 2000 (1987). Despite the replacement of the Koch by the Dinkins administration, this volume still appears to embody the general goals and strategy of the mayoral regime. The second, *Strategic Planning Advice for London: Policies for the 1990s*, resulted from a study by the London Planning Advisory Committee, consisting of representatives of the 33 planning authorities, prepared for the Secretary of State for the Environment (LPAC, 1988; see chapter 8).

The London report is a good deal more specific than its New York counterpart, reflecting the much greater traditional London commitment to planning.[3] It seeks to restrict business development to particular locations and urges borough authorities to encourage manufacturing growth through assistance to small and medium firms, the provision of well-serviced sites, and limitations on conversion of land from manufacturing to nonindustrial uses. It proposes a battery of transportation, job training, and housing programs for the benefit of disadvantaged populations. The New York document similarly declares the need for retention of manufacturing and targeted policies for low-income people. It differs from the London report by emphasizing the need to reduce welfare dependency and to lower taxes on business as methods of social improvement and growth stimulation. Neither document explains from where the revenues to support expanded programs will come.

Despite the temperate nature of the two reports, the regimes in neither city have, except for New York City's housing program, done much to implement them. Rather they seem to have equated economic growth with real estate development, assuming that if buildings are built, firms will come to occupy them. Community groups have opposed this viewpoint but have not come up with a credible alternative.

Other cities and regions within the United Kingdom and the United States have, with some success, developed programs for employment growth by targeting industries and working out coordinated strategies to attract them (e.g. Sheffield, England; Silicon Glen, Scotland; the Monogahela Valley, Pennsylvania; Research Triangle, North Carolina) (Judd and Parkinson, 1990; Peters, 1989; Eisinger, 1988; Vogel, 1985). They have tied subsidy programs for businesses to job training efforts thereby reducing the mismatch between displaced manufacturing workforces and new industries. Neither London nor New York has worked out a sectoral strategy to lessen its dependence on the financial services industry; in the meanwhile large-scale lay-offs in this industry point to the riskiness of such dependence.

Without greatly increased revenues directed to infrastructure improvement, job training, and housing there seems, however, little hope that governmental action will heal the social divisions of New York and London. This reordering of fiscal priorities requires strong political backing, but competition between social groups for new expenditure is inimical to the formation of a common program.

NOTES

1 See Pahl, 1984, which contains an important historical discussion on the changing context to work.
2 The literature attesting to the growth of inequality is voluminous. See, for example, Mollenkopf and Castells, 1991, and Rosenberg, 1989, for discussions of New York, and Harrison and Bluestone, 1988, US Congressional Budget Office, 1988, and National Urban League, 1988, for analyses of the United States. For the UK, see Townsend, 1991; for London see Townsend et al., 1987, and for comparative data on London and the UK, Buck, 1991a. Buck, 1990, provides a comparison of London and New York.
3 Despite the unanimity that surrounded the *Advice*, which had been directed at shaping the *Strategic Planning Guidance* of the Department of the Environment (UK Department of the Environment, 1989b), the latter document was extraordinarily vague in its prescriptions, limiting itself mainly to urging local authorities to encourage business by not opposing its interest in particular sites. Except for listing aggregate housing targets for the boroughs, its slim contents consisted of little but generalities (see chapter 8 and S. S. Fainstein, 1991).

Bibliography

Abercrombie, P. 1944: *The Greater London plan*. London: HMSO.

Advisory Commission on Intergovernmental Relations 1987: *Significant features of fiscal federalism, 1987 edition*. Washington, DC: ACIR.

Allen, J. 1988: "Fragmented firms, disorganised labour?," in J. Allen and D. Massey (eds), *The economy in question*. London: Sage, pp. 184–228.

Allen, J., and McDowell, L. 1989: *Landlords and property*. Cambridge: Cambridge University Press.

Allen, J., and Massey, D. (eds) 1988: *The economy in question*. London: Sage.

Attinger, J. 1990: "The decline of New York." *Time*, 136 (September 17), 36–44.

Auletta, K. 1981: *The underclass*. New York: Random House.

Austerberry, H., Schott, K., and Watson, S. 1984. *Homeless in London 1971–81*. London: ICERD, London School of Economics.

Ball, M. 1990: *Under one roof: retail banking and the international mortgage finance revolution*. Hemel Hempstead: Harvester-Wheatsheaf.

Barbanel, J. 1989a: "New Yorkers fear no mayor can solve city's top problems." *New York Times*, June 22.

Barbanel, J. 1989b: "How despair is engulfing a generation in New York." *New York Times*, April 2.

Barlow, J. 1989: "Planning the London conversions boom: flat developers and planners in the London Housing Market." *The Planner* 75(1), 18–21.

Barnekov, T., Boyle, R., and Rich, D. 1989: *Privatism and urban policy in Britain and the United States*. Oxford: Oxford University Press.

Barry, J., and Derevlany, J. 1987: *Yuppies invade my house at dinnertime*. Hoboken, NJ: Big River Publishing.

Berne, R., and Tobier, E. 1987: "The setting for school policy," in C. Brecher and R. Horton (eds), *Setting municipal priorities 1988*. New York: New York University Press, pp. 131–63.

Bhat, A., Carr-Hill, R., and Ohri, S. 1988: *Britain's black population*. Aldershot: Gower.

Birch, E. (ed.) 1987: *The unsheltered woman*. New Brunswick, NJ: Center for Urban Policy Research, Rutgers University.

Board of Trade 1911: *Cost of living in American towns*. London: HMSO.

Booth, C. 1892: *Life and labour of the people of London*. London: Macmillan.

Branson, N. 1979: *Poplarism, 1919–1925*, London.

Brilliant, E. 1975: *The urban development corporation*. Lexington, MA: D. C. Heath.

Brindley, T., Rydin, Y., and Stoker, G. 1989: *Remaking planning*. London: Unwin Hyman.

Brint, S. 1991: "Upper professionals: a high command of commerce, culture, and civic regulation," in J. Mollenkopf and M. Castells (eds), *Dual city: restructuring New York*. New York: Russell Sage Foundation, pp. 155–76.

Brown, C. 1984: *Black and white Britain*. London: Heinemann.

Brown, M., et al. 1985: *No turning back*. London: Conservative Political Centre.

Brown, R. 1990: "A flexible future in Europe?: changing patterns of employment in the United Kingdom." *British Journal of Sociology*, 41(3), 301–27.

Brownhill, S. Sharp, C., Shad, P., and Merrett, S. 1989: "Housing, employment and incomes: the inter-relationship between the housing and labour markets in London." Greater London Housing Study, Working Paper 4. London: University College.

Buck, N. 1981: "The analysis of state intervention in nineteenth century cities: the case of municipal labour policy in east London, 1886–1914" in M. Dear and A. J. Scott (eds), *Urbanization and urban planning in capitalist society*, London: Methuen, pp. 501–34.

Buck, N. 1990: "Social polarisation, economic restructuring and labour market change in London and New York." Paper presented at World Congress of Sociology, Madrid, July 9–13.

Buck, N. 1991a: "Social polarisation in the inner city: an analysis of the impact of labour market and household change," in M. Cross and G. Payne (eds), *Social inequality and the enterprise culture*. London: The Falmer Press, pp. 79–101.

Buck, N. 1991b: "Labour market inactivity and polarization. A household perspective on the idea of an underclass." Paper presented to the conference on "The idea of an underclass in Britain," Policy Studies Institute, London, February 26.

Buck, N., Gordon, I. R., and Young, K. 1986: *The London employment problem*. Oxford: Oxford University Press.

Buder, L. 1987: "Ex-Judge is accused of tenant harassment." *New York Times*, November 1.

Burr, B. 1989: "Bruce Bailey's landlords. Playing hardball with the big boys." *Village Voice*, August, 8, 10–12.

Burstein, D. 1989: "A Yen for New York." *New York*, January 16.

Business Week 1984: "The New York colossus." July 23.

Butterworth, R. 1966: "Islington Borough Council: some characteristics of single-party rule." *Politics* (Australasia) 1.

Cambridge Econometrics 1992: "Regional economic prospects." Press release 22 January 1992. Cambridge Econometrics: Cambridge.

Campaign Against Poverty 1989: *Decade of despair*. Manchester: CAP.

Caro, R. 1974: *The power broker*. New York: Knopf.

CBS News/*The New York Times* 1986: *CBS News/New York Times National and Local Survey, 1985*. Ann Arbor, MI: Inter-University Consortium for Political and Social Research.

Central Statistical Office 1987: *Annual abstract of statistics*. London: HMSO.

Cervero, R. 1986: *Surburban Gridlock*. New Brunswick, NJ: Center for Urban Policy Research, Rutgers University.

CES Ltd n.d.: *People and places: a classification of urban areas and residential neighbourhoods*. London: CES Ltd.

Chall, D. E. 1985: "New York City's 'skills mismatch'." *Federal Reserve Bank of New York Quarterly Review*. Spring, 20–7.

Chamberlayne, P. 1978: "The politics of participation: an inquiry into four London boroughs." *London Journal* 4, 49–68.

Champion, A. G., Green, A. E., Owen, D. W., Ellin, D. J., and Coombes, M. G. 1987: *Changing places: Britain's demographic, economic and social complexion*. London: Edward Arnold.

Cheshire, P. C., and Hay, D. G. 1989: *Urban problems in Western Europe*: London: Unwin Hyman.

Church, A. 1988: "Urban regeneration in London docklands: a five-year policy review." *Environment and Planning C: Government and Policy* 6, 187–208.

City Limits 1989: 12(1), January.

Clout, H., and Wood, P. (eds), 1986: *London: problems of change*. London: Longman.

Cockburn, C. 1976: *The local state*. London: Pluto.

Commission on the Year 2000, 1987: *New York ascendant*. New York: City of New York.

Cose, E. 1989: "Rape in the news: mainly about whites." *New York Times*, May 7.

Crampton, R. 1990: "Two tides." *New Society*, May 10.

Cutright, P. 1968: "Occupational inheritance: a cross-national analysis," *American Journal of Sociology* 73, 400–16.

Dahrendorf, R. 1987: "The erosion of citizenship and its consequences for us all." *New Statesman*, June 12.

Danielson, M., and Doig, J. 1982: *New York: the politics of urban regional development*. Berkeley, CA: University of California Press.

Deakin, N., and Ungerson, C. 1977: *Leaving London: planned mobility and the inner city*. London: Heinemann.

Dibblin, J. 1989: "Waving or drowning?" *Roof* 14(3), 18–21.

Drennan, M. 1991: "The decline and rise of the New York economy," in J. H. Mollenkopf and M. Castells (eds), *Dual City: Restructuring New York*. New York: Russell Sage Foundation.

Drew, D., and Gray, J. 1991: "The black–white gap in exam achievement: a statistical critique of a decade's research." *New Community* 17(2), 159–72.

Dyos, H. J. 1955: "Railways and housing in Victorian London." *Journal of Transport History*, 2, 11–21 and 90–100.

Ehrenhalt, S. 1984: "Changing configurations in the regional labor market." Paper presented at the New York City Council on Economic Education, May.

Ehrenhalt, S. 1989: "1989 mid-year report." New York: Middle Atlantic Regional Office, Bureau of Labor Statistics.

Ehrenreich, B. 1989: *Fear of falling*. New York: Pantheon.

Eisinger, P. K. 1988: *The rise of the entrepreneurial state*. Madison, WI: University of Wisconsin Press.

Fainstein, N. I. 1987: "The underclass/mismatch hypothesis as an explanation of black economic deprivation." *Politics and Society* 15, 403–51.

Fainstein, N. I., and Fainstein, S. S. 1974: *Urban political movements*. Englewood Cliffs, NJ: Prentice-Hall.

Fainstein, N. I., and Fainstein, S. S. 1982: "Restructuring the American city: a comparative perspective," in N. I. Fainstein and S. S. Fainstein (eds), *Urban policy under capitalism*. Beverly Hills, CA: Sage, pp. 161–89.

Fainstein, N. I., and Fainstein, S. S. 1987: "Economic restructuring and the politics of land use planning in New York City." *Journal of the American Planning Association*, 53, 237–48.

Fainstein, N. I., and Fainstein, S. S. 1988: "Governing regimes and the political economy of development in New York City, 1946–84," in Mollenkopf, J. H. (ed.), *Power, culture, and place*. New York: Russell Sage Foundation.

Fainstein, N. I., and Fainstein, S. S. 1989a: "New York City: the Manhattan business district; 1945–1988," in G. D. Squires (ed.), *Unequal partnerships: the political-economy of urban redevelopment in postwar America*. New Brunswick, NJ: Rutgers University Press.

Fainstein, N. I., and Fainstein, S. S. 1989b: "Economic shifts and land-use in the global city: New York, 1940–87," in R. Beauregard, (ed.), *Atop the urban hierarchy*. Totowa, NJ: Rowman and Littlefield.

Fainstein, S. S. 1990: "Economics, politics, and development policy: the convergence of New York and London," *International Journal of Urban and Regional Research* 14(4), 553–75.

Fainstein, S. S. 1991: "Promoting economic development: urban planning in the United States and Great Britain." *Journal of the American Planning Association* 57, 22–33.

Fainstein, S. S., and Fainstein, N. I., 1991: "The changing character of community politics in New York City, 1968–1988," in J. H. Mollenkopf and M. Castells (eds), *Dual City: restructuring New York*. New York: Russell Sage Foundation, pp. 315–332.

Falcon, A. 1988: "Black and Latino politics in New York: race and ethnicity in a changing ethnic context." *New Community* 14(3), 370–84.

Feinstein, C. H. 1972: *Statistical tables of national income, expenditure and output of the U.K. 1855–1965*. Cambridge: Cambridge University Press.

Finder, A. 1987: "New York City prestige outweighs lower costs in Jersey, NBC chief says." *New York Times*, December 9.

Fishman, R. 1987: *Bourgeois utopias*. New York: Basic Books.

Fiske, E. B. 1991: "New York growth is linked to immigration." *New York Times*, February 22.

Fitzgerald, M. 1988: "Different roads: the development of Afro-Caribbean and Asian political organisations in London." *New Community* 14(3), 385–96.

Florida, R. L., and Feldman, M. A. 1988: "Housing in US Fordism." *International Journal of Urban and Regional Research* 12(2), 187–210.

Forrest, R., and Murie, A. 1986: "Marginalisation and subsidised individualism: the sale of council houses in the restructuring of the British welfare state." *International Journal of Urban and Regional Research* 10(1), 46–66.

Fothergill, S., and Gudgin, G. 1982: *Unequal growth*. London: Heinemann.

Fox, D: 1982: Review of Auletta, *The underclass. Social Policy* 13(2), 60–2.

Franco, J. 1985: "NY is a third world city." *Tabloid 9*.

Frey, W., and Speare, A., Jr. 1988: *Regional and metropolitan growth and decline in the United States*. New York: Russell Sage Foundation.

Friedmann, J. 1986: "The world city hypothesis." *Development and Change* 17, 69–83.

Friedmann, J., and Wolff, G. 1982: "World city formation: an agenda for research and action." *International Journal of Urban and Regional Research* 6(3), 309–44.

Frobel, F., Heinrichs, J., and Kreye, O. 1980: *The new international division of labour*. Cambridge: Cambridge University Press.

Fujita, K. 1991: "A world city and flexible specialization: restructuring of the Tokyo metropolis." *International Journal of Urban and Regional Research* 15(2), 269–84.

Gershuny, J. 1978: *After industrial society*. London: Macmillan.

Giddens, A. 1973: *The class structure of the advanced societies*. London: Hutchinson.

Gillespie, J. 1989: "Poplarism and proletarianism: unemployment and Labour politics in London, 1918–1934," in D. Feldman and G. Stedman Jones (eds), *Metropolis London: histories and representations since 1800*. London: Routledge, pp. 163–88.

Glass, R. 1964: "Introduction," in *London: aspects of change*. London: McGibbon and Kee.

Glassberg, A. 1981: *Representation and urban community*. London: Macmillan.

Goldberger, P. 1989: "Why design can't transform cities." *New York Times*, June 23.

Gordon, I. R. 1988: "Evaluating the effects of employment changes on local unemployment." *Regional Studies* 22, 135–47.

Gordon, I. R. 1991a: "Pay, conditions and segmentalism in the London labour market." Unpublished paper, Department of Geography, University of Reading.

Gordon, I. R. 1991b: "Looking for an informal sector in the London labour market." Unpublished paper, Department of Geography, University of Reading.

Gordon, I. R., and Harloe, M. 1991: "A dual to New York? London in the 1980s," in J. H. Mollenkopf and M. Castells (eds), *Dual city: restructuring New York*. New York: Russell Sage Foundation, pp. 377–96.

Gordon, I. R., Vickerman, R. W., Thomas, A., and Lamont, D. 1983: *Opportunities, preferences and constraints on population movement in the London region*. Final report to the Department of the Environment, Urban and Regional Studies Unit, University of Kent at Canterbury.

Gosling, J. 1987: "The end of the East End." *Roof* 12(6), 20–1.

Goss, S. 1988: *Local labour and local government*. Edinburgh: Edinburgh University Press.

Gourevitch, P. 1986: *Politics in hard times*. Ithaca, NY: Cornell University Press.

Grant, C. 1988: "Making tenants foot the bill." *Roof* 13(5), 15–17.

Greater London Council 1986: *Private tenants in London 1983–4*. London: GLC.

Guardian 1988: November 12.

Guardian 1989: July 26.

Hall, P. G. 1988: *Cities of tomorrow*. Oxford: Basil Blackwell.

Hall, P. G. 1989: *London 2001*. London: Unwin Hyman.

Hall, P. G., Gracey, H., Drewett, R., and Thomas, R., 1973: *The containment of urban England*. London: George Allen & Unwin.

Hambleton, R. 1989: "Urban government under Thatcher and Reagan." *Urban Affairs Quarterly* 24, 359–88.

Hammack, D. C. 1982: *Power and society: greater New York at the turn of the century*. New York: Russell Sage Foundation.

Hamnett, C. 1990: "The spatial and social segregation of the London owner-occupied housing market: an analysis of the flat conversion sector," in M. Breheny and P. Congdon (eds), *Growth and change in a core region – the case of South-East England*. London papers 20. London: Pion, pp. 203–18.

Hamnett, C., and Randolph; B. 1986: "Terminal transformation and the flat break-up market in London: the British condo experience," in N. Smith and P. Williams (eds), *Gentrification of the city*. London: Allen & Unwin, pp. 121–52.

Harloe, M. 1985: *Private rental housing in America and Europe*. Beckenham: Croom Helm.

Harloe, M. 1990: "Great Britain," in W. van Vliet (ed.), *International handbook of housing policies and practices*. New York: Greenwood Press, pp. 85–125.

Harloe, M. 1991: "Social housing and the 'social question': the origins of housing reform," in M. P. Smith (ed.), *Breaking chains: social movements and collective action*. (*Comparative urban and community research* vol. 3.) New Brunswick, NJ: Transaction Publishers, pp. 69–107.

Harloe, M., Pickvance, C., and Urry, J. (eds) 1990: *Place, policy and politics: do localities matter?* London: Unwin Hyman.

Harris, R. 1991: "Home and work in New York since 1950," in J. H. Mollenkopf, and M. Castells (eds), *Dual City: restructuring New York*. New York: Russell Sage Foundation, pp. 129–52.

Harrison, B., and Bluestone, B. 1988: *The great u-turn: corporate restructuring and the polarizing of America*. New York: Basic Books.

Harrison, P. 1985: *Inside the inner city*. Harmondsworth: Penguin.

Harvey, D. 1990: *The condition of postmodernity*. Oxford: Basil Blackwell.

Heath, A. 1991: "The attitudes of the underclass." Paper presented to the conference on "The idea of an underclass in Britain," Policy Studies Institute, London, February 26.

Hebbert, M., and Travers, T. (ed.) 1988: *The London government handbook*. London: Cassell.

Henney, A. 1985: *Trust the tenant*. London: Centre for Policy Studies.

Hentoff, N. 1989: "The mayor of the children's graveyard." *The Village Voice*, January 24.

Herington, J. 1984: *The outer city*. London: Harper & Row.

Hills, D. 1987: In A. Walker and C. Walker (eds), *The growing divide*. London: Child Poverty Action Group.

Holcomb, B. 1989–90: "Geography and the underclass: a plea for new directions." *Transition* 17(1), 13–17.

Howe, M. 1989: "Asians in New York region: poverty amid high ambition." *New York Times*, April 17.

Hughes, J. and Sternlieb, G. 1989. *Rutgers regional report: Volume I: Job, income, population and housing baselines*. New Brunswick, NJ: Department of Urban Planning and Policy Development, Rutgers University.

Hurst, R. 1989: "A million home truths." *Search* 1 (May), 20–1.

Hymer, S. 1972: "The multinational corporation and the law of uneven development," in J. Bhagwati (ed.), *Economics and the world order from the 1970s to the 1990s*. London: Collier-Macmillan, pp. 113–40.

Ingham, G. 1984: *Capitalism divided? The city and industry in British social development*. London: Macmillan.

Inner London Education Authority, Research and Statistics Branch 1990: *Differences in examination performance*, RS 1277/90. London: ILEA.

Institute of Economic Affairs (ed.) 1990: *The emerging British underclass*. London: IEA.

Irwin, V. 1987: "After Howard Beach: time to re-examine racism in N.Y.C." *The Christian Science Monitor*, December 23.

Jeffery, T. 1989: "The suburban nation: politics and class in Lewisham," in D. Feldman and G. Stedman Jones (eds), *Metropolis London: histories and representations since 1800*. London: Routledge, pp. 189–216.

Johnson, J. H. 1964: "The suburban expansion of housing in London 1918–1939," in J. T. Coppock and H. C. Prince (eds), *Greater London*. London: Faber & Faber, pp. 142–66.

Jones, G. W., and Donoughue, B. 1973: *Herbert Morrison: portrait of a politician*. London: Weidenfeld & Nicholson.

Jowell, R. et al. 1984– , annual: *British social attitudes*. Aldershot: Gower.

Judd, D., and Parkinson, M. (eds) 1990: *Leadership and urban regeneration*. Newbury Park, CA: Sage.

Kasarda, J. 1985: "Urban change and minority opportunities," in P. Peterson (ed.), *The new urban reality*. Washington, DC: Brookings Institution.

Kasarda, J. 1990: "Urban industrial transition and the underclass." *Annals* (AAPSS) 501 (January), 26–47.

Kellett, J. R. 1969: *The impact of railways on Victorian cities*. London.

Kellner, P. 1989: "A capital example of British rot." *The Independent*, August 7.

KFR Research 1987: *Docklands: commercial and residential developments*. London: Knight, Frank and Rutley.

KFR Research 1988: *Docklands: commercial and residential developments*. London: Knight, Frank and Rutley.

King, A. D. 1990: *Global cities*. London: Routledge, Chapman & Hall.

Koch, E. 1984: *Mayor*. New York: Simon & Schuster.

Koptiuch, K. 1989: "Third worlding at home: transforming new frontiers in the urban U.S." Paper presented at the conference on "Marxism Now," Amherst, MA, December 1.

Kornblum, W., and Beshers, J. 1988: "White ethnicity: ecological dimensions," in J. H. Mollenkopf (ed.), *Power, culture, and place*. New York: Russell Sage Foundation.

Kysel, F. 1988: "Ethnic background and examination results." *Educational Research* 30(2), 83–9.

Lake, R. 1981: *The new suburbanites: race and housing in the suburbs*. New Brunswick, NJ: Center for Urban Policy Research, Rutgers University.

Lampard, E. 1986: "The New York metropolis in transition," in H. -J. Ewers, J. Goddard, and H. Matzerath (eds), *The future of the metropolis*. New York: Walter de Gruyter, pp. 27–110.

Lawless, P. 1989: *Britain's inner cities*. 2nd edn. London: Paul Chapman.

Levin, R. 1989: "Koch acts like himself and voters are tired of it." *New York Times*, Section 4, June 25.

Levine, R. 1989: "New York City's economic growth fails to curb rise of new poverty." *New York Times*, February 28.

Levy, F. 1987: *Dollars and dreams: the changing American income distribution*. New York: Russell Sage Foundation.

Lipietz, A. 1986: "New tendencies in the international division of labour: regimes of accumulation and modes of regulation," in A. J. Scott and M. Storper (eds), *Production, work, territory*. Boston, MA: Allen & Unwin.

Livingstone, K. 1987: *If voting changed anything, they'd abolish it*. Glasgow: Collins.

Llewellyn Smith, H., et al. 1931: *New survey of London life and labour*, Vol. 2. London: P. S. King.

Lloyd, P. 1980: *The young towns of Lima*. London: Cambridge University Press.

London Housing Unit 1989: *One in every hundred*. London: London Research Centre.

London Planning Advisory Committee (LPAC) 1988: *Strategic planning advice for London. Policies for the 1990s.* London: LPAC.

London Research Centre 1989a: *Annual abstract of Greater London statistics, 1987–1988.* London: London Research Centre.

London Research Centre 1989b: *London housing statistics 1988.* Statistical Series No. 70. London: London Research Centre.

London Research Centre 1989c: *The London housing survey 1986–87: full report of results.* London: London Research Centre.

Loughlin, M., Gelfand, M. D., and Young, K. (eds), 1985: *Half a century of municipal decline, 1935–1985.* London: Allen & Unwin.

Lovering, J. 1990: "Fordism's unknown successor: a comment on Scott's theory of flexible accumulation and the re-emergence of regional economies." *International Journal of Urban and Regional Research* 14(1), 159–74.

Lovering, J. 1991: "Theorizing postfordism: why contingency matters (a further response to Scott)." *International Journal of Urban and Regional Research* 15(2), 298–301.

Lowi, T. 1963: *At the pleasure of the mayor.* New York: Free Press.

Lyons, Richard D. 1987: "Lure for long commute: cheaper homes." *New York Times,* September 20.

Mabey, C. 1986: "Black pupils' achievement in inner London." *Educational Research* 28(2), 163–73.

McCormick, M., O'Cleireacain, C., and Dickson, E., 1980: "Compensation of municipal workers in larger cities: a New York City perspective." *City Almanac* 15, 1–9, 16–20.

Mackintosh, M., and Wainwright, H. 1987: *A taste of power.* London: Verso.

Magri, S., and Topalov, C. 1988. '"Reconstruire": l'habitat populaire au lendemain de la première guerre modiale." *Archives Européenes Sociologie* 29, 319–70.

Malanga, S. 1991: "N.Y. economy bottoming out, but very weak." *Crain's New York Business* 7 (June 24), 1 and 33.

Malpass, P. (ed.) 1986: *The housing crisis.* London: Croom Helm.

Malpass, P., and Murie, A. 1987: *Housing policy and practice.* Basingstoke: Macmillan.

Marcuse, P. 1981: "The targeted crisis: on the ideology of the urban fiscal crisis and its uses." *International Journal of Urban and Regional Research* 5(2), 330–55.

Marcuse, P. 1986: "Abandonment, gentrification, and displacement: the linkages in New York City," in N. Smith and P. Williams (eds), *Gentrification of the city.* London: Allen & Unwin, pp. 153–77.

Marcuse, P. 1987: "Neighborhood policy and the distribution of power: New York City's community boards." *Policy Studies Journal* 16, 277–89.

Marcuse, P. 1988: "Divide and siphon: New York City builds on division." *City Limits* 13(3), 8–11, 29.

Marcuse, P. 1989a: "Gentrification, homelessness, and the work process: housing markets and labour markets in the quartered city." *Housing Studies* 4(3), 211–20.

Marcuse, P. 1989b: "'Dual city': a muddy metaphor for a quartered city." *International Journal of Urban and Regional Research* 13(4), 697–708.

Marcuse, P. 1990: "Isolating homelessness from housing," in C. L. M. Caton (ed.), *Homeless in America.* New York: Oxford University Press, pp. 138–50.

Marcuse, P., Medoff, P., and Pereira, A. 1982: "Triage as urban policy." *Social Policy,* 12(3), 33–7.

Markusen, A. 1984: *Profit cycles, oligopoly and regional development.* Cambridge, MA: MIT Press.

Marris, P. 1987: *Meaning and action.* London: Routledge & Kegan Paul.

Marris, P., and Rein, M. 1973: *Dilemmas of social reform.* Chicago, IL: Aldine.

Massey, D. 1984: *Spatial divisions of labour.* London: Macmillan.

Masterman, C. F. G. (ed.) 1902: *The heart of the Empire,* London: T. Fisher Unwin.

Maughan, B., and Rutter, M. 1986: "'Black pupils' progress in secondary schools II: examination achievements." *British Journal of Developmental Psychology* 14, 19–29.

Mead, L. 1986: *Beyond entitlement: the social obligations of citizenship.* New York: Free Press.

Meegan, R. 1988: "A crisis of mass production?" in J. Allen and D. Massey (eds), *The economy in question.* London: Sage, pp. 136–83.

Melendez, E. 1990: "Labor market structure and wage inequality in New York City: a comparative analysis of Hispanic and non-Hispanic blacks and whites." Final report to the Committee on Public Policy Research on Contemporary Hispanic Issues, Social Science Research Council, New York.

Mingione, E. 1991: *Fragmented societies: a sociology of economic life beyond the market paradigm.* Oxford: Basil Blackwell.

Mollenkopf, J. H. 1988a: "The postindustrial transformation of the political order in New York City," in J. H. Mollenkopf (ed.), *Power, culture, and place.* New York: Russell Sage Foundation, pp. 223–58.

Mollenkopf, J. H. 1988b: "The place of politics and the politics of place", in J. H. Mollenkopf (ed.), *Power, culture, and place.* New York: Russell Sage Foundation, pp. 273–84.

Mollenkopf, J. H. 1991: "Political inequality," in J. H. Mollenkopf and M. Castells (eds), *Dual city: restructuring New York.* New York: Russell Sage Foundation, pp. 333–58.

Mollenkopf, J. H., and Castells, M. (eds), 1991: *Dual city: restructuring New York.* New York: Russell Sage Foundation.

Morgan, T. 1991: "Again, grim shelters house a rising number of families." *New York Times,* June 19.

Morokvasic, M., Phizacklea, A., and Waldinger, R. 1988: "Business on the ragged edge: immigrant and minority business in the garment industries of Paris, London and New York." Unpublished paper, Department of Sociology, City College – City University of New York.

Morris, C. R. 1980: *The cost of good intentions.* New York: W. W. Norton.

Muller, P. 1981: *Contemporary suburban America.* Englewood Cliffs, NJ: Prentice-Hall.

Murie, A. 1990: "Tenure conversion and social change: new elements in British cities." Paper presented at the European Symposium on Gentrification, Utrecht, January 25.

Murray, C. 1984: *Losing ground: American social policy, 1950–1980*. New York: Basic Books.

Murray, C. 1990: "The underclass" and "Rejoinder," in Institute of Economic Affairs, (ed.), *The emerging British underclass*. London: IEA, pp. 1–36 and 67–82.

National Urban League 1988: *The state of black America 1988*. New York: National Urban League.

Nelson, J. I., and Lorence, J. 1985: "Employment in service activities and inequality in metropolitan areas." *Urban Affairs Quarterly* 21, 106–25.

New York City Department of City Planning 1983: *City Fiscal Year 1984 Community Development Program*. New York: City of New York.

New York City Harlem Task Force 1982: *Redevelopment strategy for central Harlem*. New York: City of New York.

New York City Human Resources Administration 1989: *CHAP – Comprehensive Homeless Assistance Plan*. New York City, January.

New York City Public Development Corporaton n.d.: *1984/1985 development projects*. New York: Public Development Corporation.

New York State Department of Labor 1988: "Characteristics of job openings, New York City, December/January 1987." New York: New York Department of Labor.

Newfield, J. 1976: "How the power brokers profit," in R. E. Alcaly and D. Mermelstein (eds), *The fiscal crisis of American cities*. New York: Vintage.

Noyelle, T. J., and Stanback, T. M., Jr. 1983: *The economic transformation of American cities*. Totowa, NJ: Rowman & Allanheld.

O'Leary, B. 1987a: "British farce, French drama and tales of two cities: reorganisations of Paris and London governments." *Public Administration* 65, 369–90.

O'Leary, B. 1987b: "Why was the GLC abolished?" *International Journal of Urban and Regional Research* 11(2), 193–217.

O'Mahony, B. 1988: *A capital offence: the plight of the young single homeless in London*. London: Routledge.

Page, D. 1987: "Opening the magic money box." *Roof* 12(5), 24–5.

Pahl, R. E. 1984: *Divisions of labour*. Oxford: Basil Blackwell.

Pahl, R. E. 1988: "Some remarks on informal work, social polarization and the social structure." *International Journal of Urban and Regional Research* 12(2), 247–67.

Pahl, R. E. 1989: "Saint Matthew and the golden handcuffs." Unpublished paper, Sociology Department, University of Kent at Canterbury.

Parker, T. 1983: *The people of providence*. London: Hutchinson.

Passel, J. 1985: "Estimates of undocumented aliens in the 1980 Census for SMSAs." Memorandum to Roger Herriot, US Bureau of the Census.

Passel, J., Siegel, J., and Robinson, J. 1982: "Coverage of the national population by age, sex and race in the 1980 Census: preliminary estimates by demographic analysis." *Current Population Reports*, Series P-23, No. 115. Washington, DC: US Government Printing Office.

Passell, P. 1989: "Forces in society, and Reaganism, helped dig deeper hole for poor." *New York Times*, August 16.

Perlman, J. 1976: *The myth of marginality: urban poverty and politics in Rio de Janeiro*. Berkeley, CA: University of California Press.

Peters, A. H. 1989: *Industrial location and the electronics industry in Scotland*. Ph.D. Rutgers University, Brunswick, NJ.

Pickvance, C. 1990: "Introduction: the institutional context of local economic development: central controls, spatial policies and local economic policies," in M. Harloe, C. Pickvance and J. Urry (eds), *Place, policy and politics: do localities matter?* London: Unwin Hyman, pp. 1–41.

Piore, M. J., and Sabel, C. F. 1984: *The second industrial divide*. New York: Basic Books.

Portes, A., Castells, M., and Benton, L. (eds) (1989) *The informal economy*. Baltimore, MD: Johns Hopkins University Press.

Rasmussen, S. E. 1937: *London: the unique city*. London: Jonathan Cape.

Quante, W. 1976: *The exodus of corporate headquarters from New York City*, New York: Praeger.

Rees, G., and Lambert J. 1985: *Cities in crisis*: London: Edward Arnold.

Regional Plan Association 1929: *Regional survey of New York and its environs 1929. Vol. 2: Population, land value, and government*. New York: Regional Plan Association.

Reimers, D. 1985: *Still the golden door*. New York: Columbia University Press.

Rex, J., and Tomlinson, S. 1979: *Colonial immigrants in a British city: a class analysis*. London: Routledge & Kegan Paul.

Robertson, D. B. and Judd, D. R. 1989: *The development of American public policy*. Glenview, IL: Scott, Foresman.

Rosenberg, T. J. 1989: *Poverty in New York City, 1985–1988: the crisis continues*. New York: Community Service Society of New York.

Rosenwaike, L. C. 1972: *Population history of New York City*. Syracuse, NY: Syracuse University Press.

Royal Commission 1884–5: *Report of the Royal Commission on the housing of the working classes*. Parliamentary papers, Vol. 30. London: HMSO.

Royal Commission 1940: *Report of the Royal Commission on the distribution of the industrial population*. Cmnd. 6153. London: HMSO.

Runciman, W. 1990: "How many classes are there in contemporary British society?" *Sociology* 24(3), 377–96.

Salisbury, R. 1964: "Urban politics: the new convergence of power." *Journal of Politics* 26 (November), 775–97.

Sassen-Koob, S. 1984: "The new labor demand in global cities," in M. Smith (ed.), *Cities in transformation*. Beverly Hills, CA: Sage.

Sassen, S. 1988: *The mobility of labor and capital*. New York: Cambridge University Press.

Sassen, S. 1989: "New York City's informal economy," in R. Portes, M. Castells, and L. Benton (eds), *The informal economy*. Baltimore, MD: Johns Hopkins University Press.

Sassen, S. 1991a: *The global city*. Princeton, NJ: Princeton University Press.

Sassen, S. 1991b: "New York City's informal economy," in J. H. Mollenkopf and M. Castells (eds), *Dual city: restructuring New York*. New York: Russell Sage Foundation, pp. 79–102.

Saunders, P. 1990: *A nation of home owners*. London: Unwin Hyman.

Savitch, H. V. 1988: *Post-industrial cities*. Princeton, NJ: Princeton University Press.

Sayer, A. 1989: "Postfordism in question." *International Journal of Urban and Regional Research* 13(4), 666–95.

Scardino, A. 1986: "They'll take Manhattan." *New York Times Magazine* (December 7).

Schaffer, R., and Smith, N. 1986: "The gentrification of Harlem?" *Annals of the Association of American Geographers* 76, 347–65.

Schmalz, J. 1987: "New York reaches accord on housing." *New York Times*, December 27.

Schwartz, A. 1989: *The decentralization of advanced service industries in the New York metropolitan area*. Ph.D. thesis, Rutgers University, New Brunswick, NJ.

Scott, A. J. 1988a: *Metropolis: From the division of labor to urban form*. Berkeley, CA: University of California Press.

Scott, A. J. 1988b: "Flexible production systems and regional development: the rise of new industrial spaces in North America and Western Europe." *International Journal of Urban and Regional Research* 12(1), 171–85.

Scott, A. J. 1991a: "Flexible production systems: analytical tasks and theoretical horizons – a reply to Lovering." *International Journal of Urban and Regional Research* 15(1), 130–4.

Scott, A. J., 1991b: 'A further rejoinder to Lovering'. *International Journal of Urban and Regional Research* 15(2), 302.

Scott, A. J., and Storper, M. (eds) 1986: *Production, work, territory*. Boston, MA: Allen & Unwin.

Self, P. 1971: "Metropolitan planning." Greater London Paper No. 14. London: London School of Economics.

Shannon, H. A. 1935: "Migration and the growth of London, 1841–91, a statistical note." *Economic History Review* 5(2), 79–86.

Sheets, R. G., Nord, S., and Phelps, J. J. 1987: *The impact of service industries on underemployment in metropolitan economies*. Lexington, MA: D. C. Heath.

Shefter, M. 1985: *Political crisis/fiscal crisis*. New York: Basic Books.

Shenon, P. 1984: "22 indicted in a 'terror' plot to force tenants out." *New York Times*, May 2.

Sleeper, J. 1987: "Boom and bust with Ed Koch." *Dissent* 34, 437–52.

Smith, A. 1989: "Gentrification and the spatial constitution of the state: the restructuring of London's Docklands." *Antipode* 21, 232–60.

Smith, D. 1991: "Defining the underclass." Paper presented to the conference on "The idea of an underclass in Britain." Policy Studies Institute, London, February 26.

Smith, D. 1989: *North and south*. London: Penguin Books.

Smith, D., Gray, J., and Small, S. 1983: *Police and people in London*, Vols 1–4. London: Policy Studies Institute.

Smith, N. 1986: "Gentrification, the frontier, and the restructuring of urban space," in N. Smith and P. Williams (eds), *Gentrification of the city*. London: Allen & Unwin, pp. 15–34.

Smith, N. 1987: "Of Yuppies and housing: gentrification, social restructuring and the urban dream." *Environment and planning D: Society and Space 5*, 151–72.

Smith, N. 1990: "Lower East Side as wild wild West," in M. Sorkin (ed.), *Variations on a theme (park)*. New York: Hill & Wang, pp. 61–93.

Smith, S. 1989: *The politics of "race" and residence: citizenship, segregation and white supremacy in Britain*. Cambridge: Polity Press.

Solomos, J. 1989: *Race and racism in contemporary Britain*. London: Macmillan.

South-East Regional Planning Conference 1989: *Into the next century: review of the regional strategy*. London: SERPLAN.

Squires, G. (ed.) 1989: *Unequal partnerships: the political economy of urban redevelopment in postwar America*. New Brunswick, NJ: Rutgers University Press.

Stedman Jones, G. 1971: *Outcast London*. Oxford: Clarendon Press.

Stegman, M. 1988: *Housing and vacancy report: New York City, 1987*. New York: New York City Department of Housing Preservation and Development.

Sternlieb, G. 1986: *Patterns of development*. Piscataway; NJ: Center for Urban Policy Research, Rutgers University.

Sternlieb, G., and Hughes, J. 1975: *Post-industrial America: metropolitan decline and inter-regional job shifts*. New Brunswick, NJ: Center for Urban Policy Research.

Sternlieb, G., Roistacher, E., and Hughes, J. 1976: *Tax subsidies and housing investment*. New Brunswick, NJ: Center for Urban Policy Research, Rutgers University.

Stuart, A. 1989: *The social and geographical mobility of South Asians and Caribbeans in middle age and later working life*. LS Working Paper No. 61. London: City University.

Swanstrom, T. 1989: "Homeless: a product of policy." *New York Times*, March 23.

Tabb, W. K. 1982: *The long default*. New York: Monthly Review Press.

Taylor-Gooby, P. 1989: "Polarization, privatization and attitudes to poverty." Unpublished paper, Social Policy Department, University of Kent at Canterbury.

Temporary Commission on City Finances 1976: "The effects of taxation on manufacturing in New York City." New York: Temporary Commission.

Temporary Commission on City Finances 1977: "Economic and demographic trends in New York City: the outlook for the future." New York: Temporary Commission.

Thompson, P. 1967: *Socialists, Liberals and Labour: the struggle for London, 1885–1914*. London: Routledge & Kegan Paul.

Thrift, N., Leyshon, A., and Daniels, P. 1987: "Sexy greedy: the new international financial system, the City of London and the South East of England." Working Paper on Producer Services No. 8, University of Bristol and SIRC, Portsmouth Polytechnic.

Tienda, M. 1989: "Puerto Ricans and the underclass debate." *The Annals* (AAPSS) 501 (January), 105–19.

Tobier, E. 1979: "Gentrification: the Manhattan story." *New York Affairs 5*, 13–25.

Tobier, E. 1984: *The changing face of poverty: trends in New York City's population in poverty: 1960–1990*. New York: Community Service Society of New York.

Tobier, E. 1988: "Manhattan's business district in the Industrial age," in J. H. Mollenkopf (ed.), *Power, culture, and place*. New York: Russell Sage Foundation.

Tolchin, M. 1989: "Richest got richer and poorest poorer in 1979–87." *New York Times*, March 23.

Topalov, C. 1985: "Social policies from below: a call for comparative historical studies." *International Journal of Urban and Regional Research* 9 (2), 254–71.

Townsend, P. 1991: *The poor are poorer: a statistical report on changes in the living standards of rich and poor in the United Kingdom 1979–1989*. Bristol: Bristol University Statistical Monitoring Unit.

Townsend, P. 1990: "Underclass and overclass: the widening gulf between social classes in Britain in the 1980s," in G. Payne and M. Cross (eds), *Sociology in action*. Basingstoke: Macmillan.

Townsend, P. 1989: "Slipping through the net." *Guardian*, November 29.

Townsend, P. 1979: *Poverty*. Harmondsworth: Penguin.

Townsend, P., Corrigan, P., and Kowarzik, U. 1987: *Poverty and labour in London*. London: Low Pay Unit.

Traub, J. 1990: "Fernandez takes charge." *New York Times Magazine* (June 17), 23–25; 52–4, 58.

Tyree, A., Semyonov, M., Hodge, R. W., 1981: "Gaps and glissandos: inequality, economic development and social mobility in 24 countries." *American Sociological Review* 44, 410–24.

Uchitelle, L. 1990: "New York City is hurt but still has reserves." *New York Times*, November 12.

UK Department of Employment 1976: "The pattern of pay, April 1976: key results of the New Earnings Survey", *Department of Employment Gazette* 84, October, 1100–44.

UK Department of Employment 1986: "Patterns of pay: early results of the 1986 New Earnings Survey", *Employment Gazette* 94, December, 482–4.

UK Department of Employment 1988a: "Ethnic origins and the labour market." *Employment Gazette*, March, 164–77.

UK Department of Employment 1988b: "Ethnic origins and the labour market." *Employment Gazette,* December, 633–46.

UK Department of Employment 1991: Unpublished tabulation.

UK Department of Employment and Central Statistical Office, various dates: *Family expenditure survey.* London: HMSO.

UK Department of the Environment 1989a: *Draft strategic planning guidance for London.* London: DoE (March).

UK Department of the Environment 1989b: *Strategic planning guidance for London.* London DoE (July).

UK Department of the Environment, various dates: *Housing and construction statistics.* London: HMSO.

UK Home Office 1983: "Crime statistics for the metropolitan police divisions analysed by ethnic groups." *Statistical Bulletin* 22/23.

UK House of Commons 1990: *Low income statistics, fourth report of the Social Services Select Committee, 1989–90.* London: HMSO.

US Bureau of the Census 1982: *Annual housing survey, 1976 (United States): SMSA files.* Ann Arbor, MI: Inter-University Consortium for Political and Social Research.

US Bureau of the Census 1985a: *Annual Housing Survey, 1983 (United States): SMSA Files.* Ann Arbor, MI: Inter-University Consortium for Political and Social Research.

US Bureau of the Census 1985b: *1980 census of population: general social and economic characteristics: New York,* Vol. 1, Chapter C. Washington, DC: US Government Printing Office.

US Bureau of the Census 1986: *State and metropolitan area data book 1986.* Washington, DC: US Government Printing Office.

US Congressional Budget Office 1988: *Trends in family income: 1970–1986.* Washington, DC: US Government Printing Office.

US Department of Commerce 1966–1979, 1982, 1988: *Statistical yearbook of the Immigration and Naturalization Service.* Washington, DC: US Government Printing Office.

US Department of Commerce 1989: "Employment by county, 1969–1987." Unpublished computer printouts, Bureau of Economic Analysis. April.

US Department of Labor n.d.: Nonagricultural establishment employment. Unpublished data, Bureau of Labor Statistics.

Valentine, C. A. 1968: *Culture and poverty.* Chicago, IL: University of Chicago Press.

Vogel, E. 1985: *Comeback.* New York: Simon & Schuster.

Vogel, D. 1988: "The future of New York City as a global and national financial center." Paper prepared for the Committee on New York City, Social Science Research Council.

Waldinger, R. 1989: "Race and ethnicity," in C. Brecher and R. Horton (eds), *Setting municipal priorities 1990.* New York: New York University Press, pp. 50–79.

Waldinger, R., and Lapp, M. 1989: "Back to the sweatshop or ahead to the informal economy?" Unpublished paper, Department of Sociology, City College – City University of New York.

White, J. 1986: *The worst street in north London*. London: Routledge & Kegan Paul.

Williams, R. 1973: *The country and the city*. London: Chatto & Windus.

Williams, W. 1987: "Rise in values spurs rescue of buildings." *New York Times*, April 4.

Wilson, W. J. 1980: *The declining significance of race*. 2nd edn. Chicago, IL: University of Chicago Press.

Wilson, W. J. 1987: *The truly disadvantaged: the inner city, the underclass and public policy*. Chicago, IL: University of Chicago Press.

Wilson, W. J. 1990: "The underclass: issues, perspectives and public policy." *Annals* (AAPSS), 501 (January), 182–92.

Wilson, W. J. 1991: "Studying inner-city social dislocations: the challenge of public agenda research." *American Sociological Review* 56 (February), 1–14.

Witte, A. 1987: "The nature and extent of unrecorded activity: a survey concentrating on recent U.S. research," in S. Allesandrini and B. Dallago (eds), *The unofficial economy*. Brookfield, VT: Gower, pp. 61–81.

Wohl, A. S. 1977: *The eternal slum: housing and social policy in Victorian London*. London: Edward Arnold.

Wolfe, T. 1987: *The bonfire of the vanities*. New York: Farrar, Strauss & Giroux.

Yates, D. 1974: "The urban jigsaw puzzle: New York under Lindsay." *New York Affairs* 2 (Winter), 3–19.

Young, K., and Garside, P. L. 1982: *Metropolitan London: politics and urban change; 1831–1981*. London: Edward Arnold.

Young, K., and Kramer, J. 1978: *Strategy and conflict in metropolitan housing: the suburbs versus the GLC*. London: Heinemann.

Zipser, A. 1989: "Gimme shelter." *Wall Street Journal*, May 9.

Zukin, S. 1982: *Loft Living*. Baltimore, MD: Johns Hopkins University Press.

Zukin, S. 1992: "The city as a landscape of power: London and New York as global financial capitals," in L. Budd and S. Whimster (eds), *Global finance and urban living: the case of London*. London: Routledge, pp. 195–223.

Index

abandonment, 156, 182
Abercrombie Plan (1944) *see* Greater London Development Plan
African-Americans *see* blacks
agglomoration economies, 107, 244, 246, 251
American Labor Party, 45
Asians *see* immigration; minorities

banking, employment in, 98; New York, 100–1; *see also* employment; financial industry
Barlow Report, 48
Battery Park City Authority, 55, 188, 192, 218, 219, 224, 241, 261
Beame administration, 209
Big Bang, 75, 98, 109, 121
Birmingham, 70
blacks, London, 133–4, 157–61, 164–6, 169–71, 191, 243, 266; London and New York, 136–46, 151–2, 161–2, 171–3; New York, 42, 51, 54, 56, 62, 115–16, 123–4, 133, 152–7, 162–4, 167–9, 208, 220, 240; *see also* ethnicity; minorities
Board of Estimate, New York City, 206, 207
Bristol, 101
Bronx *see* New York City, boroughs

Brooklyn, *see* New York City, boroughs
built environment, London, 223–6; New York, 31, 44, 218–20

Canary Wharf *see* Docklands
Castells, M., 20, 254–5, 261
Central London, 57, 68, 74, 78, 81, 98, 101, 111, 252; definition, 24–5; employment, 88; luxury housing, 174
centralization; in Britain, 39
Channel Tunnel, 212, 223, 225
Chase Manhattan Bank, 55, 219
Cheshire, P. C., and Hay, D. G., 3, 21
Chicago, 99, 154, 157, 237
Chinatown (New York), 156
City of London, 45, 57, 98, 223, 225; financial role of, 36, 74–5, 78, 120–1
City University of New York, 209, 222
civil rights movement, 52
class, 6, 8–13, 200, 233, 249, 251, 255, 262; consciousness, 21; definition of divisions, 256–9; London, divisions in, 37–8, 39–41, 62–3, 107; New York, politics of, 33–4; *see also* poverty, underclass